POCKET *A*DVENTURES

VIRGIN ISLANDS

Lynne Sullivan

HUNTER

HUNTER PUBLISHING, INC,
130 Campus Drive, Edison, NJ 08818
732-225-1900; 800-255-0343; fax 732-417-1744
www.hunterpublishing.com

Ulysses Travel Publications
4176 Saint-Denis, Montréal, Québec
Canada H2W 2M5
514-843-9882, ext. 2232; fax 514-843-9448

Windsor Books
The Boundary, Wheatley Road, Garsington
Oxford, OX44 9EJ England
01865-361122; fax 01865-361133

ISBN 978-1-58843-629-0
© 2007 Lynne M. Sullivan

Cover photo: Colorful buildings, St. Croix © FotoSearch
Index: Mary Ellen McGrath
Photos: All photos provided courtesy of USVI Tourist Board and
BVI Tourism Board unless noted otherwise.

Maps by Kim André & Lissa K. Dailey unless noted otherwise
© 2007 Hunter Publishing, Inc.

1   2   3   4

About the Author

Lynne Sullivan is passionate about Caribbean islands. As the author of a dozen best-selling travel guides to islands throughout the eastern Caribbean, she spends much of her time hopping from one place to another scouting out a variety of activities, attractions, shops, accommodations and restaurants. Her goal is to steer independent vacationers on any size budget to the best each island has to offer.

www.hunterpublishing.com

N

Hunter's full range of guides to all corners of the globe is featured on our exciting website. You'll find guidebooks to suit every type of traveler, no matter what their budget, lifestyle, or idea of fun.

Adventure Guides – There are now over 40 titles in this series, covering destinations from Costa Rica and the Yucatán to Tampa Bay & Florida's West Coast, Rome and the Alaska Highway. Complete information on what to do, as well as where to stay and eat, *Adventure Guides* are tailor-made for the curious traveler, with a focus on cultural and physical adventures – dance lessons, hiking, biking, language courses, canoeing, horseback riding, skiing, watersports, festivals and all other kinds of fun.

Alive Guides – This ever-popular line of books takes a unique look at the best each destination offers: fine dining, jazz clubs, first-class class hotels and resorts. In-margin icons direct the reader at a glance. Top-sellers include *The Cayman Islands, St. Martin & St. Barts,* and *Aruba, Bonaire & Curaçao.*

One-of-a-kind travel books available from Hunter include *Best Dives of the Caribbean; A Traveler's Guide to the Galapagos Islands; London A-Z* and many more.

Full descriptions are given for each book, along with reviewers' comments and a cover image. You can also view the table of contents and sample pages. Books may be purchased on-line via our secure transaction facility.

Contents

◆ Maps

The Islands

The United States and United Kingdom share an extraordinary mix of islands sprinkled along the northern curve of the Lesser Antilles just east of Puerto Rico. Known collectively as *The Virgin Islands,* they offer some of the world's most beautiful scenery and idyllic weather. The major islands are amazingly diverse, and each has a well-defined personality, while the 100 or so minor islands (most uninhabited and no larger than prominent rocks) provide privacy and space for anyone who cares to seek it (and can afford it).

St. Thomas, **St. John** and **St. Croix** (the three main US Virgins) are more like disparate kin than siblings. Only two miles of water separate St. Thomas and St. John, and visitors often ferry between the strikingly handsome pair. St. Thomas is the cosmopolitan capitalist, St. John the rugged environmentalist.

Many visitors say that St. Croix, 40 miles to the south, is a combination of the best of St. Thomas and St. John. But I believe the island marches to the beat of a different drummer, flaunting its Danish past flamboyantly and asserting its originality. Of the three, it's the least American, the most Caribbean in atmosphere.

Among the sparsely developed British Virgins, **Tortola** is the largest and most populated island. Visitors are drawn to its green mountains, sheltered bays, and easygoing lifestyle, but few are content to stay put for long. Most hop about by ferry or speed boat to The Baths on **Virgin Gorda**, the coral-sand beaches on **Anegada**, Foxy's famous bar on **Jost Van**

Dyke, the caves on **Norman Island** and the sea turtle playgrounds on **Peter Island**.

If you can't decide which island to call home base, charter a live-aboard boat, so you can change location on a whim. While it's tiresome to clear Customs each time you cross the international boundary that zigzags invisibly between St. John and Tortola, you'll enjoy the freedom of visiting two countries and countless islands in one vacation.

Of course, you may prefer to pick one island and explore it thoroughly at a leisurely pace. All of the major islands offer enough creature comforts and diversions to keep travelers content for at least a week, and each one offers fabulous sun, sea and sand.

A Dozen Reasons to Visit

- ❖ Duty-free shopping.
- ❖ Endless powder-soft sand and a marked underwater snorkel trail on Buck Island, St. Croix.
- ❖ Hiking trails on Sage Mountain, Tortola and in the national park on St. John.
- ❖ Picnics on deserted islands.
- ❖ Snorkeling among the massive boulders at The Baths on Virgin Gorda.
- ❖ Romantic dining at award-winning waterfront restaurants.
- ❖ Outstanding scuba diving among coral reefs and ancient shipwrecks.
- ❖ Ruined and restored sugar plantations to explore.
- ❖ Sunrise at Point Udall on St. Croix, the easternmost spot in the United States.
- ❖ Sailing through the Sir Francis Drake Channel.
- ❖ Lively nightlife in Cruz Bay on St. John.
- ❖ The five-foot rock iguanas and the flamingo colonies on remote Anegada.

Tips on Using This Book

❖ General Caribbean travel information and facts that apply to all the Virgin Islands is covered at the front of this convenient, take-along guide.

❖ Specific information about each of the islands follows in separate sections.

❖ If you plan to visit only one or two of the islands, rip out just the relevant sections from this book, place them inside a zip-lock bag and tuck them

into your carry-on bag. Leave the unneeded
pages at home.

❖ Most attractions, hotels and restaurants have
websites, which we list in the contact details.
Use them to gather additional information or
make reservations.

❖ Prices change seasonally in the Caribbean, so
use our figures as a guide to recent high-season charges for double accommodations. Expect to pay less during low season.

❖ Check *Island Facts & Numbers* sections for important information that will be helpful both during the trip-planning stage and once you arrive
on the island.

❖ Every listing in this book is recommended and
considered above average in its category. Listings with one star (☆) are highly recommended, and those earning two stars (☆☆)
are considered to be exceptional. A few resorts
and restaurants rate three stars (☆☆☆),
which means the establishment is worthy of a
special occasion splurge.

A Historical Timeline

710 BC: Earliest archeological evidence of nomadic
tribesmen, probably from South America, inhabiting
some of the Virgin Islands.

100 AD: **Taino/Arawak Indians** live peacefully in villages, cultivate the land and hold religious celebrations
on many of the Virgin Islands.

1300: Hostile tribes of **Carib Indians** migrate from South
America, establish settlements and raid Arawak villages
for food and brides. These rival tribes live in separate
communities on many islands for more than a century.

1493: **Christopher Columbus** and his crew sail into Salt
River Bay on **St. Croix** and find the island inhabited by

Carib Indians. The explorers sail north, through a cluster of islands that they call *Las Virgines* in honor of the virgin followers of St. Ursula, a religious order that was slaughtered by the Huns during the fourth century.

1500s: Spain declares ownership of the entire West Indies by right of discovery, and no other governments have the resources or power to challenge the

This late 19th-century engraving is one of many conjectural images of Columbus.

claim. The islands serve as a stopover point for cargo ships moving goods between the Americas and Europe, but no permanent settlements are established.

Paintings of Drake were in great demand after he became famous.

1572: Englishman **Francis Drake** defeats Spanish troops on Panama and returns home with two ships loaded with silver and gold. This launches the age of piracy, and legend maintains that numerous pirates set up bases in the Virgin Islands.

1625: Dutch and **English** settlers colonize St. Croix. They are soon joined by the **French West Indies Company**, and **Denmark** establishes communities on St. Thomas and St. John, while the British take over Tortola. Ownership of the islands changes frequently over the years as European countries vie for control as the Virgins become a significant supplier of sugarcane. The islands began to make rum from the sugar crop, which was popular in Europe and America. In addition, a thriving slave market developed, creating what is known as the **triangle trade**. (Ships sail from North America, stop in the Virgin Islands to buy rum from European plantation owners, then sail to Africa, where they trade the rum for slaves. Returning from Africa, the ships stop again in the Virgin Islands to exchange some of the slaves for more rum before heading back to America loaded with both slaves and rum.)

1672: The English remove the ruling Dutch population from Tortola, and, two years later, from Anegada and Virgin Gorda. By the end of the 1600s, England ruled all the islands that make up the present day BVI. The Danes gained control of St. Thomas in 1672, St. John in 1694, and St. Croix (bought from France) in 1733.

1834: Slavery is abolished on all the British islands. Denmark frees slaves on Danish islands in **1848.** During this same time period, sugar beet was introduced in Europe and prices for island-produced sugarcane fell. Many plantation owners were financially ruined and returned to Europe, leaving the islands in the hands of former slaves.

1917: Denmark sells St. Thomas, St. John and St. Croix to the United States for $25 million, and the islands become known collectively as the US Virgin Islands. Subsequently, Tortola, Virgin Gorda, Anegada, Jost Van Dyke and their outer islands officially become the British Virgin Islands.

1927: Residents of the USVI are granted United States citizenship.

1960: Separate colony status is granted the BVI .

1967: The British islands become autonomous.

Today, residents of both the US and British Virgin Islands enjoy a high standard of living. The economy is stable, due in part to the government's commitment to ecology-based sustainable tourism and favorable tax conditions for island-based corporations.

The Islands At A Glance

◆ Location

St. Thomas, the most western of the Virgin Islands, is located about 1,000 miles south of Miami and 75 miles east of Puerto Rico. The other Virgins extend in an upward-swinging curve to the east, excluding St. Croix, which lies 40 miles to the south. Most of the islands are bounded by the Atlantic on the north and the Caribbean on the south, except for St. Croix, which is entirely in the Caribbean, and Anegada, which is entirely in the Atlantic.

The Virgins are divided into two groups, with the US islands to the west and the British islands to the east. St. Thomas, St. John and St. Croix are the major US islands. Tortola, Virgin Gorda, Anegada and Jost Van Dyke are the prominent British islands. All are connected by ferry, seaplane or small airplane service, and their close proximity makes for an ideal island-hopping itinerary.

Most of the Virgin Islands are separated by less than five miles (the exceptions are St. Croix, 40 miles south, and Anegada, 15 miles north). All but Anegada are hilly and volcanic in origin, and each is fringed with gorgeous beaches.

USVI

St. Thomas covers 32 square miles and is 13 miles long and four miles wide at its broadest point. Hills run almost the entire length of the island, which means you must go up and

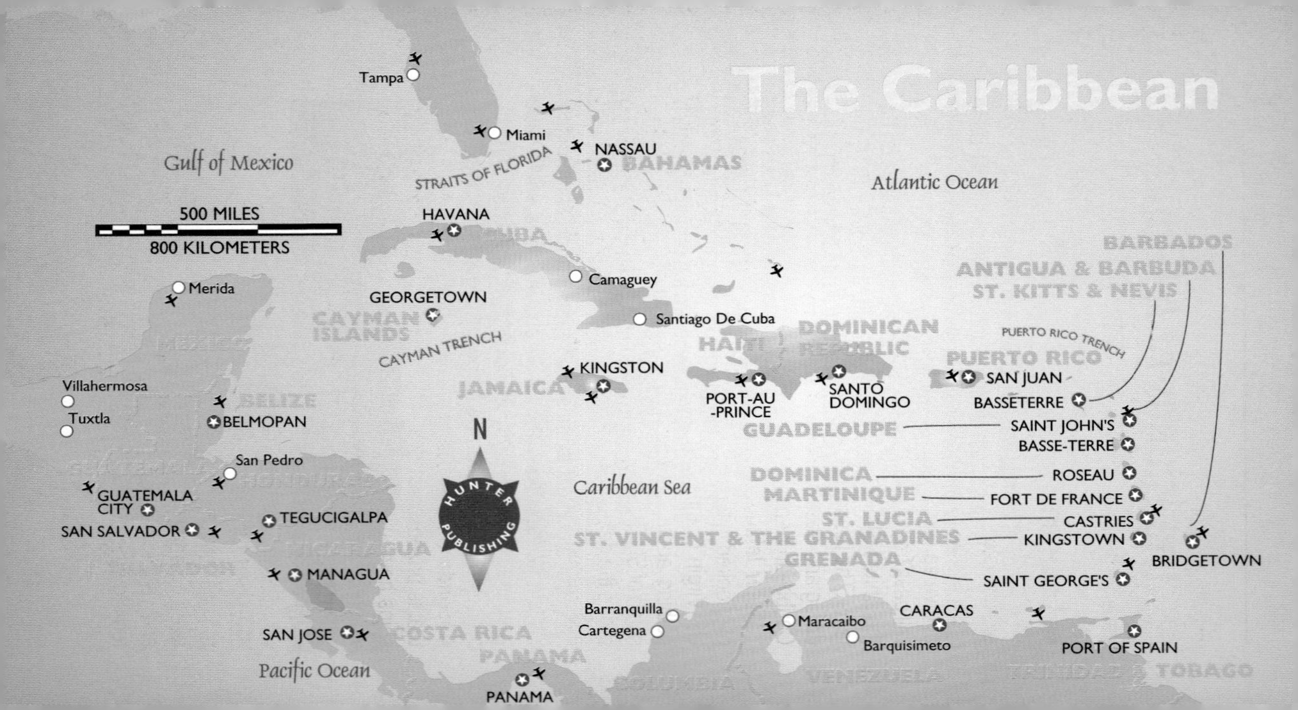
The Caribbean
Gulf of Mexico
500 MILES
800 KILOMETERS
Tampa
Miami
STRAITS OF FLORIDA
NASSAU
BAHAMAS
Atlantic Ocean
HAVANA
CUBA
Camaguey
Merida
GEORGETOWN
CAYMAN ISLANDS
CAYMAN TRENCH
Santiago De Cuba
HAITI
DOMINICAN REPUBLIC
PUERTO RICO TRENCH
PUERTO RICO
SAN JUAN
BASSETERRE
BARBADOS
ANTIGUA & BARBUDA
ST. KITTS & NEVIS
JAMAICA
KINGSTON
PORT-AU -PRINCE
SANTO DOMINGO
Villahermosa
Tuxtla
BELIZE
BELMOPAN
GUADELOUPE
SAINT JOHN'S
BASSE-TERRE
N
HUNTER PUBLISHING
San Pedro
GUATEMALA CITY
SAN SALVADOR
TEGUCIGALPA
NICARAGUA
MANAGUA
Caribbean Sea
DOMINICA
ROSEAU
MARTINIQUE
FORT DE FRANCE
ST. LUCIA
CASTRIES
ST. VINCENT & THE GRANADINES
KINGSTOWN
GRENADA
BRIDGETOWN
SAINT GEORGE'S
SAN JOSE
COSTA RICA
Pacific Ocean
PANAMA
Barranquilla
Cartegena
Maracaibo
Barquisimeto
CARACAS
PORT OF SPAIN
VENEZUELA
TRINIDAD & TOBAGO

over to get from one side to the other. White-sand beaches encircle the tropically rugged landscape.

St. John's 20 square miles is two-thirds Virgin Islands National Park and surprisingly undisturbed despite its 5,000 residents and popularity with tourists. Hiking trails and campgrounds make the park highly accessible, and its pristine beaches and clear water draw all types of water sports enthusiasts.

St. Croix is the largest of the Virgins, with 84 square miles of diverse countryside. Visitors who drive its 28-mile length will pass from the dry, rocky east tip (the easternmost point of the United States) to a lush rain forest in the western mountains. The island has fantastic white-sand beaches, and both diving and deep-sea fishing are excellent in the surrounding Caribbean Sea.

Water Island is the smallest, least developed and most overlooked in the USVI cluster. It was not officially one of the US Virgin Islands until 1996, and many travelers still know nothing about this 492-acre tract that lies just a half-mile south of St. Thomas. Most visitors are day trippers who enjoy biking the deserted roads, hiking over the low hills, exploring abandoned Fort Segarra, and relaxing on one of the secluded white-sand beaches.

BVI

Anegada is a flat 15-square-mile limestone and coral island that is prized for its deserted sandy shores. More than 200 ships have wrecked on the reefs that surround the island, which makes it popular with scuba divers.

Tortola is the largest and hilliest of the BVI. It covers 21 square miles and offers extraordinary beaches on its northern shore and fantastic outlooks from its hilltops. The capital city, Road Town, is a bustling place with a wide assortment of regional and international restaurants and shops. Its sheltered harbor is popular with the international yachting crowd, and visitors often use the island as a base for day trips by ferry to other locations in the Virgin Islands.

The Virgin Islands

ANEGADA

Necker Island

VIRGIN GORDA

Prickly Pear Island

Mosquito Island

The Dogs

Scrub Island

Beef Island

Great Camanoe Island

Guana Island

TORTOLA

Fallen Jerusalem

Ginger Island

Cooper Island

Salt Island

Dead Chest

Peter Island

Norman Island

Sir Francis Drake Channel

Caribbean Sea

Atlantic Ocean

Little Jost Van Dyke

Jost Van Dyke

Great Thatch

ST. JOHN

Great Tobago

Little Tobago

Thatch Cay

Hans Lollick Islands

Brass Islands

ST. THOMAS

Water Island

US VIRGIN ISLANDS | BRITISH VIRGIN ISLANDS

St. Thomas to St. Croix - approx. 40 miles

INSET

ST. CROIX

St. Thomas to St. Croix - approx. 40 miles

10 MILES

10 KM

N

HUNTER PUBLISHING

Virgin Gorda is only seven miles long, but it has one of the most popular geological sites in all the Virgin Islands – **The Baths**. These massive boulders at the southwestern tip of the island form underwater caves and concealed swimming pools which provide infinite adventures for snorkelers. High hills in the north and central parts of the island have been set aside as national parks (Gorda Peak and Little Fork), so much of the island's natural beauty is protected from development.

Jost Van Dyke is a mere four miles in length, but its tall hills make it an impressive sight. Day-trippers

The Baths.

make the four-mile trip from Tortola to enjoy the fabulous white-sand beaches on the south coast.

Norman Island is known for its four caves and is said to be the breathtakingly beautiful setting of Robert Louis Stevenson's *Treasure Island*.

Climate

Year-round sun, balmy trade winds and relatively low rainfall make the Virgin Islands' climate monotonously perfect. Weather patterns are remarkably stable, and when an occasional storm does kick up, it usually moves on to the north before it becomes strong enough to do much damage.

CLIMATE CHART		
MONTH	AVG. TEMP. (°F)	AVG. RAINFALL (inches)
January	77.1	3.34
February	76.9	2.47
March	77.6	2.64
April	78.6	3.70
May	80.2	5.72
June	81.8	3.36
July	82.5	4.29
August	82.4	5.83
September	82.0	6.56
October	81.5	6.27
November	79.9	6.08
December	78.1	4.12
ANNUAL	79.9	54.38

Temperatures range from the 70s at night to the 80s during the day, with rare and brief periods of higher heat on a few summer afternoons. Even during the rainy season, which runs from late summer through autumn, most days are sunny, and only 40 to 50 inches of rain fall each year.

Visitors who enjoy sailing and windsurfing can depend on a steady 15- to 20-knot northeast trade wind during the winter and a slightly weaker southeast breeze during the summer.

Caribbean hurricanes get a lot of press, but the truth is that the Virgin Islands have fewer severe tropical storms than the eastern United States. Those that do blow through develop slowly, so residents and visitors have plenty of time to prepare or evacuate.

Wildlife

Don't expect to see a lot of critters roaming around the Virgin Islands. While there are plenty of insects, birds and fish to see, most of the land-dwelling wildlife is hidden under rocks or plants.

The **white-tailed deer** is the largest mammal found on the islands. This species was brought here late in the 18th century to provide game for hunters, but only a few can now be found. Pesky **wild donkeys** wander the hills on St. John rummaging through picnic supplies, ripping into trash bags and creating havoc for local gardeners. Don't mistake them for tame pets – they bite. **Wild pigs** also present a problem on St. John. While they rarely bother people, they eat the roots of plants and cause environmental damage.

Another annoying animal is the **mongoose**, which can be seen scurrying from place to place. Mongooses were imported from India in the 19th century to devour the burgeoning rat population. The rats had originally arrived as stowaways on European ships and were destroying the sugar cane fields. Since rats are nocturnal and the mongoose hunts for food during the day, the two rarely came into contact. Instead, this squirrel-like predator is responsible for eliminating many of the islands' reptiles and ground-nesting birds.

Several types of **lizards** live on the islands and most locals encourage them to come right indoors, since the little reptiles have an insatiable appe-tite for mosquitoes and other bugs. The most commonly seen is the anole tree lizard, which does a comical push-up routine while inflating a flap in its throat. When they're not working out, they can be recognized by their pointed noses. Geckos are another familiar lizard on the islands. They are distinguished by their long, sticky toes, which they use to scamper up walls and trees.

Juvenile green iguana.

Iguanas, the large prehistoric-looking lizards, have been known to grow up to five feet in length. Unfortunately, they are almost extinct on the islands, but they are sometimes seen sleeping in trees or lumbering about in protected areas. Some resorts and outdoor restaurants encourage them to hang out in garden areas by planting blooming hibiscus trees, the iguanas' favorite treat, and setting out plates of fruit and vegetable scraps for the reptiles.

◆ Marine Life

Ghost crabs never leave the beach. They tunnel into the sand, then dart out of their holes, zip a few feet across the wet beach, then burrow down again and disappear. At night, they emerge to feed, and during a full moon hordes of them can be seen scooting around the beach.

One of the most popular shelled creatures in the Caribbean is the **Conch** (pronounced Konk). Its meat is the key ingredient in many island recipes, and collectors covet the large shells, which have a pearly pink interior and echo the sound of ocean waves. It's not unusual to see islanders cleaning and selling the more perfect shells near busy piers.

Hermit crabs live on land but lay their eggs in water, so during spawning season, hundreds of them dash down the hillsides to become parents on the coast. After the baby crabs hatch, they spend a few months in the

A hermit crab peaks out of its shell.

ocean before trudging onto land, carrying enough water in their shells to sustain themselves for a while. When they grow too big for their backpack homes, they look about for larger dwellings – sometimes killing and eating other hermits so they can steal the shell. If a suitable shell isn't available, they will move into almost any kind of container. Hermit crabs will eat almost any kind of garbage, including sewage.

Sea turtles are fascinating creatures, and several endangered species are protected by law in the Virgin Islands. Females come ashore at night on remote beaches to dig their nests and lay eggs. After burying the eggs with a thin layer of warm sand, the female returns to offshore waters, and the eggs incubate for six to nine weeks, depending upon the type of turtle. The youngsters hatch at night and instinctively turn toward the sea where they live and grow to maturity. A female turtle can take up to 50 years to reach reproductive maturity, at which point she returns to her place of birth to lay eggs.

Leatherbacks, the largest of the sea turtles, are an endangered species. They have a leather-like skin over their backs instead of a shell. The largest leatherback ever recorded measured 10 feet from tip to tail, but the average length is five feet. A mature leatherback weighs upward of 1,000 pounds. Poachers seek out leatherbacks' eggs, thus threatening the dwindling population. In addition, many of them die when they eat discarded plastic bags, which they mistake for jellyfish, their favorite food.

© Thomas Doeppner

A close-up of the hawksbill's unique beak.

Hawksbills, also endangered, have a hawk-like beak and grow to about three feet in diameter and average 130 pounds. They live around warm-water reefs and primarily eat other sea creatures, such as crabs and snails, but also dine on encrusted organisms that they scrape off rocks with their pointed noses.

Green turtles have a rounded head and also grow to be about three feet around, but are usually much heavier than a hawksbill. They prefer to live in the tall grasses that grow on the ocean floor where they graze like cattle. During nesting season, hundreds of them come ashore to lay their eggs in the sand.

From December until May, migrating **whales** move through the water around the Virgin Islands. Lucky passengers sometimes spot the whales on boat trips, and playful **dolphins** are known to swim alongside ferries as they shuttle between the islands.

 See pictures of Caribbean sea creatures in *Marine Life of the Caribbean*, a Caribbean Natural History Series paperback by Alick Jones, or *Guide to Marine Life: Caribbean* by Marty Snyderman.

◆ Birdlife

Dozens of species of tropical birds breed on the islands. The **yellow breast** (*Coereba flaveola*) is the official national bird of the Virgin Islands and visitors recognize it by its bright yellow feathers. Islanders also call the yellow breast the **banana bird** because of its color, or the **sugar bird** because of its love for sweets.

The yellow breast is the national bird of the Virgin Islands.

Many birds migrate to the islands for the winter, and the national parks provide safe nesting grounds for native species. Frigates, pelicans, brown boobies, parakeets and sparrow hawks are year-round residents on most islands. Kingfishers, sandpipers and warblers come for the winter.

Anegada has a 1,100-acre bird sanctuary where flamingos, ospreys, herons and terns find shelter. More than 160 species of birds live on St. John, and birdwatchers enjoy spotting unusual varieties such as the yellow-billed cuckoo and the West Indian whistling duck.

 Serious birders may want to pick up a copy of ***Birds of the West Indies*** by Herbert Raffaele, a Princeton Field Guide paperback.

Plants

Hundreds of species of trees, shrubs, flowers and plants grow on each island. More than 800 different species flourish in the Virgin Islands National Park on St. John.

The indigenous **yellow elder** or **yellow cedar** is the official flower of the US Virgin Islands and it blooms all year long. Most of the islands have flowering **flamboyant** and **frangipani** trees. In the summer, the flamboyant is covered with brilliant red flowers, while the frangipani has white or pink flowers.

Seagrape trees, common on beaches, can grow as tall as 30 feet, and the female bears clusters of fruit that turn purple when they are ripe. These grapes are edible, but most people

Seagrape.

© Hans Hillewaert

prefer them sweetened in jams or desserts. **Coconut palms** also are common on the beaches, and they can grow in sandy areas where few plants survive. Islanders call the immature coconut fruit a **jelly nut,** and enjoy drinking the liquid from the shell before eating the soft meat inside.

Other indigenous trees include the **bay rum,** whose dark-green aromatic leaves produce an oil that once was made into a cologne on St. John; the **kapok**, whose silky fiber is used as filler in life jackets; and the **calabash**, whose fronds make excellent brooms.

Manchineel trees typically grow along the coast, and most are identified by signs or red paint on the trunk.

> **CAUTION:** *The sap and small fruit of the manchineel are poisonous and cause intense stinging if they come in contact with the skin. Illness or death can result from eating the fruit.*

In the forests, **evergreens** grow as high as 75 feet, providing shade for shrubs, vines, ferns, mosses and bromeliads. Drier areas produce turpentine trees, white cedars and a variety of cacti.

The water-rooted **mangrove** trees thrive along the coasts, where they provide shelter for marine animals and birds.

Coral Reefs

A reef is a living community of various organisms and must have sunlight, oxygen and food to survive. The reef itself is a rock-like structure built from coral and algae. Worms, fish and other sea creatures break down and rearrange the growth, creating a more solid base for additional development. Reefs grow slowly, and "branches" of the structure may increase by only three or four inches each year. Large brain corals are

Star coral, Montastrea cavernosa.

often hundreds of years old. Unfortunately, careless swimmers, divers and boaters often cause harm to the easily-damaged reefs through carelessness.

Many animals live on and around a reef, including moray eels, starfish, urchins, crabs, sponges, lobsters and anemones. Coral reefs often draw parrotfish, tangs, snappers, angels and squirrel fish.

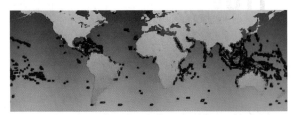

Locations of coral reefs throughout the world.

FACT: *Coral polyps feed at only during the night. They gather food by extending tentacles from their skeletal homes to capture plankton from the water.*

Reefs develop best when water temperatures are between 70 and 80°. Most sand is actually tiny fragments of broken-down coral that are carried to shore by waves, tides and currents. When reefs are prevented from growing and breaking down naturally, there is no new sand, and, therefore, no replenished beaches. Reefs also defend beaches from powerful ocean waves. Coasts that are not protected by reefs are usually rocky and craggy.

TIP: *You can see a natural coral reef without getting wet at Coral World on the north coast of St. Thomas (see page 67).*

 Serious nature lovers will want to order a copy of **Island Peak to Coral Reef** from the University of the Virgin Islands, written by researchers Toni Thomas and Barry Devine. Available at island bookstores and by mail from the university. ☎ (340) 693-1057, pr@uvi.edu.

Travel Information

When to Go

Everyone imagines being on a Caribbean island during the winter when the weather is miserable most everywhere else. While winter is an ideal time to visit the Virgin Islands, summer, spring and fall have advantages, too.

◆ Island Celebrations

Since temperatures remain steadily in the 80s year-round, smart travelers often prefer to come here during the summer off-season, when more bargains are available. The islands celebrate a variety of holidays and events during the April-October off-season. For the exact dates of specific festivals and celebrations, contact the government tourist offices listed in the *Island Facts & Numbers* section at the end of each island chapter.

> **NOTE:** *If a legal holiday falls on a Sunday, the following Monday becomes the official holiday.*

Public Holidays - US Virgin Islands

■ **JANUARY**

1st	New Year's Day
6th	Three King's Day
15th	Martin Luther King's Birthday

▧ FEBRUARY
Third Monday . . . . Presidents' Day

▧ MARCH
31st. . . . . Transfer Day
Celebrates the transfer of island ownership to the US in 1917.

▧ APRIL
March or April . . . . Holy Thursday

March or April . . . . Good Friday

March or April . . . . Easter Monday

▧ MAY
Last Monday . . . . Memorial Day

▧ JUNE
Third Monday . . . . Organic Act Day
Commemorates adoption of the USVI constitution.

▧ JULY
3rd . . . . West Indies Emancipation Day
Emancipation announced in Frederiksted, St. Croix, in 1848.
4th. . . . . Independence Day

Fourth Mon. . . . . Supplication Day
A day of prayer asking that no hurricanes hit the islands.

▧ SEPTEMBER
First Monday. . . . . Labor Day

▧ OCTOBER
Second Monday . . . . Columbus Day &
Puerto Rico Friendship Day
A boat trip is made to Puerto Rico to express friendship.
Third Monday . . . . Local Thanksgiving Day
Celebrates the end of hurricane season.

▧ NOVEMBER
1st. . . . . Liberty Day
Also known as D. Hamilton Jackson Day, a memorial to a St. Croix citizen who contributed greatly to the advancement of fellow VI residents.

11th . . . . Veterans Day

Fourth Thursday. . . . . Thanksgiving Day

▦ **DECEMBER**

25th . . . . Christmas Day

26th . . . . Christmas Second Day

Public Holidays - British Virgin Islands

▦ **JANUARY**

1st. . . . . New Year's Day

▦ **MARCH**

First Monday . . . . H. Lavity Stoutt's Birthday
*Commemorates the memory of the longest serving
Chief Minister of the BVI (three terms, totaling 15
years), who died in 1995.*

Second Monday . . . . Commonwealth Day

▦ **APRIL**

March or April . . . . Holy Thursday

March or April . . . . Good Friday

March or April . . . . Easter Monday

▦ **MAY**

First Monday. . . . . Labor Day

▦ **JUNE**

Late May/early June. . . . . Whit Monday

Second Saturday. . . . . Queen's Birthday

▦ **JULY**

Beginning of July . . . . Territory Day
*Celebrates the day in 1956 when the islands gained
territorial status and the right to administer their government.*

▦ **AUGUST**

First Monday-Wednesday . . . . Carnival

▦ **OCTOBER**

Around 21st. . . . . St. Ursula's Day
*Celebrates the feast day of the Christian saint and her
maids who were killed by the Huns in Germany. Columbus named the islands in their honor.*

■ **NOVEMBER**

1st. . . . . Independence Day
15th. . . . . . . Birthday of heir to the throne of England,
Prince Charles.

■ **DECEMBER**

25th. . . . . Christmas Day
26th. . . . . Boxing Day

Travel Documents

The best advice when traveling outside the continental boundaries of your home country is to carry a valid passport, even if you think you don't need one. Since regulations are subject to change, it's always a good idea to check with the tourist office of the country you'll be visiting for current visa requirements. The toll-free number for the **US Virgin Islands Division of Tourism** is ☎ 800-372-8784. To contact the **British Virgin Islands Tourist Board**, ☎ 800-835-8530. (See *Island Facts & Numbers* for additional contact information.) US citizens can get current information about travel documents on line at www.travel.state.gov (click International Travel). Canadians will find information at www.ppt.gc.ca, and British nationals may obtain passport services at www.ukpa.gov.uk.

◆ Passports & Paperwork

As of December 31, 2006, a passport is required for all US citizens traveling by sea or air to and from the Caribbean, Bermuda, Canada, Mexico, Central America and South America. By December 31, 2007, a valid passport will be required for all sea, air and land crossings into the US. Citizens of other countries should check with their own governmental agencies for passport and visa requirements.

Immigration officials in the Caribbean may ask visitors to present an ongoing ticket off the island and to provide the name of prearranged accommodations, as well as prove that they have adequate money to support themselves during their stay. While all officials do not routinely request such information, it's best to be prepared. Remember that you must carry required documentation when you travel between the USVI and BVI.

> **TIP:** *Make two copies of all documents, tickets, confirmation numbers and other important data before you leave home. Leave one copy with a reliable friend and carry the other separately from the originals.*

Customs & Duty-Free

◆ Allowances

Basic regulations allow citizens of foreign countries to enter the USVI and BVI with 200 cigarettes, 50 cigars, a liter of alcohol and unlimited gifts valued at less than $100 each. Rules vary between the US and British islands, but visitors who stay within these limits will have no problems.

Returning American citizens who have been out of the country for at least 48 hours may claim $1,200 worth of duty-free goods from the USVI every 30 days. This is double the amount of goods allowed back duty-free from other islands covered by the Caribbean Basin Initiative (CBI), of which the BVI are members. If a single vacation includes both the USVI and other islands that are part of the CBI, the duty-free allowance is still $1,200, but only $600 worth of items may come from the CBI countries. In other words, any purchases valued at more than $600 will be dutiable unless you bought them in the USVI.

DUTY-FREE BARGAINS

A duty-free shop is one that has not paid import duties on the merchandise it is selling. This may mean that the merchant will pass the savings on to the consumer, but that's not always the case. Check prices before you leave home so that you'll recognize a bargain when shopping in the islands.

Customs regulations are complex and varied. Citizens of countries other than the US and all travelers who plan to make expensive or unusual purchases should check with the appropriate agency before leaving on vacation.

US Customs . . . . . ☎ 877-CUSTOMS; 202-354-1000

Revenue Canada . . . . ☎ 800-461-9999

HM Customs (UK citizens) . . . . ☎ 0845-0109000

Getting There

Several major airlines have flights to the Virgin Islands, either directly or through another Caribbean island. Since schedules change faster than we can update our books,

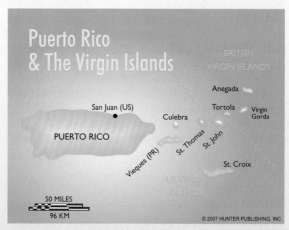

© 2007 HUNTER PUBLISHING, INC

check with an experienced travel agent, your favorite airline or one of our recommended websites for up-to-date information. The following charts provide toll-free telephone numbers and Internet addresses for travel planning. Each island section lists local contact data.

AIRLINE CONTACT INFORMATION	
■ **INTERNATIONAL AIRLINES**	
Air Canada	☎ 888-247-2262 (US, Canada); www.aircanada.ca
American Airlines	☎ 800-474-4884 (Carib), 800-433-7300 www.aa.com
British Airways	☎ 800-247-9297; www.britishairways.com
BWIA (British W. Indies Air)	☎ 800-538-2942; www.bwee.com
Continental Airlines	☎ 800-525-0280; www.continental.com
Delta Air Lines	☎ 800-221-1212; www.delta.com
JetBlue	☎ 800-JETBLUE, 800-538-2583; www.jetblue.com
Northwest Airlines/KLM	☎ 800-225-2525; www.nwa.com
Spirit Airline	☎ 800-772-7117, www.spiritair.com
United Airlines	☎ 800-241-6522; www.united.com
US Airways	☎ 800-622-1015 (Carib), 800-428-4322 (US) www.usairways.com

AIRLINE CONTACT INFORMATION	
■ **REGIONAL AIRLINES**	
Air St. Thomas	☎ 877-776-4315; www.airstthomas.com
Air Sunshine	☎ 800-327-8900; www.airsunshine.com
American Eagle	☎ 800-433-7300; www.aa.com
BWIA	☎ 800-538-2942; www.bwee.com
Cape Air	☎ 800-352-0714; www.flycapeair.com
Caribbean Sun	☎ 866-864-6272 ; www.flycsa.com
Clair Aero	☎ 284-495-2271; www.clairaero.com
Fly BVI	☎ 866-819-3146 (US); 284-495-1747 (local) www.fly-bvi.com
LIAT	☎ 800-780-5733 (US, Canada); 284-495-1187 (local); 00-800-11-20-11-40 (Europe); www.liat.com
Seaborne Aviation	☎ 888-359-8687; www.seaborneairlines.com
WINAIR	☎ 866-466-0410 (US, Canada); www.fly-winair.com

Government regulated airports are located on St. Thomas, St. Croix, Beef Island (Tortola), Virgin Gorda and Anegada. Transportation to St. John and the smaller islands is by private or commercial boat service.

Island Hopping

Jumping from one Virgin Island to another is fun and easy. Airplanes, seaplanes, hydrofoils, ferries and private boats regularly travel among the larger US and British islands, and tour operators offer day-trips to the smaller islands. Many visitors prefer to charter a boat for inter-island jaunts.

The Virgin Islands.

Courtesy NASA/JPL-Caltech

Seaborne Seaplane, ☎ 888-359-8687, www.seaborne airlines.com, is a great way to travel between San Juan, St. Thomas, Tortola and St. Croix. Passengers get a superb aerial view of the islands as they fly low-level from one to another. The seaplane takes off and lands in the harbor, so there is no airport hassle. Round-trip fares are about $100. Ticket kiosks are located at the harbors in Charlotte Amalia on St. Thomas, Christiansted on St. Croix and Road Town on Tortola.

Island Lynx Ferry Company, operated by Southerland Tours and located in the Caravelle Arcade on the waterfront in Christiansted, offers two trips from Gallows Bay, St. Croix to Charlotte Amalie, St. Thomas on Monday, Wednesday,

Thursday and Friday at 7 am and 4 pm. The ferry makes a reverse trip from St. Thomas to St. Croix at 9:30 am and 6:30 pm. On Saturdays and Sundays, all trips leave the dock one hour later: St. Croix at 8 am and 5 pm; St.Thomas at 10:30 am and 7:30 pm. The 90-minute trip costs $44 one-way or $78 round-trip for adults and $39 one way or $68 round trip for children ages two-11. A day trip from St. Croix to St. Thomas, including ferry tickets and a three-hour land tour of St. Thomas, is $138 per person. Confirm departure times and buy tickets in advance, ☎ 800-260-2603 or 340-773-9500, www.southerlandtours.com/islandlynx/.

Caribbean Maritime Excursion operates the **British Virgin Islands Fast Ferry** between Charlotte Amalie and both West End and Road Town on Tortola. The trip takes about an hour. Round-trip fares are $40 for adults and $22 for kids. ☎ 866-903-3779 (toll free), 340-777-2800 (St. Thomas), 284-494-2323 (Tortola).

Dohm's Catamaran powerboats run from Red Hook on St. Thomas to St. John, St. Croix or any of the British Virgin Islands. Make reservations at ☎ 340-775-6501, www.watertaxi-vi.com.

Ferries travel between several points in the archipelago. Schedules change seasonally, but frequent service is provided year-round between both Red Hook and Charlotte Amalie on St. Thomas to both West End and Road Town on Tortola as well as to Cruz Bay on St. John. Additional ferry service includes:

- Passenger ferry from Crown Bay (Charlotte Amalie) to Phillip's Landing (Water Island).
- Car and passenger-only ferries between Red Hook on St. Thomas and Cruz Bay on St. John.
- Passenger ferries between Christiansted on St. Croix and Charlotte Amalie on St. Thomas.
- Passenger ferries from Tortola to Jost Van Dyke, Cooper Island, Virgin Gorda and Peter Island.
- Passenger ferries from St. Thomas to Tortola.

NOTE: *Visitors must clear Customs each time they travel between the USVI and the BVI. See Passports & Paperwork, page 24, for information on documentation.*

Schedules and information are available at harborside kiosks; tickets may be purchased just before departure. Additional inter-island travel details are given in each island section of this guide. See *Regional Airline Contact Information* on previous page for inter-island air service.

FERRY SERVICE	
Native Son, Inc.	☎ 340-774-8685; www.nativesonbvi.com
Smith's Ferry	☎ 340-775-7292
Inter-Island Ferries	☎ 340-776-6597
Transportation Services	☎ 340-776-6282
Boyson, Inc. (car ferry)	☎ 340-776-6294; www.smithsferry.com
Island Lynx Ferry Co	☎ 340-773-9500 www.southerlandtours.com/islandlynx/
Varlack Ventures	☎ 340-776-6412; www.varlackventures.com
Republic Barge (car ferry)	☎ 340-779-4000; www.captvicvi.com
Speedy's	☎ 284-495-5240; www.speedysbvi.com

Getting Around

◆ By Car

Rental cars offer the most freedom and flexibility for getting around. Several companies operate on all the major islands, and each chapter gives details on renting all types of transportation – cars, bikes, motorcycles.

However, consider the following before you opt to rent a vehicle here:

- ❖ Driving is UK-style, on the left side of the road.
- ❖ Rental cars have US-style right-hand drive, with the steering wheel on the left.

- Traffic can be heavy in the towns.
- Locals are known to turn without signaling and to stop without warning to greet friends.
- The one-way street system in Charlotte Amalie can be confusing.
- Roads often are narrow and winding, especially in the countryside.
- Many locals drive without insurance.

On the positive side, a valid driver's license from the US, Canada or the UK is good in the USVI for 90 days. On the British islands, you must purchase a temporary permit from the rental-car agency for $10. Most roads on all the islands are paved and in fair to good condition.

Island Driving Signals

- Two quick beeps of the horn mean: *thanks*; *hi*; *go ahead*; *I'm passing*; or *watch out, I'm just around the curve.*
- A flash of the headlights means: *go ahead, I'll wait.*
- One long blast of the horn means: *get out of the way*; *hurry up*; *don't drive like a tourist.*

◆ By Taxi

The Virgin Islands Taxi Commission sets standard rates for point-to-point trips on the US islands. However, taxis are not metered, so visitors should ask about rates before they get into the vehicle. Charges vary with the number of passengers, and drivers add additional fees for luggage and trips between midnight and six am.

> **TIP:** *If you have questions or problems concerning taxi service or a specific cab driver, contact the **Taxi Commission** weekdays from 8 am to 5 pm at ☎ 340-776-8294.*

TRAVEL INFORMATION

On the British islands, Tortola and Virgin Gorda have several taxi operators. The smaller islands have less dependable service. See each island chapter for specifics.

◆ By Bus

Limited public bus service is available on St. Thomas and St. Croix. While the routes aren't structured for tourist travel, you can easily get to several major destinations.

On St. Thomas, air-conditioned VITRAN buses run regular routes from the airport to Charlotte Amalie about every 45 minutes from 6 am until 9:30 pm. These city buses also provide service in the downtown area and to the shopping center at Tutu Mall. The charge is 75¢. The country buses ($1) travel round-trip from Charlotte Amalie to Red Hook on the east coast and Bordeaux on the west coast between 5:30 am and 8:30 pm.

On St. Croix, VITRAN buses mostly stick to the residential areas, but visitors can travel between the major towns of Christiansted and Frederiksted for $1 per trip. For schedules and information, contact **VITRAN**, ☎ 774-5678 (on St. Thomas); ☎ 773-1290 (St. Croix).

See "Getting Around" in each island's chapter for taxi and car rental companies, sample rates and contact information.

Accommodations

The larger US and British Virgin Islands offer a number of lodging choices from camping to all-inclusive luxury resorts. Many options are detailed in the *Where to Stay* section of each island, but a few generalities apply:

> ◆ Most hotels discount rooms from mid-April through mid-December, with the lowest rates available during the summer months.

- Small establishments may close annually during off-peak months, and larger hotels often schedule renovations at that time.
- New resorts frequently run tempting specials to bring in guests.
- Government taxes and service charges will be added to quoted prices unless specifically stated otherwise.

Dining

People eat well in the Virgin Islands. The land and sea produce a bounty of fresh foods that are flavored with island spices and cooked with West Indian flair. Fast-food restaurants supply plenty of burgers and fried chicken on some islands. Near-perfect weather makes it possible for restaurants to offer open-air seating, and many sit right on the water. Unusual island specialties include:

- **fungi** (pronounced foon-GEE), a seasoned cornmeal-and-okra dumpling
- **kallaloo** or callaloo, soup made with a vegetable similar to spinach
- **gunga**, a type of pea that is often mixed with rice
- **souse**, a lime-flavored stew made with the head, tail and feet of a pig
- **maubi**, a drink made from tree bark and ginger root

More recognizable island dishes include curried goat, fresh fish cooked a multitude of ways, johnnycakes (fried bread dough) and sweet potato pie. Many hotel restaurants serve a West Indian buffet once a week with live entertainment. This is an excellent opportunity to sample several unfamiliar dishes at one meal.

Most restaurants in large towns accept major credit cards, but local cafés may not. On smaller islands and in the countryside, expect to pay cash. The *Where to Eat* section of each island chapter suggests the best eateries in a variety of price ranges and a selection of specialties.

Money Matters

The US dollar is the official currency on all the US and British Virgin Islands. ATMs are conveniently located at banks and in tourist areas throughout the islands. Most large hotels, shops and restaurants on the main islands accept major credit cards. However, most gas stations require cash, and credit cards will not be taken on many of the smaller islands.

Time

All the Virgin Islands are on Atlantic Standard Time, which is four hours earlier than Greenwich Mean Time and one hour later than Eastern Standard Time. The islands do not observe daylight savings time.

Taxes

The British Virgin Islands charge a $20 departure tax for visitors leaving by air and a $5 departure tax for those leaving by sea. A $5 departure tax is included in airline ticket prices to the US Virgin Islands, and no additional tax is charged for departure by sea.

Hotels add a 7% tax to rooms in the BVI and an 8% tax to rooms in the USVI. In addition, a 10% service charge is added to BVI room rates, and USVI hotels may add a 10% energy charge.

The US Virgin Islands

It's easy to love the US Virgin Islands. **St. Thomas**, **St. John** and **St. Croix** have all the amenities and indulgences you'd expect to find in a tropical paradise, plus a breathtaking Caribbean setting and just enough "foreign" quirks to convince you that you've left the mainland.

Menus are written in English, but the choices are exotically West Indian. Traffic travels on the left side of the road, but cars have state-side-designed steering. Mocko jumbies march in the Fourth of July parades, and you'll pay US dollars for locally made Africa-inspired art sold from an 18th-century Danish warehouse.

Together, the 60 or so islands and cays in the USVI offer something for every type of vacationer. The small outer islets are mostly uninhabited and appeal to day-trippers in search of lazy hours under a palm tree on a secluded beach. Each of the main islands have enough differences to make them interesting destinations on their own. **St. John** lures nature lovers, **St. Thomas** draws high-energy shoppers and doers, and **St. Croix** attracts those who relish a bit more history and architecture with their sun and fun.

St. Thomas and St. John are separated by a two-mile gap of water called **Pillsbury Sound.** Most of the other volcanic islets and cays that make up the unincorporated US territory are clustered nearby, and the British Virgin Islands begin just

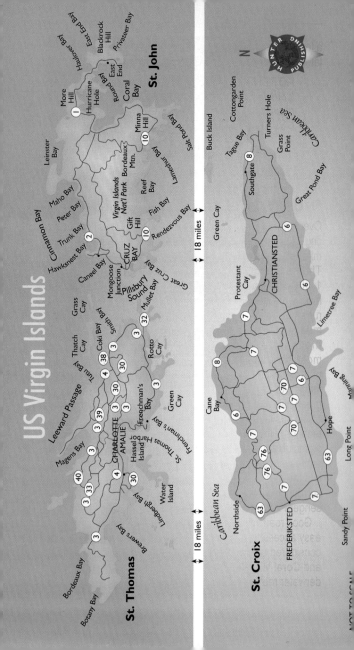

a few miles to the east. St. Croix, the largest US Virgin, is isolated 40 miles to the south.

> **NOTE:** *The area code for all of the US Virgin Islands is 340. Use it the same way you would a regular state-side area code. You can dial the USVI direct from the States.*

St. Thomas

◆ Overview

Over forty beaches ring the 32-square-mile island of St. Thomas, and a 1,500-foot-high mountain ridge runs down its 13-mile length. Although it's the most developed of the Virgin Islands, you're never far from pristine white sand, spacious green hills and endless turquoise-blue water.

Magen's Bay is one of the prettiest beaches in the island chain.

The bustling capital of **Charlotte Amalie** (ah-MAHL-yah) is teeming with duty-free shops, upscale restaurants, trendy nightclubs and lovely old Danish buildings with graceful arches and shaded courtyards. A gondola transports visitors into the hills above the city for killer views of the harbor and surrounding countryside, and the *Reefer* ferry whisks passengers from town to nearby **Morningstar Beach**.

Good roads circle the island and cut across interior hills for easy access to major sites such as glorious **Magen's Bay**, considered one of the most beautiful beaches in the world, and **Coral World** at **Coki Point**, where visitors view an underwater reef without getting wet.

ST THOMAS

Outside the capital, St. Thomas is relatively peaceful, but homes and businesses spread in every direction. Only the rugged western end remains primarily undeveloped. Most of the luxury resorts and large hotels are located along the eastern coast, and many of the best restaurants and bars are found at **Red Hook** and **Frenchtown**, a neighborhood on Charlotte Amalie's west end.

The northern side of St. Thomas is wetter and greener, with giant ferns growing up under tall banana trees and flowering poincianas. On the drier south side, bougainvillea and hibiscus bushes produce colorful blooms, and succulents such as aloe grow up the hillsides. Beautiful beaches, some with facilities and watersport rentals, are found on almost every stretch of coastline.

One of Charlotte Amalie's pretty streets.

Remnants of Denmark's 200-year rule are visible all over the island. Streets have names such as Droningens Gade and Kongens Gade. Houses and churches retain their colorful architecture. **Fort Christian** still stands beside the harbor. **Bluebeard's Castle** and **Blackbeard's Castle** are nestled into the hills above the capital.

The auction blocks at **Market Square**, where slaves were once sold, have been turned into stalls for selling local produce and spices. Outside the city, **Drake's Seat**, said to be a lookout point for the famous seaman, Sir Frances Drake, is the perfect spot for viewing Magens Bay.

Opposite: View of Charlotte Amalie

ST THOMAS

◆ Getting There

By Air

Several international carriers fly directly from major US airports to modern Cyril E. King International Airport, ☎ 340-774-5100, three miles west of the capital of Charlotte Amalie on St. Thomas. The Caribbean islands of Puerto Rico and St. Martin serve as hubs for flights connecting from North and South America and Europe. Regional carriers provide service within the Caribbean.

Tourist information kiosks are located near the baggage claim and car rental area at the airport. Taxis, ranging from subcompacts to open-air buses, meet all flights and fares to hotels are regulated. Expect to pay about $6 per person to locations near Charlotte Amalie and $9 per person to East End hotels. An additional 75 cents is charged for each piece of luggage. If you prefer the bus, **VITRAN,** ☎ 340-774-5678, picks up about every 20 minutes from the posted stop outside the terminal. Be sure to have the exact 75-cent fare, because drivers often don't have change.

For contact details of local and regional airlines servicing Charlotte Amalie, see page 27.

By Seaplane & Fast Ferry

Seaborne Aviation ☆ (☎ 888-359-8687 or 340-773-6442; www.seaborne airlines.com) offers frequent seaplane flights from the harbor at Old San Juan (Puerto Rico), Charlotte Amalie (St. Thomas) and Christiansted (St. Croix). From the British Virgin Islands, Seaborne flies from the ferry terminal in Road Town and West End (Tortola) to Charlotte Amalie.

Native Son (☎ 340-774-8685) and **Smith's Ferry** (☎ 340-775-7292) will take you from Road Town or West End (Tortola) to the harbor in Charlotte Amalie in just under an hour for about $40 round trip.

Island Lynx Ferry Company (☎ 800-260-2603 or 340-773-9500, www.southerlandtours.com/islandlynx/), located in Christiansted, offers two trips from Gallows Bay, St. Croix to Charlotte Amalie on Monday, Wednesday, Thursday and Friday. See page 28 for details. The 90-minute trip costs $44 one-way or $78 round-trip for adults and $39 one way or $68 round-trip for

Christiansted's waterfront.

children ages two-11. A day trip from St. Croix to St. Thomas, including ferry tickets and a three-hour land tour of St. Thomas, is $138 per person.

By Cruise Ship

More cruise ships stop in St. Thomas than any other island in the Caribbean. It's not unusual to see five large ships in the Charlotte Amalie harbor at one time, which explains why the little town is sometimes described as overcrowded. Smaller ships can dock right at King's Wharf's Crown Bay Marina on the city's western waterfront. The Virgin Islands Port Authority is currently overseeing a multi-million dollar project to build a second passenger-friendly port at **Subbase** on the city's west side to increase capacity and accommodate some of the largest cruise vessels in the Caribbean. When it is completed (the schedule calls for all work to be completed in time for the 2007-2008 tourist season), a new waterfront promenade will include restaurants, coffeehouses and fast-food eateries. Shops will feature brand-name clothing, designer jewelry and duty-free liquor, cosmetics and art.

Most ships still pull into the **West Indian Dock** (shown above) at Havensight on the capital's east side. Here, passengers are within easy strolling distance of 100 shops at Havensight Mall. A shuttle bus makes continuous loops through the shady streets to transport shoppers and their

A cruise ship tows over Charlotte Amalie's streets.

bags from point to point. While many cruisers find everything they want right at the dockside shops, some opt for a brisk walk or quick taxi ride into the center of town. Others rent a car from Budget, located in the Havensight Mall, or take a guided tour of the island by taxi or hop over to a neighboring island on a motorboat or catamaran.

Taxis and minibuses continuously travel to and from both ports when ships are docked, and the quick ride into town costs $3.50-$4 per person. Private guides offer two-hour island tours for $40 per person for one or two passengers; groups of three or more pay $20 per person. Trips to single sites around the island range from $7 to $15, and drivers carry a copy of regulated fares.

> **TIP:** *While some price negotiation is worthwhile if you're using a taxi guide, it's more important to ask about the guide's experience and knowledge of island history (or whatever your field of interest is). Personality should also be taken into consideration before you climb into the car.*

◆ Getting Around

By Car

If you're going to be on the island for more than a few days, consider renting a car. It's possible to get around by taxi and, to a limited extent, by public bus, but a car allows you the freedom to go anywhere at any time. A valid driver's license from home is all you need.

> **TIP:** *Remember, islanders drive on the left and are usually aggressive, with little regard for space constraints on the narrow roads. Most visitors from right-hand-drive countries quickly adapt.*

National and local companies rent compact cars for around $50 per day or $235 per week. Jeeps run about $65 per day. Check with your travel agent, airline and hotel about special package deals. Most major rental companies have pick-up facilities at the airport as well as at offices around the island. Some will arrange to meet you at the cruise-ship pier or your hotel, but during peak demand periods, service is known to be unreliable. The following are recommended as dependable choices.

TIP: *Be aware that some car rental agencies require customers to sign a contract stating they will not take their car off St. Thomas. If you plan to do so, check around for an agency that allows it.*

RENTAL CAR AGENCIES	
Avis	☎ 800-230-4898 or 774-1468; www.avis.com
Budget ☆	☎ 800-626-4516, 776-5774; www.budgetstt.com
Dependable	☎ 800-522-3076, 774-2253 www.dependablecar.com
Discount	☎ 877-478-2833, 776-4858; www.discountcar.vi

TIP: *Look for a bargain rate from **St. Thomas Car Rental Guide**, ☎ 877-282-2574, www.stjohn.rentalcargroup.com. They display rates from major companies on St. Thomas, often at a discount.*

By Taxi

Multi-destination taxi vans wait for passengers outside the airport terminal. If you prefer a private taxi, make arrangements in advance or call one of the services listed below as soon as you land. Taxi, minibus and open-air jitney service is available at the ship docks. Rates are regulated and based on destination, rather than distance. Drivers usually carry a copy of point-to-point rate sheets, and you should confirm the price before you enter the cab or bus.

TIP: *A few drivers may try to charge the single-person rate for each passenger, but the Commission sets lower charges for additional passengers traveling to the same destination. Be sure to ask for the better rate.*

It's common practice for a driver to fill his vehicle before leaving, so look for one that's almost full to avoid a wait. Even at hotels this practice is common. Occupy the time chatting with the driver. Chances are, you'll pick up some good tips or learn about a new entertainment spot.

Ride only in taxis with an official Taxi Association sign (usually displayed on the roof) and the letters *TP* on their license plate. Other cabs are not official and do not abide by the Taxi Commission guidelines and rates.

You may call for a private cab to pick you up anywhere on the island. The dispatcher will give you the license number of the cab being sent for you, so there will be no mix-up about the arrangements. It's always a good idea to jot down the number so you can report lost items or unprofessional service to the Taxi Commission ☎ 340-776-8294.

Accessible Travel is available for tourists and locals with disabilities. ☎ DIAL-A-RIDE to arrange transportation or tours, ☎ 340-776-1277, Monday-Friday, 7 am-6 pm.

TAXI COMPANIES	
East End	☎ 888-484-TAXI (888-484-8294), 340-775-6974
VI Radio Dispatch	☎ 340-774-7457
VI Taxi Association	☎ 340-774-4550
24-Hour Dispatch	☎ 340-776-0496

By Bus

Air-conditioned (☎ 340-774-5678) **VITRAN** buses travel the streets of Charlotte Amalie and connect the town with the airport, Red Hook and Bordeaux. In-town buses run from 6:15 am to 10:15 pm and charge 75¢ per passenger. Country buses run from 5:15 am to 8 pm and charge $1 per passenger. Carry the exact fare, since many drivers don't carry or won't give change.

By Ferry

A 26-passenger ferry known as *The Reefer* runs from the waterfront in Charlotte Amalie, across from the Rolex shop, to Marriott's Frenchman's Reef hotel on Morningstar Beach between 8:30 am and 5 pm, Monday through Saturday. The fare is $5 each way for adults, $3 for kids. During the week, the ferry leaves from town every hour on the hour; from the

Marriott on the half-hour. On Sundays, service is from 9 am until 4:30 pm and the schedule reverses, with the ferry departing from the hotel on the hour and from Charlotte Amalie on the half-hour. Call to confirm the schedule, ☎ 340-776-8500, ext. 6814.

It's also possible to go by ferry from Charlotte Amalie to Water Island, St. Croix, St. John and Tortola, in the British Virgin Islands. You'll find current schedules posted on the ferry dock and in the free weekly publication St. Thomas This Week. **Seaborne Aviation** ☆ offers a faster alternative: 18-passenger seaplane service to and from Charlotte Amalie's harbor and the main towns on St. Croix, Tortola and Puerto Rico. Make reservations by phone or online, ☎ 888-359-8687 or 340-773-6442, www.seaborneairlines.com.

> **TIP:** *You must have a passport to enter and return from Tortola in the British Virgin Islands.*

The **Water Island Ferry** operates frequent service Monday through Saturday between Crown Bay (west Charlotte Amalie) and Phillip's Landing (Water Island) from 6:30 am until 6 pm. Sundays and holidays, the ferry makes three round trips at 8 am, noon and 5 pm. On most Friday and Saturday nights, you can go over or return on the late ferry, which makes one round trip around 9 pm. Adult tickets for daytime trips are $5 one-way or $9 round trip, and children pay $3 one-way or $5 round trip. Tickets for the night ferry are $10 per person each way. ☎ 340-690-4159, 340-690-4446, 340-775-5770.

© VINow.com

Ferry arriving at Water Island.

The east-end town of Red Hook is separated from Cruz Bay, St. John by only three miles of water. Ferries travel back and forth daily, leaving Red Hook at 6:30 am and 7:30 am, then hourly from 8 am until midnight. Return boats leave Cruz Bay every hour from 6 am until 11 pm. The trip takes only 20 minutes, and the one-way fare is $5 for adults, $1 for children under 12, $1.25 for people over age 65.

> **NOTE:** *The marine terminal at Red Hook was undergoing major renovations at press time. When it is finished, the $8 million project will include an 8,000-square-foot passenger area with ticket counters, concession booths and restrooms. More than a hundred additional spaces are being added to the parking lot, and the ferry dock is being expanded to accommodate up to four vessels at the same time. A separate dock is being constructed east of the passenger terminal for cargo vessels. During construction, park in the lot west of Ivanna E Kean High School, across from the National Park Dock.*

Some ferry service is seasonal. Always call or check current island publications for up-to-date times and fares.

Ferry service is also available from Red Hook to Tortola, Jost Van Dyke, and Virgin Gorda in the British Virgin Islands. Ticket kiosks are set up at the harbor in Red Hook, and everyone must have a passport to enter and return from the British Virgin Islands.

Dohm's Water Taxi ☆ provides on-demand ferry service point-to-point within the US and British Virgin Islands. You specify the dock and pick-up time. You also can charter one of the three motor-powered catamarans for a private party, wedding, or a day of island hopping. Call for rate information and reservations, ☎ 340-775-6501, www.watertaxi-vi.com.

One of Dohm's boats.

ST THOMAS

FERRY SERVICE	
SERVICE	OPERATORS
Charlotte Amalie, St. Thomas - Christiansted, St. Croix *$68 round-trip; 1hr 30 min*	**Island Lynx Ferry Co** ☎ 340-773-9500 or 800-260-2603 www.southerlandtours.com/islandlynx
Red Hook - Cruz Bay *Passenger ferries,* *$7 round-trip ; 20 min* *Car ferries,* *$40 round-trip; 25 min*	*Passenger ferries* **Transportation Services** ☎ 340-776-6282 **Varlack Ventures** ☎ 340-776-6412 *Car ferries* **Republic Barge Service,** ☎ 340-779-4000 **Boyson,** ☎ 340-776-6294 **Roanoke,** ☎ 340-779-1739
Charlotte Amalie-Water Island *$9 round-trip; 15 min*	**Water Island Ferry,** ☎ 340-690-4159/4446 or 775-5770
Red Hook-West End, Tortola *$40 round-trip, 30-45 min*	*Native Son* (see below) **Smith's Ferry** (see below)
Red Hook-Virgin Gorda via Cruz Bay *$50 round-trip; 1hr 15 min*	**Inter Island Boat Service** (Tues and Sun), ☎ 340-776-6597
Red Hook-Virgin Gorda via Road Town *$50 round-trip; 1hr 30 min*	**Speedy's** (Tues, Thurs, Sat only) ☎ 284-495-5240, 284-495-5235; www.speedysbvi.com
Charlotte Amalie-West End & Road Town, Tortola *$40 round-trip; 45 min to/from West End, 1hr 30 min to/from Road Town*	*Native Son*, ☎ 340-775-3111, www.nativesonbvi.com **Smith's Ferry,** ☎ 340-775-7292, www.smithsferry.com **British Virgin Island Fast Ferry** *$40 round-trip, 50-60min (to/from Road Town only)*, ☎ 866-903-3779 (toll free), 340-777-2800 (St. Thomas), 284-494-2323 (Tortola), www.tortolafastferry.com
Red Hook-Jost Van Dyke via Cruz Bay *$40 round-trip; 45 min*	**Inter Island Boat Service** (Fri, Sat, Sun), ☎ 340-776-6597
Cruz Bay-West End, Tortola *$35 round-trip; 30 min*	**Inter Island Boat Service** (above)

◆ Touring the Island

Guided Tours

First-time visitors will want to take a guided tour of St. Thomas. Once you've had an overview of the island, head back to your favorite spots to spend more time. Your hotel or cruise ship can arrange everything for you, or call one of the companies listed below.

The Virgin Island Taxi Association runs **Tours and Travel, Inc.**, a company that offers a two-hour trip through Charlotte Amalie and around the island with stops at scenic overlooks. Expect to pay about $29 per person for a two-hour tour private tour, ☎ 340-774-4550, www.vitaxi.com.

As the name suggests, **Air Force 1 Fun** is a jovial group of knowledgeable guides. They offer sightseeing tours, beach outings and shopping jaunts in a bright red, open-air bus that holds up to 20 passengers. Plan on paying $25 per person for a combination sightseeing-beach bumming four-hour outing. Add a two-hour shopping trip for about $5 per person more. Check the website or call to schedule the combination tour of your choice, ☎ 800-501-0122 or 340-774-8342, www. havefunwithus.com.

Hamblet's Island Paradise Taxi and Tour Service does double duty as both a taxi company and a tour agency. Since their rates are regulated by the taxi commission, you'll pay standard rates for airport transfers and point-to-point transportation. Two-hour island tours make stops at major historical sites and scenic overlooks; cost is $20 per person based on a group of four. Add a stop at the beach or include a little shopping for an extra $5 per person per stop; join a tour, beach and shopping group for $35 per

A Hamblet's bus.

ST THOMAS

person . See St. John and snorkel at Trunk Bay during an eight-hour tour priced at $75 per person. Expect to pay a bit more if you prefer a private tour with fewer than four people. Make reservations well in advance, ☎ 340-513-8535, 340-777-4530, www.hambletsislandparadise.com.

On **Tropic Tours'** half-day, $30 per-person shopping-and-sightseeing tour, you'll visit Estate St. Peter Greathouse and Botanical Gardens, Mountain Top and Drake's Seat. Afterwards, the bus stops at Havensight Mall, near the cruise-ship dock in Charlotte Amalie, where you'll be turned loose for some duty-free shopping. This is an okay trip, especially if you don't have a car. Make reservations a day or two in advance for either tour by calling the Tropic Tours office, ☎ 800-524-4334 or 340-774-1855, www.tropictours-virginislands. com.

VI Scenic Tours runs a similar, but somewhat more personal, tour. Islander Burlie Simeine enjoys showing off her little piece of paradise to visitors. She starts with shopping and ends at the beach of your choice. A long tour runs $25 per person. ☎ 340-777-5077, www.viscenictours.com.

Members of the **St. Thomas Historical Trust** lead walking tours of some of the island's key historic and architectural sights in and around Charlotte Amalie. Guides are remarkably knowledgeable and enjoy sharing their stories about the island's past while leading you from Blackbeard's Tower to Haagensen House, then down the hill past Hotel 1829 to Emancipation Garden. If you want to stroll this route on your own, pick up a copy of the Trust's self-guided tour (about $2), available at most souvenir shops in town. Get more information or make reservations by calling the Historical Trust, ☎ 340-776-2726.

You don't need reservations to join **Cindy Born** for a walking tour of the town's historic sites. Simply show up at the entrance to Fort Christian at 9:30 am Monday through Friday. Cindy is an energetic walker and knowledgeable guide, so wear comfortable shoes and be prepared to spend about 2½ hours trekking though the streets and alleys. Cost is $20 per adult, $15 for students, and kids under 15 can come along free with a paying parent. If three or more sign up in advance, Cindy will lead the same tour again at 12:30 weekdays or on Saturday mornings, ☎ 340-714-1672.

Self-Guided Tours

A WALKING TOUR OF CHARLOTTE AMALIE

> **TIP:** *To sound like a local, say "ah-MAHL-yah."*

The capital of St. Thomas and the US Virgin Islands is best seen on foot. You can spend all day and most of the night sightseeing, shopping, dining and bar-hopping without driving or hailing a cab. If you become tired or overloaded with purchases, hop in a cab or open-air jitney bus. The town is listed in the National Register of Historic Places because of its 300-year history and thick-walled Danish architecture.

CITY TRIVIA

Charlotte Amalie is the capital of the US Virgin Islands and home to one of the Caribbean's best and busiest harbors. The town was founded as a Danish colony in 1672 and, 20 years later, was named for the Queen of Denmark, the wife of King Christian the Fifth.

> **NOTE:** *The following sites and attractions are recommended. Those with one star (☆) are worthy of a detour, and you should consider allowing extra time for those marked with two stars (☆☆).*

Begin your walking tour at **Fort Christian** ☆. The red brick structure, which was named for Denmark's King Christian V, sits near the waterfront on the east end of town, across from the Vendors' Plaza on Veterans Highway (Waterfront Drive). If you have a car, park in the large public lot on the east side of the fort off Fortet Strade. Parking fees run 50¢ per hour or $4 per day from 6 am to 6 pm weekdays. On weekends and evenings, parking is free.

Fort Christian was constructed between 1666 and 1671 by Danish settlers and is the oldest building still in use in the Virgin Islands. The structure was intended to defend the harbor, but in the early years, it also served as the seat of government, a meeting hall and a church. Later, it became a jail, and today the dungeon houses **The Virgin Islands Museum**.

Fort Christian is the oldest standing structure in the Virgin Islands.

Each room in the museum focuses on a period of the islands' history and various displays depict the region's culture, plants, wildlife and art. A gift shop, located in an area that once served as the police station, sells books, maps and souvenirs. The museum is open 8:30 am to 4:30 pm Monday through Friday. Admission is free, but donations are appreciated. ☎ 340-776-4566.

It's impossible to miss the bright green **Legislative Building** with the red roof southeast of the fort on Veterans Highway (Waterfront). The Virgin Islands Senate conducts sessions in the upstairs chamber. Those interested in the territory's politics are invited to sit in. Danish colonists built the two-story structure in Italian Renaissance style around 1874 to house the police force. After the US bought the islands in 1917, the Marine Corps moved in and the building was later used as a school. Open to the public weekdays from 8 am until 5 pm, ☎ 340-774-0880.

Now a shopping arcade known as **Grand Galleria**, the buildings were formerly the prestigious Grand Hotel, which was built in 1839, opened in May 1940, and closed as a hotel more than 30 years ago. The original courtyard now provides outdoor seating for several restaurants. The central building, which faces Main, has a sunlit atrium. A gallery in the second floor overlooks Emancipation Gardens and the harbor.

The oldest church on the island is located north of Emancipation Garden, across from the Galleria, at 7 Norre Gade (Main Street). Lutheran is the official religion of Denmark, and **Frederick Lutheran Church** was built in the Gothic Revival style in 1820 to replace the church's original sanctuary that burned. A massive altar made of local mahogany dominates the interior of the brick structure. The church's treasures include a gold-plated silver chalice that was given to the congregation by Danish royalty in 1713. Services are held at 8 am and 10:30 am each Sunday, but the church doors are open Monday through Saturday from 8 am until 5 pm, ☎ 340-776-1315.

Continue your walking tour by heading north toward **Government Hill** and the famous **99 Steps** ☆. Steep stairs are built into the hillsides all over town to connect parallel streets, but this set leading up from Kongens Gade (King Street) is the most renowned.

> **FACT:** *99 Steps has 103 steps. No one seems to know why they are known by a lesser number, but you won't care once you are climbing!*

Several interesting sites are located on Government Hill near the 99 Steps. At the bottom, to your left as you face the stairs, take the time to admire the Spanish-style iron work and coral-colored walls of **Hotel 1829**, which was built as a town home by a Frenchman named Lavalette in, of course, 1829. ☎ 340-776-1829.

Government House is on the east side of the 99 Steps, to your right as you face the stairs. It's an elegant three-story structure built between 1865 and 1867, which now serves as offices for the governor of the US Virgin Islands. The ground

ST THOMAS

floor is open to visitors and features local mahogany stair-cases and various historical paintings. If you wish to see the reception rooms on the second floor, call ahead for an ap-pointment or locate one of the officials and ask for a tour after you arrive. Upstairs, you'll see a lovely ballroom, some small paintings by Camille Pissarro (who was born on St. Thomas in 1830) and a gorgeous view of the harbor from the terrace. Gov-ernment House is open free of charge Monday through Friday, 8 am to noon and 1 pm to 5 pm, ☎ 340-774-0001.

Government House.

At the top of the 99 Steps you'll see a green gate that opens into the courtyard of **Haagensen House,** an early 19th-cen-tury mansion that recently has been restored by the owners of Hotel 1829. Inside, the furniture and decorations look as they did when the 11-member family of Danish banker Hans Haagensen lived there. His wife, Sarah Julia Magens, was a relative of the Magens whose plantation was located on the now famous Magens Bay Beach. The house features ele-ments of the Greek revival style and has a marble-tile stair-case on the outside to connect the two floors. Five exhibit rooms, managed by the St.Thomas Historical Trust, display West Indian antiques, which will give you an idea of how well the island's merchant class lived during the pre-emancipa-tion days of the 1800s. A detached kitchen sits behind the main house and labeled Caribbean plants grow in the ter-raced garden. The garden gift shop stocks souvenirs, rum and cigars, and an antique print gallery offers maps and pho-tos. Open daily 9 am to 1 pm, admission to the house is $8 for adults and $4 for children and senior citizens, ☎ 340-774-5541.

Opposite: 99 Steps.

Haagensen House sits on a hill dominated by **Fort Skytsborg** ☆, better known as **Blackbeard's Tower.** The five-story tower was built in 1678 (well before any other structure still standing on the island) of native volcanic stone

called blue bitch. Listed on the National Register of Historic Places, the tower is said to have been used as a lookout by Edward Teach, the infamous pirate known as Blackbeard. Today, a small hotel called The Inn at Blackbeard's Castle surrounds the tower and a restaurant offers diners gourmet meals and dazzling views of the town and harbor. ☎ 340-776-1234.

18th-century lithograph of Edward Teach, Blackbeard.

If you have time to see yet another piece of Danish history and architecture, go back down to Kongens Gade (King Street) and turn east. A short distance past Government House you'll find an odd little place called **Seven Arches Museum** on a narrow alleyway behind the Lieutenant Governor's office. You must ring the bell on the iron gate for admission; the couple (Philibert Fluck and Barbara Demaras) who restored and run the museum live on the first floor of this 19th-century home. When you enter the house, built of ballast bricks from Denmark, you will see a fine collection of antique mahogany furniture. You'll be invited to enjoy a complimentary fruit punch in the original kitchen or out in the courtyard where iguanas roam about looking for hibiscus flowers to eat. A $5 donation is requested. The museum is open 10 am to 3 pm, Tuesday through Saturday. ☎ 340-774-9295.

FACT: *The United States bought the US Virgin Islands from Denmark in 1917 for $25 million, but many of the original Danish place names are still in use. Dronningens Gade (Queen Street) is the official post office address of the capital's main street. The sign on King Street reads Kongens Gade. When you see Kronprindsens Gade, know it translates as Crown Prince Street.*

The oldest synagogue in continuous use on US soil is located on the north side of a street named Crystal Gade. From Government Hill, walk west to a set of steps that lead down to Garden Street. Turn right and walk north a short distance to 15 Crystal Gade.

St. Thomas Synagogue received the National Trust for Historic Preservation Honor Award in 2004, after extensive restorations. Completed in 1833 to replace two earlier temples that were built on the same spot, the structure also is listed on the National Register of Historic Places and is recognized as a National Historic Landmark. Sand on the floor of the stone and brick building symbolizes the Jews' exodus from Egypt and a time during the Inquisition when Spanish Jews were forced to hide in unfinished basements. Furniture and most of

St. Thomas Synagogue.

the fixtures date from 1833, and the Holy Ark on the east wall hides six scrolls of the Torah, three of them over 200 years old. A small museum next to the synagogue covers the history of Jews on the island. You can visit the **Weibel Museum**

Monday through Friday from 9 am to 4 pm, ☎ 340-774-4312. Sabbath services are held in the synagogue on Friday evenings and visitors are welcome there Monday through Friday, 9 am to 4 pm. The gift shop features locally made objects such as soder plates and signed art prints. It's open 10 am to 3 pm Monday through Friday. ☎ 340-774-4312.

East of the synagogue, find Raadet's Gade and take it down the hill one block to Vimmelskaft Gade (Back Street). A right turn will take you west to **Market Square**, site of what was once the largest slave market in the West Indies. The old auction blocks are now covered by a metal roof that came from a 19th-century European railway station, and local vendors use the stalls to sell fruits and vegetables. This is a good place to find fresh-squeezed juices, coconuts that will be hacked open by a machete expert so you can drink the milk inside and colorful tie-dyed T-shirts. The market is busiest on Saturday mornings, the traditional market day.

The south side of the market is bordered by Dronningens Gade (Main Street), which you can take two blocks east to **Camille Pissarro's Birthplace** in the town's historic district. The Impressionist artist was born July 10, 1830, and lived on the second floor of the building at 14 Dronningens Gade for 12 years before moving to Paris. He died a Danish citizen in 1903. Pissarro left behind a collection of recently-discovered paintings of Caribbean life. The place where he lived on St. Thomas is now home to an art gallery, with one room displays his paintings. Traveling exhibits are featured at various times. ☎ 340-774-4621.

The area between Dronningens Gade and the waterfront is a network of parallel alleys lined with historic warehouses that have been turned into attractive shops selling everything from imported luxury merchandise to local made crafts. If one or more jumbo ships are in port, expect the narrow passageways to be packed with bargain-hunting tourists. Escape the madness by taking the Marriott Frenchman's Reef Hotel Ferry from the waterfront (across from the Rolex store) to Morningstar Beach for a swim.

Hassel Island

The tiny island located near the shore in Charlotte Amalie Harbor is **Hassel Island**, a 135-acre spit of land less than a quarter-mile from the bustling capital. Most of it is protected by the Virgin Islands National Park System, ☎ 340-776-6201, but little has been done to improve or maintain its assets. A few houses cluster along the coast, the ruins of a fort stand at one end, remains of an old steam-powered marine railway hide in overgrown grass, but otherwise the island is vacant; a serene getaway for anyone who wishes to escape the city.

Hassel Island.

Since there are no hotels, restaurants or other amenities on Hassel, bring a picnic and spend only a morning or afternoon strolling along the rocky shore and exploring the deserted ruins. If you don't have your own boat, check with the water taxis and ferries serving the Charlotte Amalie harbor about getting a ride out to Hassel Island during one of their regular runs.

At one time, Hassel was a peninsula attached to St. Thomas at the western edge of Charlotte Amalie's harbor. Pre-Colombian tribes settled on the peninsula, later, pirates hid their loot there, and even later, Danish and British military troops built fortresses on the highest hill (267 feet) to protect the harbor.

In about 1840, a marine railway and ship-repair facility was built on Hassel Peninsula by Danish businessmen. At the time, St. Thomas was a major trade center for the Caribbean, and the anchorage provided an out-of-water slip where international merchant ships could be cleaned, painted, patched and refueled. Late in the 19th century, an islander named

Henry Creque bought the operation, which has since been known as the **Creque Marine Railway.**

Hassel Peninsula became Hassel Island in 1865 when the narrow spit of land connecting it to the main island was severed to improve water circulation and facilitate marine traffic in the harbor. The US Army Corps of Engineers widened the watery gap after the United States purchased the Danish Virgin Islands in 1917. For awhile, the US Navy manned a base on Water Island, and the Army quartered troops in barracks there during World War II.

Over the years, the military and shipping structures were abandoned and left to deteriorate, but the ruins are considered important historical sites. Four of the buildings are listed on the National Historic Places Registry: **Cowell's Battery, Fort Willoughby, Garrison House**, and **Creque Marine Railway**. Today, the Virgin Islands National Park System owns all but a tiny part of the island; the Virgin Island Port Authority controls a patch of land on top of **Signal Hill**, which includes old military structures and a signal tower that's been in use for centuries.

Neither the Park System nor the Port Authority has immediate plans to conserve the island's historical sites. However, a community activist, Edward Killebrew, and a group called Friends of the Virgin Islands National Park (☎ 340-779-4940) host clean-up expeditions, train tour guides, and solicit funds for conservation work. If history, architecture and wild open spaces interest you, Hassel is well worth a visit.

> **NOTE:** *The other island in Charlotte Amalie's harbor is **Water Island**. Details about this fourth US Virgin Island start on page 131.*

Charlotte Amalie to Red Hook

An end-to-end driving tour of St. Thomas will take you to scenic overlooks, superb beaches, interesting historical sites and unusual attractions. You'll be driving on the left side of the road (British style) in a car with left-side steering (American style), but you'll be surprised at how quickly you get the

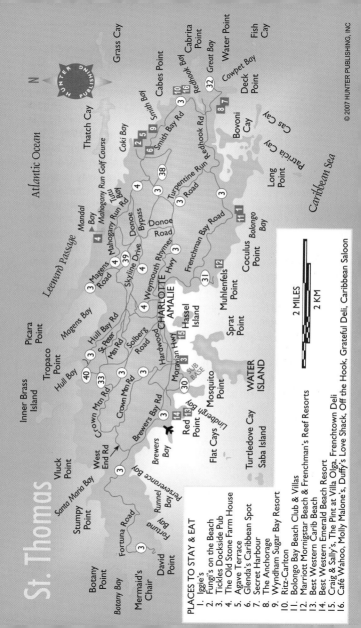

St. Thomas

© 2007 HUNTER PUBLISHING, INC

PLACES TO STAY & EAT
1. Iggie's
2. Fungi's on the Beach
3. Tickles Dockside Pub
4. The Old Stone Farm House
5. Agave Terrace
6. Glenda's Caribbean Spot
7. Secret Harbour
8. The Anchorage
9. Wyndham Sugar Bay Resort
10. Ritz-Carlton
11. Bolongo Bay Beach Club & Villas
12. Marriott Morningstar Beach & Frenchman's Reef Resorts
13. Best Western Carib Beach
14. Best Western Emerald Beach Resort
15. Craig & Sally's, The Pint at Villa Olga, Frenchtown Deli
16. Café Wahoo, Molly Malone's, Duffy's Love Shack, Off the Hook, Grateful Deli, Caribbean Saloon

hang of it. This left-left system is especially beneficial when you're hugging the edge of one of the island's steep, winding roads.

Starting from Fort Christian on the eastern edge of Charlotte Amalie, head east on Veterans Highway (Route 30) toward the West Indian Company Dock, where most large cruise ships tie up. **Havensight Mall** ☆, ☎ 340-777-5313, www.havensight mall.com, a 100-store complex selling many of the same goods found in the downtown shops, is adjacent to the dock, and **Paradise Point Tramway** is directly across the street. Tickets for Paradise Point Tramway are $18 per adult, $9 for kids age six-12, and it runs continuously from 9 am to 5 pm daily during the November to April high season. It's closed on various days from May to October, especially when cruise ships are not in port. Call for the off-season schedule and late-night closings throughout the year. ☎ 340-774-9809, www.stthomasskyride.com.

You can drive to the lookout at **Paradise Point** on top of **Flag Hill** by taking the road directly in front of the entrance to Havensight Mall, but the **Tramway's** modern Swiss-built gondola is an enjoyable alternative. The 700-foot ascent takes seven minutes, and you'll have a breathtaking view of Charlotte Amalie, the harbor, and nearby islands on the way up and from the observation deck at the top. Indoor shops sell a variety of island-style merchandise; snacks and drinks are available at the bar. A marginally interesting nature trail winds through the foliage on the peak, and a free tropical bird show takes place at 10:30 am, 1:30 and 3:30 pm daily. Even though the setting is an obvious "tourist trap," you should go for the views, which are especially spectacular at sunset. ☎ 340-777-4540.

Route 30 continues south a short distance then curves toward the east near the junction with Route 315, which leads to **Morningstar Beach**. If you're ready for a swim, detour toward this golden stretch of sand. Two recently renovated Marriott resorts – Frenchman's Reef and Morning Star Beach – sit near the calm water, and you can rent sports equipment and lounge chairs from their vendors.

Opposite: Paradise Tramway.

TIP: *Cruise passengers often take* The Reefer *ferry from Charlotte Amalie to Morningstar to enjoy the beach, watersports and snack bars, so expect a crowd if ships are in port. At other times, the beach is relatively quiet, and a fine place to take a break while touring the island.*

Back on Route 30 traveling east from Morningstar, you'll notice secondary roads leading to south-shore beaches. At one point the main road dips south and passes directly in front of **Bolongo Bay** and its popular stretch of sand, then skirts the **Marine Sanctuary** at **Mangrove Lagoon**. (See *Adventures On Water*, page 93, for information about exploring the lagoon sanctuary by kayak.)

Red Hook.

Route 30 meets Route 32 just east of the lagoon, and a turn to the right will take you to **Red Hook** ☆. This busy harbor town is the prime departure point for inter-island ferries, fishing boats and charter yachts. All types of marine-related businesses are located here, along with a variety of restaurants, bars and shops that line both sides of the main road. It's worth a stop.

Directly to the south of town, Route 322 leads out to a small spit of land rimmed with some of the most spectacular bays and beaches on the island. Several hotels and restaurants cater to snorkelers, windsurfers and sailors who favor the fine sand and rolling surf of **Secret Harbour** ☆, **Cowpet Beach** and **Great Bay**.

Cowpet Beach.

Red Hook to Magens Bay

North of Red Hook, Route 38 passes a lineup of some of the island's finest resorts with access to choice northeast beaches. Make a stop at **Kilnworks Pottery & Art Gallery** (see *Shopping* for more information) to browse among shelves full of top-quality pottery made by local artisans, then continue on to Route 388, which leads to **Coki Point** and **Coral World Ocean Park and Observatory** ☆.

Don't make the mistake of dismissing this showy geodesic-domed complex as an overpriced tourist trap. It's not. The main observation room at Coral World is built 100 feet off-shore directly over a coral reef. Even certified divers enjoy descending, dry and fully clothed, 15 feet into this underwater room to gaze at the profusion of sea creatures swimming and feeding in their natural habitat of sea plants and coral. Unlike traditional aquariums that exhibit a limited number of captured fish, Coral World's waterproof glass gives visitors a 360° view of marine creatures who are free to come and go as they please. A 50,000-gallon Predator Tank holds some of the fiercer critters, and you can watch as divers enter the tank to feed the adult sharks and eels.

Above ground is the Observatory Tower, which offers a stunning view of nearby islands, seabirds and, during the winter, migrating humpback whales. Elsewhere in the four-acre compound, individual pools contain young sharks, green sea turtles and stingrays. Twenty-one tanks in the Marine Gardens hold the most delicate marine species, such as seahorses and rare corals. A more diverse selection of exquisite marine life is housed in an 80,000-gallon tank at the Caribbean Reef Encounter. In addition, take time to stroll along the Tropical Nature Trail that includes plants from the Caribbean's dry and wet zones, and peek through the underwater viewing window of the Mangrove Lagoon. You'll be intrigued by this look into the remarkable beauty and fragile balance of the Caribbean ecosystem.

© Coral World Ocean Park

Sea turtle.

Talks and feedings take place in various areas of the park between 9:45 am and 4 pm each day. The schedule changes occasionally, so call ahead if you're interested in a specific exhibit. Coral World is open daily, 9 am until 5 pm, during high season, and summer hours may vary. Ticket prices are $18 for adults and $9 for children, and discount coupons are available from the website and visitor publications. Route 388, Coki Point, St. Thomas. ☎ 340-775-1555.

Coki Beach, adjacent to Coral World, is famous for excellent snorkeling and shore diving, and you can rent equipment from several waterside vendors. The beach itself is small and you should expect a crowd on weekends and days when cruise ships are docked in Charlotte Amalie. However, if you visit late in the day or off-season, you may have the whole place to yourself. (See *Beaches* and *Adventures On Water* for more information.)

Coki Beach, with Coral World in the background.

TIP: *While this isn't the most tranquil spot on the island, the view of nearby Thatch Cay is lovely, and the rolling surf sings a solicitous song after the crowds leave in the evening. It's a great place for night dives and romantic strolls.*

Back on Route 38, head west up the hill to Route 42, which parallels the scenic northeast shore and leads to Magens

ST THOMAS

Bay Road (Route 35). The long, palm-lined, white-sand beach at **Magens Bay** ☆ is considered one of the most beautiful in the world. Nestled between lush green hills, the two-mile-deep crescent-shaped bay offers incredible scenery, calm water for swimmers and a variety of amenities.

Arial view of Magens Bay.

Just inland, acres of former plantation land surrounding the beach contain donkey paths, ruined mills and an arboretum of exotic trees. Arrive early or late in the day for the best chance of avoiding crowds of tourists. Unlike other beaches on the island, Magens charges a fee for admission and parking between 8 am and 5 pm. It's $1 per vehicle, $3 per adult and 25¢ per child under 12. (See *Beaches* and *Adventures On Water* for more information.)

Above Magens Bay

From Magens Bay, go back along Route 35 to the junction with scenic **Skyline Drive** (Route 40) and the spectacular view from **Drake's Seat.** An actual stone seat is positioned on the hill above the road, and legend says that Sir Frances Drake used the spot as a lookout for Spanish ships approaching St. Thomas. Most tourists ignore the hilltop and cluster in the parking area with local vendors and a photo-op donkey to admire the stunning view of Magen's Bay and offshore islands. Plan to visit late in the afternoon, just before

Drake's Seat.

sunset, to enjoy the panorama in solitude.

Follow Route 40 west as it becomes St. Peter Mountain Road. Make a stop at **Fairchild Park**, where you'll have more stunning views. This small, wooded, mountaintop retreat is named for Arthur Fairchild, a wealthy publisher and philanthropist who donated Magen's Bay and its adjacent acreage to the public in 1950. Try to visit on a clear day when you'll have a 360° panoramic view of St. Thomas, including the north and south coasts, and neighboring islands. It's much quieter at Fairchild Park than at Drake's Seat, and you most likely will have an entire park bench to yourself.

Next, stop at **Estate St. Peter Greathouse and Botanical Gardens** ☆. Again, the mountaintop views are breathtaking. The estate sits on land that was part of Plantation St. Peter during the 19th century. Records show that in 1938 Lawrence W. Cramer, then governor of the USVI, bought the property from a man named Thomas Berry for a mere $400. During the 1960s, the Johnson & Johnson Corporation purchased the estate for a retreat center and later sold it to Sylvie and Howard DeWolfe, who began developing the botanical gardens. Hurricane Hugo demolished the property in September 1989, but the estate was rebuilt immediately.

Allow time to see the luxurious Greathouse, which exhibits an excellent collection of local art. From the observation deck you can gaze at the panoramic view and then stroll along the labeled nature trails that wind through beautifully landscaped gardens. Admission to the estate on St. Peter Mountain

Road (Route 40) is $10 for adults and $6 for students. Open daily, 9 am to 4:30 pm, ☎ 340-774-4999; www.greathouse-mountaintop.com.

At the risk of sensory overload, make one more scenic stop at **Mountain Top.** Ignore the tourist-trap packaging and come for the cool air and spectacular view from the outdoor

observation deck. This is the highest point in the island at 1,547 feet, and the view of Magens Bay is beyond description. Because of its height, the mountaintop was used by the government as a signal station in the 1940s. The indoor snack bar has a six-foot mahogany bar, from which it has served more than six million banana daiquiris. You'll find a good selection of island products in the enclosed air-conditioned mall, and the talking parrots at the entrance will keep the kids occupied while you shop. Mountain Top is open daily, 9 am to 5 pm. ☎ 340-774-3400, www.greathouse-mountaintop.com.

◆ Adventures on Water

The combination of ideal weather and crystal-clear water makes St. Thomas the perfect setting for a watersports enthusiast's dream vacation. Boating, deep-sea fishing, windsurfing, snorkeling and scuba diving are some of the options offered by the island's professional instructors and outfitters. Visitors who prefer less strenuous activities may choose to relax on one of the picturesque beaches or sign on for a tour of the offshore reefs in a submarine.

Best Beaches

With more than 40 beaches, St. Thomas has three or four to suit everyone. All are open to the public, even if the only access is through a resort, and only one, Magens, charges an entrance fee. The following are descriptions of the most popular beaches, running counterclockwise around the island from Charlotte Amalie. Beaches with a star (☆) are recommended; those with two stars should not be missed.

> **TIP:** *If you favor secluded spots, head to the less populated west coast. If you prefer lots of amenities, look for a beach along the popular northeastern shore.*

Morningstar Beach is easily accessible from Charlotte Amalia. If you don't have a car, just hop aboard *The Reefer* ferry for the short ride from the capital's waterfront. The trip costs $5 each way, leaving from in front of the Rolex store every hour on the hour from 8:30 am to 5 pm daily, with a reverse schedule on Sundays, ☎ 340-776-8500, ext. 6814.

Since Marriott's Frenchman's Reef and Morning Star Resorts are here, you can get meals and drinks at the beachside bars and rent lounge chairs, umbrellas and watersports equipment. Locals come here to play sand volleyball and body surf, and the water is usually full of colorful Sunfish and windsurfer sails. Snorkeling is fairly interesting around the rocks at both ends of the beach.

Resort eateries are set right on Morningstar Beach.

Bolongo Beach draws a young, active crowd that enjoys snorkeling in the bay and lounging around the white sand with a cold drink from the laid-back bar that's connected with the Bolongo Bay Beach Club, ☎ 340-775-1800. The St. Thomas Diving Club is located here, and you can rent snorkeling equipment and book scuba trips through them. ☎ 340-776-2381 or 877-538-8734 (toll free).

Bolongo Beach.

Scott Beach is off Route 32 at the Compass Point turnoff. You can rent lounge chairs and umbrellas for a day on the beautiful beach, but watch out for the strong surf and deep drop-off a short distance from shore.

Secret Harbour Beach ☆, behind the resort with the same name, is off Route 322 just south of Red Hook. Palm trees provide shade. Rent some snorkeling equipment to explore the offshore reef to the left, below the rocky area.

> **TIP:** *Several good beaches rim the piece of land that juts out into the sea south of Red Hook. Take the rather-rough secondary road out to calm, often-deserted* **Vessup Bay** *on the north side, or follow Route 322 to tranquil* **Bluebeard's Beach** *east of the Ritz Carlton.*

Sapphire Beach ☆ is a half-mile of fine sand off Route 38 around the northern corner from Red Hook. It's popular for all types of watersports including parasailing, windsurfing and sailing. The view of nearby islands is terrific.

You can get refreshments and rent equipment from the sports hut connected with the Sapphire Beach Resort and

Marina, and scuba trips are arranged through **Dive In!**, ☎ 866-434-8436 or 340-777-5255. Snorkelers can join the diving trips or try the close-in sites along the reefs at both ends of the beach. On Sundays, the resort hosts a popular beach party with live entertainment.

> **TIP:** *Several resorts line the gorgeous beaches along Water Bay off Smith Bay Road (Route 38) between Sapphire Beach and Coki Beach. You can rent Jet Skis, pedal boats, windsurfers, Sunfish and snorkeling equipment from various vendors, and there's no shortage of beach bars and full-service restaurants.*

Coki Beach ☆ is terrific for snorkeling and scuba diving. Turn onto Route 388 off Route 38 and look for parking along the narrow road that's lined with vendors and snack shacks. This busy spot is a favorite for novice divers because of the interesting coral and fish near the shore, and **Coki Beach Dive Club**, ☎ 340-775-4220, offers instruction and equipment rental right on the beach. (The Coral World Underwater Observatory is built above the reef around the eastern curve of the beach.) There's only a small area of open sand for relaxing, but you'll likely want to spend most of the time in the water anyway. Bathroom facilities are rustic and food choices are limited.

Magen's Beach ☆☆ is so nearly perfect that it's listed by *Condé Nast Traveler* and *National Geographic* magazine as one of the world's 10 most beautiful. Green hills dip down to the mile-long, sugar-white sand beach lining a bright blue bay that cuts deep into the island's north coast. Shady Route 35 dead-ends at the popu-

Magen's Beach.

ST THOMAS

lar beach, which is surrounded by a park donated to the public by publisher Arthur Fairchild in 1946. It's worth the $1 per car, $3 per adult and 25¢ per child fee to get in. Changing rooms, rest- rooms, snack bars, a gift shop and picnic tables are located at one end. You can rent watersports equipment, lounge chairs, rafts, lockers and towels. The water here is calm with a smooth, sandy bottom, so swimming is great but snorkeling is a waste of time.

> **TIP:** *The majority of visitors to Little Magens Beach are gay men, and nudity is tolerated, but not officially allowed. You're not likely to come across the beach by accident, but locals can direct you there, should you wish to go. It's secluded on the east side of Magens Bay (to the right as you face the water), past the rocky shoreline at the end of the main beach.*

Hull Beach, at the end of Route 37 just west of Magens, is the island's best surfing beach because the western end is wide open to rough Atlantic waves. Local fishermen anchor their brightly-colored boats here. The water tends to be calm enough for swimming near the shady beach. The **Hideaway Bar** serves a variety of refreshments and features live music on Sunday afternoons, ☎ 340-777-1898.

Brewers Beach, near the University of the Virgin Islands on the south coast west of Charlotte Amalie, is great for swimming and watching planes arrive and depart from the airport. The beach is especially busy on the weekends, but you can watch the sun set in relative solitude most evenings. Watersports equipment is available for rent and snack trucks show up most afternoons.

Lindbergh Beach is named after Charles Lindbergh, who landed on the island during his around-the-world flight in the 1920s. It's adjacent to the airport. You can rent watersports equipment from vendors at several beachside hotels. The water is calm with a sandy floor – ideal for swimming. The beach is long enough for leisurely strolls.

Submarine Tour

A voyage aboard the submarine *Atlantis*, out of Charlotte Amalie, is a novel way to see the fantastic underwater world surrounding St. Thomas. This is a true submarine diving into the depths of a real ocean, so the experience is better than the glass-bottom boat trip or aquarium tour.

Marine life around St. Thomas is varied and colorful.

The sub is 50 feet long, 13 feet wide and weighs 49 tons. It was specifically designed for tourists and is air conditioned and roomy (seven feet in diameter). Both sides are lined with flat viewing windows that allow you to see through several ports as the sub dives 90 feet below the water's surface.

Once submerged, the vessel slowly cruises about 1½ miles past coral reefs that draw a variety of fascinating marine life. The trip is narrated, so all the most interesting sites and creatures are identified.

> **TIP:** *The light is usually strong enough to allow photographs using a fast-speed film (ASA 400 or higher), but a flash won't work.*

ST THOMAS

The excursion departs from the Havensight Cruise Ship Dock Monday through Saturday, but the timetable varies, so call ahead for the current schedule. Allow a total of two hours, which includes the tender ride to and from the submarine and the one-hour underwater tour. Tickets are $84 per adult and $45 per child (must be over 36 inches tall). ☎ 340-776-5650 or 866-546-7820. Discount tickets and additional information are available at www.atlantisadventures.com.

Scuba Diving & Snorkeling

Experts rate the Virgin Islands among the best sites in the world for both novice and experienced divers. The clear waters often offer visibility up to 150 feet, and the average year-round water temperature is 80°. Inexperienced divers and snorkelers can explore a variety of close-in shallow reefs that serve as feeding grounds for colorful fish. Expert divers have an even larger choice of fascinating sites located within easy boating distance from shore.

> **NOTE:** *The RL Schneider Hospital on St. Thomas has a hyperbaric chamber,* ☎ *340-776-8311; www.rlshospital.org.*

Many visitors head to **Coki Beach** on the north coast for snorkeling, scuba instruction and shore diving. If you have your own equipment, you can set out solo (air fills are available from Coki Beach Dive Club). Otherwise, snorkeling gear is available for rent from beachside vendors. Certification courses or introduction dives can be arranged through Coki Beach Dive Club.

The rocks and coral along the east side of the bay, near Coral World's Underwater Observatory, harbor an abundance of sergeant majors and parrotfish that have become accustomed to eating from human hands. It is great fun, but environmentalists take a dim view of this, calling it "habitat adulteration." Farther out from shore, you may see yellowtail snapper, tarpon and stingrays. Along the western side of the bay, you'll find fewer people and better coral.

TIP: *The best place on the island to buy snorkeling equipment is **Mask and Fin** at 42 Norre Gade in Charlotte Amalie. ☎ 340-774-7177. They also have a list of good snorkeling spots.*

Other good snorkeling beaches include **Sapphire**, **Hull** and **Brewers.** Most dive operators will allow snorkelers to go along on scuba trips, if there's room on the boat. The best dive sites for snorkelers are **Cow** and **Calf**, in **Jersey Bay** off the southeast coast, and the waters off **St. James Island**, across from the southeastern tip of St. Thomas. Both these areas have coral, caves and abundant fish at depths of five to 25 feet, which is easily visible to snorkelers.

If you're interested in viewing a sunken ship, St. Thomas has some of the best in the Caribbean. Two **Navy barges**, in fairly shallow water, are perfect for beginners. They are home to colorful dense sponges. The **Wit Shoal**, a 300-foot World War II cargo ship, lies upright in 25 to 90 feet of water, providing divers of various skills the opportunity to explore its decks. The truly intrepid enjoy plunging head-first down the smoke stacks, which are encrusted with coral. Night divers favor the **Kennedy Barge**, which is home to manta rays, lobsters and sea turtles.

Experienced divers have a choice of 30 excellent sites within a 20-minute boat ride from St. Thomas. Those on the north side of the island are favored for the bounteous numbers of fish that are carried by the currents at the confluence of the Atlantic Ocean and the Caribbean Sea. Waters off **Thatch Cay** and **Congo Cay** offer boulders, tunnels and arches. **Coki Beach** is known for great night diving.

South of St. Thomas, **French Cap Cay** has a fascinating reef with caves and tunnels. Colorful sponges, corals and sea fans grow along the reef and draw a variety of sea creatures. Other good dives sites include the canyons just off **Capella Island,** a bit east of Buck Island, and the giant underwater boulders off **Saba Island**, west of Water Island.

> **FACT:** *According to volunteer surveyors for REEF (Reef Environmental Education Foundation), approximately 284 species of marine life inhabit the waters surrounding the Virgin Islands.*

DIVE OPERATORS

The following recommended dive shops on St. Thomas offer first-class PADI instruction, multi-level certification, guided dive trips and equipment rental. Most operators schedule two boat trips daily and arrange instruction courses to suit. Those with a star (☆) beside them are highly recommended for friendliness, experience or special amenities.

Expect to pay $70 for a one-tank dive, $90 for a two-tank dive, about $70 for an introductory resort-course dive and $385 for an open-water certification course.

Coki Beach Dive Club ☆ is one of the most convenient dive operations on the island. They are located right on Coki Beach, just steps from the water. The staff specializes in making beginners feel at ease in the water, whether they are snorkeling or diving, and the PADI instructors offer guided trips from the beach. Equipment can be rented on-site at excellent prices (snorkeling sets are $10, tanks rent for $10), there are lockers for your valuables, snack shacks serve refreshments, and they'll even pick you up at the cruise-ship dock if you call in advance. Certified divers will want to sign

Opposite: Diver with coral.

up for the $60 night dive or the $50 guided tour of one of two reefs located right off the beach. ☎ 800-474-2654 or 340-775-4220, www.cokidive.com.

St. Thomas Diving Club is a five-star PADI center located at Bolongo Beach Resort. The staff enjoys every aspect of diving, from training first-time snorkelers to guiding experienced divers and leading instructor classes. Trips go out mornings and afternoons for two-tank dives in one of two custom-outfitted boats with six to 10 divers; night dives are scheduled weekly. When room allows, snorkelers are welcome on the dive boat at a cost of $40. If you plan to dive several times during your vacation, ask about the multi-dive packages. ☎ 340-776-2381 or 877-538-8734, www.stthomas divingclub.com.

Aqua Action, located at Secret Harbour Beach Resort, is a remarkable five-star PADI facility and watersports center. Carl Moore, the owner, is certified by the Handicapped Scuba Association (HAS) to train divers with disabilities. In addition, he is licensed by the US Coast Guard as a Master Captain and by PADI as a Master Scuba Instructor and equipment specialist. He and his staff run PADI sanctioned *Bubblemaker* and *Seal Team* programs for kids, offer free snorkeling classes, take certified divers on night dives every Friday, and specialize in customized beach and boat dives for small groups of two to 10. The sports center rents kayaks, canoes, Sunfish sailboats and snorkeling gear. ☎ 340-775-6285 or 888-775-6285; www.aadivers.com.

Chris Sawyer Diving Center ☆ is known among experienced divers for full-day trips to the sunken HMS *Rhone* and night dives at the wreck. In addition, the five-star PADI center organizes dive packages for guests of Colony Point Pleasant, Renaissance Grand Beach and Wyndham Sugar Bay Beach Resorts. Chris, who started diving 30 years ago as a student at UCLA, and his staff are serious about both the safety and fun of diving. Thorough pre-dive instruction and site briefings are given as each small group heads out on one of two 42-foot custom-built dive boats. A well-stocked store is located at American Yacht Harbor in Red Hook, ☎ 340-777-7804; 877-929-3483; fax 775-9495; www.sawyerdive.vi.

Dive In! ☆ is often recommended by divers who enjoy individual attention and expert instruction. Owners Bobbie and Bruce Pachta run the full-service PADI shop, which offers beginning resort courses through advanced training and schedules both beach and boat dives. Trips go to more than 40 spots located off both the north and south shores and include many sites off St. John. You can bring home a picture or video of yourself taken underwater. Located at Sapphire Beach Resort & Marina, between Coki Beach and Red Hook, ☎ 340-777-5255 or 866-434-8346; www.diveinusvi.com.

ST THOMAS

Blue Island Divers is a five-star PADI facility run by Sean and Aitch, who both hold instructor and first-class diver certification from the British Sub-Aqua Club (BSAC). The center is located on the waterfront at Crown Bay Marina, near Tickles Dockside Pub and only a 10-minute drive from the airport. In addition to offering every imaginable dive trip and instruction class, Blue Island has a fully-stocked retail shop and is the winner of the Environmental Achievement Award. If you book a six-dive package, the crew will wash down and store your equipment each day and have it set up on the boat, *Island*

Diver, the next day. ☎ 866-728-2284; www.blueislanddivers. com.

Snuba

Snuba offers underwater exploration for those who want to go deeper than a snorkel allows without all the equipment and training required for scuba diving. Basically, you breathe through a hose hooked to an air tank that floats on the surface above you. Anyone over the age of eight can do it, and the air hose is long enough to allow dives up to 20 feet deep. The cost is $68 for adults and $65 for kids under age 12 (kid fees include a pass to Coral World). You'll find Snuba excursions at Coral World on Coki Bay. Make a reservation and your guide will meet you at the entrance booth. ☎ 340-693-8063; www.visnuba.com.

BOB

You may have seen BOB on the Today Show. It's a Breathing Observation Bubble that allows you to sit on your own yellow scooter-like vehicle, with your head and shoulders inside an air-fed helmet-style device, while you zoom around underwater. The helmet is attached to the scooter, so you have no additional weight to support. A certified dive master guides you along coral reefs, but you don't need any dive experience to feel comfortable inside BOB. Call ahead to make a reservation for this half-day adventure ($99 per person) that begins with a boat trip out to the reefs and ends with snorkeling time. The office is at Port of Sale Mall across from the ship dock at Havensight. ☎ 340-715-0348, www.bobusvi.com.

Boating & Sailing

St. Thomas is known as a center for charter boat operations, and with good reason. Year-round balmy weather and calm, clear seas draw visitors who crave hidden coves, deserted beaches and dependable sun, matched with trouble-free anchorages and full-service marinas.

Regattas are held in the Virgin Islands throughout the year. One of the largest and best known is the **Rolex Cup Regatta**, held at St. Thomas Yacht Club each spring. ☎ 340-775-6320; www.rolexcupregatta.com.

You can rent everything from a small dinghy to a huge oceanworthy yacht, either bare-boat or with a full crew and provisions. Experienced yachtsmen may compete in various regattas throughout the year, and novices like to try their hand at handling a day rental. Those who truly want to do nothing but relax may opt for a half- or full-day catered sail along the coast or out to a neighboring island.

The following companies are a few of the best who operate out of St. Thomas. Many have stateside offices, toll-free numbers and websites for easy contact. Those listings with a star (☆) for their friendly staff, knowledgeable crew or outstanding boats.

DAY-CRUISE OPERATORS

Rates run around $95-$110 per person for full-day excursions that include unlimited drinks and lunch. Prices for half-day and sunset sails vary depending on the type of refreshments served and the length of the trip. Power boat tours are more expensive; their prices vary depending on the vessel size and the duration of your trip. While you probably can't make a bad choice among the many operators on St. Thomas, the following have a reputation for excellence.

New Horizons is a 65-foot sloop (two-masted sailboat) with a cushioned sundeck. All cruises begin with fresh-baked pastries, and choices from the open bar include soda, juice and a variety of alcoholic drinks. The all-day cruise includes a buffet lunch with hot entrées and desserts. Choose from full-day, half-day and sunset trips. *New Horizons II,* a 44-foot speedboat, takes passengers on a day-long tour of four British Virgin Islands. The office is located in suite 16 at Red Hook Plaza, ☎ 340-775-1171; 800-808-7604; www.newhorizonsvi.com.

Yacht Nightwind, a 50-foot oceangoing yawl (two-masted sailboat with a small jigger mast on the stern), sets out from Sapphire Marina every morning at 9 am for St. John. The friendly crew, headed by Steve Marsh, tells tales and points out sites along the way, and the bar is always open. During the day, you'll anchor twice in tranquil bays where you can snorkel or swim. Early afternoon features entertainment and a buffet lunch, including champagne and to-die-for chocolate desserts. Located on Sapphire Bay, just north of Red Hook, ☎ 340-775-4110; www.sailnightwind.com.

© Nightwind

Nightwind *under full sail.*

Morningstar ☆ is a 42-foot Cheoy Lee sailboat captained by Jake Morganstern. On a full-day cruise, you will be taken to secluded little spots where you can swim, snorkel and sunbathe. On your way out, enjoy a drink from the open bar, rest in the shade of the canopy, spread a towel on deck for a nap or help with the sailing. Mid-day you'll be served a cooked-on-board lunch accompanied by a chilled bottle of champagne. ☎ 340-775-1111; www.morningstarcharter.com.

CUSTOMS CLEARANCE

If you go by boat to one of the British Virgin Islands, you must clear Customs. Be prepared to present a valid passport and pay the $15 fee (included in some cruise rates).

Captain Nautica ☆ uses a motor-powered hard-hull raft to take up to 15 passengers on a sightseeing excursion spiced with island legends and pirate tales. Known as the "No Snooze Cruise," this high-energy trip leaves from Red Hook and includes two snorkeling stops off the British Virgins, Caribbean music, snacks and drinks. You buy your own lunch during a stop in Tortola. ☎ 340-715-3379; www.captain nautica.com.

© Captain Nautica

Daydreamer and *Coconut* are trimarans that provide smooth sailing and plenty of room. Their shallow draft allows them to anchor close to secluded beaches for snorkeling, swimming and relaxing. Both boats are staffed by a friendly crew and there's plenty of shade, an open bar and great snacks. Passengers may use the high-quality snorkeling gear, floats, life vests and freshwater deck shower. At lunchtime, the boats anchor off Jost Van Dyke in the BVI for a meal at a

© Daydreamer

beachside restaurant followed by a stop at the Soggy Dollar Bar for one of their famous "Painkiller" drinks. Half-day, sunset and St. John trips are also available. ☎ 340-775-2584; www.daydreamervi.com.

Fantasy ☆, crewed by Captains Pam and Brian Heath, allows you to try out your sailing skills (if you have none, the captains will teach you), or simply sit back and enjoy the day. Snorkeling equipment, floats, fishing gear, meals and open bar are included. Two to six guests are aboard for each day sail. ☎ 340-775-5652; www.daysailfantasy.com.

© SailJester.com

Jester, captained by California transplant Jim, is a 38-foot sloop that cuts through the water like a shark. Up to six people can lounge on the cushioned deck or help pilot from the shaded cockpit as the boat cruises the islands. Jim, a licensed PADI rescue diver and US Coast Guard captain, mixes unique drinks along the way. ☎ 340-513-2459; www.sailjester.com.

BOAT CHARTERS

Bare-boat and fully-crewed charters are available for a day, a week or longer from more than a dozen companies based in St. Thomas. Expect crewed rates to be in the range of $1,000 to $1,500 per week, depending on season, length of charter, type of boat and extra features. Bareboat rates start at $2,000 per week; you pay for food and gas. The following are suggested based on their excellent reputation among yachtsmen, longevity and number of available rentals.

Admiralty Yacht Vacations, owned by Hal and Anne Borns, offers catamarans, trimarans, single-hulls and power boats in all sizes. They are based at Admiral's Inn, Villa Olga,

Frenchtown, ☎ 340-774-2172 or 800-895-5808; fax 340-340-774-8010 ; www.admirals.com.

CYOA has more than 100 fully crewed and bareboat yachts in the Virgin Islands. Located at Frenchtown Marina, near Charlotte Amalie, ☎ 340-777-9690 or 800-944-2962; www.cyoacharters.com.

V.I.P. (Virgin Island Power) Yacht Charters rents luxury power and sail crafts with features such as queen-size beds, microwaves, televisions and VCRs. You can choose to captain your own yacht or hire an experienced crew to pamper you with gourmet meals and watersports instruction. Their yachts are based at Compass Point Marina on the east coast. ☎ 340-774-9224 or 866-847-9224; fax 866-847-3293; www.vipyachts.com.

Nauti Nymph ☆ has a large fleet of 25- to 29-foot boats powered by single or twin Yamaha engines. All boats have full bimini tops, large cushioned sun platforms, built-in ice coolers and freshwater showers. Charter bare boat or fully crewed from their base at American Yacht Harbor, Red Hook, ☎ 340-775-5066 or 800-734-7345; www.st-thomas.com/nautinymph/.

© Nauti Nymph

Paradise Connections, owned and operated by expert sailors Bob and Sheila Wise, is known to have a knack of match-making. You tell them what you want to do, what kinds of experiences you're looking for and how many people will be going along, and Bob and Sheila will pair you with the ideal boat and crew. Contact them online, or drop by the office at Saga Have Marina, ☎ 340-513-2858 or 877-567-9350; www.paradiseconnections.com.

Awesome Powerboat Rentals ☆, located at the dock in Red Hook, has twin-engine catamarans for rent by the day and half-day. You can take the boats out alone, if you know

ST THOMAS

what you're doing, or arrange for an experienced captain to accompany you. The 22-footer is comfortable for six, and the 26-foot catamaran will hold up to 10 passengers. With freedom to go anywhere in the Virgin Islands except St. Croix (it's too far), and Anegada (too tricky to navigate), you'll have an awesome day at sea. ☎ 340-775-0860 or 340-779-2717; www.powerboatrentalsvi.com.

> **TIP:** *If you want to learn to sail, **Fair Wind Sailing School** gives "Instant Bareboater" lessons. Check them out at www.fairwindsailing.com, ☎ 866-380-SAIL.*

Fishing

Even if you're not a fisherman, consider spending at least half a day on a deep-sea fishing boat. More than 20 world fishing records have been won in the Virgin Islands due to their prime location near the world famous **North Drop**, part of the six-mile-deep **Puerto Rico Trench**, which is the deepest spot in the Atlantic Ocean. Some of the largest sport fish in the world swim in these waters, including marlin, dolphin fish, wahoo and tuna. Nearer the shore, kingfish, bonefish, tarpon, amberjack, grouper, mackerel and snappers are abundant year-round.

Many deep-sea fishing operations based on St. Thomas are owned and operated by record-holding fishermen who enjoy sharing their knowledge and skills with others. Don't be intimidated if you're a novice. Most outfitters can match you with boats and captains that will make you look like a pro.

> **NOTE:** *You don't need a license to fish from shore, and deep-sea licenses are included in the cost of boat charters.*

Expect to pay around $500-$600 per boat for a half-day charter and double that amount for a full-day outing. You can split the cost with up to five other anglers.

Opposite: Deep sea fishing.

FISHING ETIQUETTE

Catch-and-release fishing is the norm in the Virgin Islands. In addition, fishermen often tag their catch before releasing them so that researchers can track and study various species.

One of the best ways to find a boat and captain that match your fishing skills and expectations is to stroll along the docks or call the offices at **American Yacht Harbor** in Red Hook, ☎ 340-775-6454, or **Sapphire Beach Marina** on the northeast coast in Sapphire Bay, ☎ 340-775-6100 or 800-524-2090. Many fishing charters are based at these marinas and the staff can give you inside information to help you choose the right charter. One to try is **Water's Edge**, American Yacht Harbor, ☎ 340-771-7356, www.stthomasboatrentals.com.

ANGLING OPERATORS

Also consider one of the following reputable outfitters:

Marlin Prince ☆ is a 45-foot Viking with twin-diesel engines, air conditioning, tournament equipment and a tuna tower. Captain Eddir Morrison can lead you to the best spots for marlin, tuna and wahoo. Ask about fly-fishing for blue marlin. Docked at American Yacht Harbor Marina, ☎ 340-693-5929; www.marlinprince.com.

Fish Hawk II is a 43-foot boat captained by Al Petrosky, a native of New Jersey who has a reputation for pulling in record catches. Find Captain Al at Fish Hawk Marina on the lagoon in Frydenhoj on the southeast shore, ☎ 340-775-9058.

Reel Therapy may be just what the doctor ordered. The 28-foot Pro-line fishing boat goes out under the command of Captain Gene Smith, who is known for providing excellent service and hospitality to island visitors. ☎ 340-715-0472 or 800-508-1048, www.reel-therapy.com.

Abigail III docks at Sapphire Beach Marina and is a 44-foot air-conditioned and customized Sportfisherman certified to carry up to six passengers. Call Captain Red for information and reservations, ☎ 340-775-6024; www.sportfishvi.com.

Double Header Sportfishing specializes in live-bait fishing and runs two 32-foot diesel boats with T-top coverings that provide shade. They also have a new 40-foot Dorado that seats six. The boats are docked at Sapphire Beach Marina and pick up at several locations on St. Thomas and St. John. ☎ 340-777-7317; www.doubleheadersportfishing.net.

The Peanut ☆ at Peanut Gallery Sportfishing is a 28-foot catamaran customized for sportfishing. Docked at Crown Bay Marina, the boat is ideal for cruise-ship passengers on a tight schedule. Captain Steve Malpere is an experienced fisherman with plenty of tales to keep passengers entertained. ☎ 340-775-5274; www.fishingstthomas.com.

FEELING COMPETITIVE?

If you want to participate in or observe one of the annual sportfishing tournaments, contact the USVI Tourist Bureau, ☎ 800-372-USVI or The American Yacht Harbor, ☎ 340-775-6454.

Eco-Tours

Mangrove Adventures leads kayak and snorkel expeditions through the mysterious and intriguing **Mangrove Lagoon and Marine Sanctuary** off the southeast shore. This protected area is filled with egrets, heron, iguanas, seahorses and juvenile reef fish. The only way to see it up close is on one of these guided nature tours. A marine biologists or trained naturalist will go along to point out and explain interesting sights as you head out on a two-man sit-on-top kayak.

The kayaks are stable and easy to operate, so even children can join the tour. The first hour is spent paddling through the protected waters with frequent stops to observe the mangrove thicket and discuss the ecological importance of the area. You can snorkel in shallow water at the mouth of the lagoon. Expect to see large groups of young parrotfish, herring, snappers, stingrays and barracudas.

ST THOMAS

TIP: *Ask about going out to Cas Cay, a 50-acre island off the southeast shore. It is undeveloped and under the protection of the Department of Natural Resources, but you may rent an inflatable boat or powerboat from Mangrove Adventures to make the journey. Bring a picnic and wear water shoes. The shore is rocky, so ask about the best place to dock. A 10-minute walk from shore will bring you to a blowhole and warm-water tidal pool at the base of 100-foot-tall cliffs.*

Call ahead for reservations because this is a popular tour that books up quickly during high season. The cost ($65 per adult and $35 for kids) includes snorkeling gear, safety vest, water-proof storage bag and bottled water. Virgin Islands Ecotours is off Route 32 at Estate Nadir, ☎ 340-779-2155; www. viecotours.com.

Surfing & Windsurfing

The best waves are found from November through March at the west end of **Hull Bay** on the north coast. Experienced surfers come here to ride the wild roll of the Atlantic. This is also the beach with the strongest winds for windsurfing, but

most enthusiasts prefer calmer seas around the east end of the island.

Many resorts and some public beaches have windsurfing boards for rent for about $20 per hour, with an hour of instruction priced at around $50. **West Indies Windsurfing,** ☎ 340-775-6530, at Bluebeard's Beach (Vessup Bay) on the south side of Red Hook, is a well-known outfitter. Local windsurfers often come to this area for informal competitions. Other popular windsurfing beaches include **Sapphire**, where you can get instruction on a simulator, and **Brewers**, which is favored by local college students.

Parasailing

Most waterside resorts offer parasailing right off their beach through their own watersports center. In addition, **Caribbean Parasail and Watersports,** ☎ 340-775-9360, will arrange to meet you on almost any beach or pick you up at the cruise-ship dock. Their boats are custom designed for dry take-offs and landings, so you can get a seagull's view of the island without getting wet. Find them at Pirate's Cove Marina on the East End, near Red Hook.

Sky Pirates, at the Coral World docks abutting Coki Beach, has hourly parasailing tours every day beginning at 9 am. You do a dry take off and landing on the boat, if you want, or plunge into the sea after your ride for a breath-taking cool down. Kids as young as five can do this safely when riding tandem with an adult. Rates are $50 for adults and children (plus Coral World admission of $18 for adults and $9 for kids). Make a reservation, especially during high season, ☎ 340-690-2262.

> **TIP:** *Standard rates for a basic parasail tour start at $55 per person. You often can find discount coupons in tourist publications, and you may get a reduced combo rate if you also purchase tickets to Coral World or book through your resort.*

◆ Adventures on Foot

While most of the adventures in St. Thomas happen on, in and under the water, there's still plenty to do on dry land.

Hiking

Serious hikers probably will want to head for St. John, but casual walkers can find a number of places to stroll. Meandering along any of the gorgeous beaches is fun, especially early in the morning or after sunset when the crowds leave. Another possibility is the waterfront in Charlotte Amalie.

The mountain ridge that runs east-west through the center of the island offers superb views. Unfortunately, there are no maintained trails, so walkers must travel along busy roadways – not a good idea. Plan to drive along Crown Mountain (Route 33) or Fortuna (Route 30) and stop at the turnoffs and parking areas where you can stretch your legs and admire the fabulous views.

Tennis

Two lighted public tennis courts are available at **Sub Base**, just west of Charlotte Amalie near the Water and Power Authority complex. In addition, most resorts will allow non-guests to play or take lessons for a reasonable fee. Call ahead for reservations.

Bolongo Bay Beach Club and Villas charges $10 per hour per court for non-quests who wish to use one of the two unlighted courts. ☎ 340-775-1800.

Marriott Frenchman's Reef and **Morning Star Beach Resort** share four lighted seaside courts. Non-guests may reserve a court for $10 per hour, and one-hour lessons are available for $39. ☎ 340-776-8500, ext. 6818.

Wyndham Sugar Bay Resort ☆ has the island's only court with stadium seating for tournament play. Five additional lighted courts may be used by non-guests at a charge of $10 per hour. Reserve a court by phoning the resort, ☎ 340-777-7100.

Opposite: Parasailing by C-foto/Dreamstime

Golf

St. Thomas has one spectacular golf course, **Mahogany Run**. Tom and George Fazio designed this 18-hole championship masterpiece and multimillion-dollar renovations have kept it in world-class condition. The 6,022-yard, par-70 course sprawls over rolling hills on the north side of the island overlooking the Atlantic Ocean.

Mahogany Run is known for its demanding Devil's Triangle, formed by the 13th, 14th and 15th fairways, which are angled on towering cliffs 150 feet above the ocean. Golfers often find their attention wandering to the pounding surf below or the tiny islands in the distance.

PRACTICE TIME

Just want to practice your swing? The public is allowed to putt and drive at the no-holes, no-facilities range on the campus of the University of the Virgin Islands in Brewer's Bay, ☎ 340-693-1230.

Island visitors and cruise-ship passengers are invited to play the course, which is considered one of the best in the Caribbean. Green fees fluctuate by season, but usually run about $140 per person for 18 holes and a half-share of the mandatory golf cart. Right- and left-handed rental clubs are available for $40 if you're playing 18 holes, and $20 if you're playing nine. Ask about reduced green fees after 2 pm.

Mahogany Run also features a driving range, putting green, 19th-hole snack bar, a grill and terrace bar and a fully stocked pro shop. The course is open daily with tee times from 7 am until 4:50 pm; Pro shop hours are 7 am to 5:30 pm; and the grill serves 11 am until 7 pm. Call in advance for tee times. ☎ 340-777-6006 or 800-253-7103; www.mahogany rungolf.com.

◆ Adventures in the Air

Flightseeing

Sightseeing from the air is one of the most exciting adventures in the Caribbean. Costs vary, but expect to pay around $80-$110 per person for most air tours.

Air Center Helicopters will take you on a unique tour with a birds-eye view of some of the most beautiful parts of the US and British Virgin Islands, or arrange a day-trip to Peter's Island or Anegada. Helicopters are also available for transfers to hotels on neighboring islands. Get all the information on tours and inter-island transportation from the office at the air-
port. ☎ 340-775-7335; www.aircenter helicopters.com.

© Air Center Helicopters

◆ Shopping

St. Thomas is famous as a duty-free bargain paradise. While some of the claims are overblown, you can find terrific buys on imported merchandise and local products. Since goods are free of state and city taxes, and each US citizen can bring back up to $1,200 worth of purchases duty-free, the final cost of many items is much less than if you'd bought it at home.

ST THOMAS

Liquor, European china and crystal, and jewelry are some of the best buys, and you can ship large or heavy items home at US postal rates.

> **TIP:** *If you're serious about getting a good bargain on specific merchandise, check prices and quality at shops and discount outlets near your home, so you'll come to St. Thomas as an informed shopper.*

Charlotte Amalie

St. Thomas became the center of trade in the Caribbean back in 1764 when Denmark's king proclaimed it a free port. Local merchants (and allegedly, pirates) did business from warehouses that opened up onto the harbor to provide easy access to the ships that transported their goods around the world.

Today, many of these old warehouses have been transformed into trendy shops selling luxury goods from many countries. Even if you're not a shopper, it's fun to stroll along the narrow alleys and people-watch. On quiet days, you'll almost have the streets and shady courtyards to yourself. But on cruise-ship days, you'll be shoulder-to-shoulder with frenzied shoppers bent on scooping up bags full of bargains before their ship sails.

> **TIP:** *If you want to avoid the masses, check the cruise-ship schedule printed on the front of "St. Thomas This Week," a bright-yellow freebie available everywhere including resorts, car rental offices, the airport and tourist offices.*

Most stores in Charlotte Amalie are open Monday through Saturday, 9 am until 5 pm, but many extend their hours and open on Sunday if a large number of cruise-ship passengers are expected.

Vendors' Plaza is the only spot in town where street merchants can legally sell their goods. (Food vendors are excluded from this city ordinance.) Peddlers begin setting up under brightly-colored umbrellas around 7:30 each morning,

Vendor's Plaza.

Monday through Saturday, and stay until 5:30, or whenever business falls off. They offer a variety of T-shirts, crafts, jewelry and knock-off luxuries. Don't miss the flavor of this shopping area on the waterside in front of Emancipation Park, between Fort Christian and the center of town.

EASY-GOING HASSLE

While street vendors are prohibited from approaching visitors outside their designated area, taxi drivers, tour organizers and time- share salesmen are not. However, most are friendly, easy-going fellows who will leave you alone after you just say no. You won't have problems with people trying to sell you drugs or stolen junk.

The main shopping area is located along narrow blocks of parallel alleyways between **Waterfront Highway** on the south and **Main Street** on the north. More than 400 stores are tucked

ST THOMAS

into these passageways that are bordered by Tolbad Gade on the east, near Vendors' Plaza, and Market Square on the west. A few more notable shops are located on **Back Street**, which runs parallel to and one block north of Main.

Don't worry about street names. Most are Danish and difficult to pronounce, and most aren't marked by a street sign, anyway. Simply know that the alleyways run north-south between Waterfront and Main, and locals depend on landmarks, such as large banks and public buildings, when giving directions. If you want to find a specific store, look for the easy-to-follow shopping map in the centerfold of *St. Thomas This Week*, available everywhere.

Large, big-name shops put out so much advertising and are so easily recognized, their listings aren't necessary in this guide. A walk up Main Street will bring you to **Columbian Emeralds, A.H. Riise, Cardow's** ☆ and **Little Switzerland** ☆. The following is intended to help you find lesser-known stores with unique merchandise.

DECODING THE STARS

This Pocket Adventure Guide trims the list of shops on St. Thomas to a manageable roster of those with special features, outstanding service or superior products. All are recommended, but those with one star (☆) deserve particular notice, and a two-star (☆☆) award means "you just gotta browse there."

JEWELRY, ARTS & CRAFTS

The Bernard K. Passman Gallery ☆☆ features the work of this world-famous sculptor who designs black coral jewelry and objets d'art. Most of his pieces are beyond the price range of the average shopper, but you can enjoy viewing them at 38A Main Street. ☎ 340-777-4580, or at the Havensight Mall, ☎ 340-715-5328; www.passman. com.

Native Arts and Crafts Cooperative ☆ is a collection of work by more than 90 local artisans. You'll find straw bags and hats, spice racks and household items made from native shells and woods. Visit this vast shop on Tolbod Gade, across from Emancipation Park. ☎ 340-777-1153.

Gallery St. Thomas, owned by Claire Ochoa, has two Charlotte Amalie locations featuring Virgin Island and Caribbean artwork: 2A-2C Garden Street at Government Hill and at Grand Galleria above the crystal shop on Main Street. Both shops display a wide assortment of original oils, watercolors, ceramics and prints. ☎ 340-777-6363 or 877-797-6363; www.gallerystthomas.com.

Year after year, **Gold Corner** wins recognition as one of the best places on the island to buy gold jewelry. A recent visit uncovered good prices on gold chains and pendents (an endless selection hangs from the walls), but the more interesting offerings were the West Indian bangles and hibiscus-flower earrings. Stop by, even if you just want to browse, and ask for the friendly owner, Chris Kanusing, if you need help. Located on the waterfront at Trompeter Gade in Drake's Passage Mall, ☎ 340-776-1676.

FUN STUFF

The Tradewinds Shop on the waterfront near the Royal Dane Mall carries a variety of things from around the world. Look for jewelry, model ships and airplanes, sculpture, note cards and art. A pair of Naot sandals makes the perfect souvenir or gift. ☎ 340-774-9977 or 888-244-9782; www.tradewindsshop.com.

Tropical Memories will lure you in with the smell of flavored coffees. Stick around to browse through the gourmet foods, local artwork and Caribbean cookbooks. Customers especially like the imaginative doorstops made of scrap mahogany, brightly painted paper mâché sculptures and the silk sun catchers. Look for the shop in the Royal Dane Mall, ☎ 340-776-7536.

Caribbean Chocolate is, as they say, to die for. David Dawson whips up batches of killer confections at his shop every day, and the aroma of chocolate and rum will lure you in. Try several of the specialties, then pick up a gift box of goodies for friends back home. If you're planning an island wedding, ask about the chocolate tower topped with bows. Follow your nose to 1 Trompeter Gade, ☎ 340-774- 6675.

Zora became famous in the '60s for her handmade leather sandals, but her whimsical animal-shaped canvas bags and backpacks are more fun and more affordable. Everything in the shop is top quality, including the recently added line of handmade jewelry. Located at 34 Norre Gade (east end of Main), ☎ 340-774-2559; www.zora-vi.com.

ANTIQUES

Carson Company Antiques proves that one man's junk is another man's treasure. Come here to rummage through a diverse mix of rare old books, early maps, pottery and jewelry from all parts of the world. You're sure to turn up a true gem. Located on the west side of Royal Dane Mall's narrow alley of shops. ☎ 340-774-6175.

WATCHES, CAMERAS & ELECTRONICS

Boolchand's ✪ has been around since the 1930s with multiple stores on several islands in the Caribbean. Savvy shoppers check the merchandise and prices here before they purchase anything electronic, especially multi-system products. The staff knows their stuff, so stop in to pick their brains about the latest cameras, video equipment and home entertainment systems. Two stores on St. Thomas: 31 Main in Charlotte Amalie, ☎ 340-776-0794, and in Building II at Havensight Mall, ☎ 340-776-0302; www.boolchand.com.

Royal Caribbean ✪ stocks all the big names such as Nikon, Panasonic, Sony and Seiko. In addition you'll find Lladró figurines, Mont Blanc pens, Dunhill lighters and Mikimoto pearls. The thing that makes Royal Caribbean unique is its large selection of so many famous brands. You'll probably cut down on your shopping time for specific items if you stop here first. The main store is at 33 Main Street, and another is located at the Havensight Mall. ☎ 340-774-1767 or 340-776-4110; www.royalcaribbean.vi.

> **TIP:** *Compare prices at Boochland's and Royal Caribbean before you buy a big ticket item.*

EYEWEAR

Davante carries 70 brands of glasses and sunglasses, so if you can't find something here, it probably isn't made. The staff is trained to help you choose the correct frame style for your face shape and lifestyle. Owner Marvin Freeman has 30 years experience in the eyewear business, and he stocks his store with the latest trends and most popular designs from around the world. Davante shops are also located in the US and France; the Caribbean shop is in the A.H. Riise Mall on the waterfront, ☎ 340-714-1220.

INTIMATE APPAREL

Lover's Lane sells seductive lingerie, steamy swimsuits and erotic playthings. Just the place to find a little goodie to give your vacation an exciting jump-start. This fun-to-browse shop is up a narrow flight of stairs on the Waterfront at 33 Raadets Gade. ☎ 340-777-9616. If you get hooked on this sort of thing, you can order a catalog by calling ☎ 800-266-9016 or check out their website, www.loverslane.com.

FASHION

Look for designer fashions by Fendi, Polo Ralph Lauren and DKNY in their own stores along Palm Passage. Nicole Miller is on Main Street at Palm Passage. Tommy Hilfiger has a store on the Waterfront at Royal Dane Mall. The two stores below carry a variety of top-name designers.

Cosmopolitan caters to repeat customers looking for labels such as Gottex of Israel, Bally of Switzerland and Paul & Shark of Italy. Shoes, handbags and men's and women's upscale fashions and beachwear are displayed in the two-level shop on the Waterfront at Drake's Passage, ☎ 340-776-2040.

ST THOMAS

Janine's Boutique still is considered a well-kept secret by stylish men and women who have patronized her shop for more than 20 years. They come to save 20-30% off US prices on their favorite designer wear from YSL, Cardin, St. John and Escada. Discover the secret among the other designer shops on the west side of Palm Passage, ☎ 340-774-8243.

FUN CLOTHES

Local Color shows off wearable art. Popular Jams World prints and hand-painted originals by local artists such as Sloop Jones fill the store. Men, women and children are sure to find the perfect island design to bring home as a souvenir. Located on the waterfront in the Royal Dane Mall, ☎ 340-774-2280.

PERFUME

Tropicana Perfume Shoppe ☆ will solve all your problems with which fragrance to buy at the best price. The skilled staff at this outlet will guide you through a huge stock of famous-name perfumes, colognes and aftershaves, including Dior, Chanel and Estee Lauder. The shop also sells cosmetics and skin care products in brands such as Clinique, Clarins and Lancôme. Browse through the historical building on the north side of Main Street across from Colombian Emeralds. ☎ 340-774-0010 or 800-233-7948.

LINENS

Mr. Tablecloth is the place to find imported tablecloths, place mats, runners and bed linens. Jeannie, the owner, searches for the best quality products made of cotton, Irish linen, poly-blends and organdy, and carries a wide range of sizes. Expect to pay about half of US retail prices. While linens are the obvious draw here, take a look at the handmade dresses and children's outfits. The shop is at 6 Main Street across from Hibiscus Alley, ☎ 340-774-4343.

NEWSPAPERS & MAGAZINES

Island Newsstand sells magazines and newspapers from the States along with novels, travel guides and snacks. Find it on the south side of the Grand Hotel complex across from Emancipation Park, ☎ 340-773-9109.

MUSIC

Parrot Fish has reggae, steel drum and other Caribbean sounds along with popular music from the US and Europe. A CD of island music makes a great souvenir. You'll remember the warm sun when you play it again and again on cold winter nights at home. Pick up your favorite tunes at 2 Store Tvaer Gade at Back Street, ☎ 340-776-4514; www.parrot fishmusic.com.

Havensight Mall

Havensight Mall is a complex of red-roofed buildings near the West Indian Dock. It was constructed for the convenience of cruise-ship passengers and its 100-plus shops include many of those found in the main shopping area in Charlotte Amalie. While the prices are the same, the in-town shops usually have more inventory. Avid shoppers will want to go into town, others will want to do a high-speed pass through Havensight before they hit the beach.

In addition to the expected retailers, you'll find an ATM, restrooms, pay phones, a post office, tourist information and a grocery mart. A few stores that are not found in town and are worthy of a visit include:

Caribbean Rum Balls have been a popular island treat since the 1970s when rum from St. Croix was added to an old family recipe for German candy. You can watch the confections being hand rolled at the modern Havensight factory (the staff rolls about 10,000 each day), then pick up a gift pack to take home. ☎ 340-775-6616; www.caribbeanrumballs.com.

Music Shoppe, owned by former state-side DJ Norman Grey. The store offers all types of music and musical instruments, including steel drums and steel pan music. There are

ST THOMAS

private listening stations where you can listen to tapes and CDs before you buy. ☎ 340-774-1900.

Dockside Bookshop is the place to stop for best-selling hardbacks and popular paperbacks. You'll also find travel guides, cookbooks and historical or fictional books written by Caribbean authors. ☎ 340-774-4937.

Around the Island

RED HOOK

Shops and restaurants line both sides of the main street (Route 32) that runs through Red Hook and past the dock where ferries leave for St. John. You don't need directions or an address since all storefronts face a short stretch of road. American Yacht Harbor is on the water side. Red Hook Plaza is across the road. You also can enter many of the waterside businesses from the harbor walkway.

Chris Sawyer Diving Store, American Yacht Harbor, has beachwear and diving gear. ☎ 340-777-7804.

Marina Market, Red Hook Plaza, is possibly the best, but not the largest, upscale grocery store on the island. They also make fresh take-out food. ☎ 340-779-2411.

Dolphin Dreams ☆ is packed with colorful clothing, unique jewelry (including the famous Caribbean Hook Bracelet) and local art. Owner Kathy Zeller paints glassware, which makes a great souvenir or gift. We couldn't resist the dainty jewelry holders and a couple of bracelets to display on them. Look for the shop at American Yacht Harbor, ☎ 340-775-0549.

Keep Left, at American Yacht Harbor, is a great place to pick up NAOT sandals, Patagonia dresses and Quicksilver swimsuits. The roomy store is also stocked with sun hats, sunglasses and original t-shirts. ☎ 340-775-9964.

UNUSUAL ARTWORK OFF THE BEATEN TRACK

Art lovers will want to make side trips to three outstanding sites that offer something special.

The Color of Joy ☆, near the Ritz-Carlton in the American Yacht Harbor complex, is owned by artist Corinne Van Rensselaer and is full of local artwork. The hand-painted birdhouses and island-style sarongs make great gifts or souvenirs. ☎ 340-775-4020; www.thecolorofjoy.com.

Tillett Gardens ☆ in the Tutu Estates on Route 38 is a real treat. This shady artists' complex was created from an old Danish farm in 1959 by the late artist Jim Tillett. Studios, galleries, workshops and restaurants surround the tree-filled natural garden where iguanas wander in search of Hibiscus-flower snacks.

Master craftsman Sonny Thomas invites you to watch him and other artists and craftsmen at work on projects that include paintings, silk-screen, stained glass, pottery and jewelry at the Tillett Studio, ☎ 340-775-1929. Prices are terrific. Quality is top-notch. The garden's ambience is calm, quiet and cool – a welcome break from the downtown bustle. Ask about the special arts and music festivals that are held in the gardens several times each year. Tillett Garden is open Monday through Saturday, 9 am until 5 pm, ☎ 340-775-1929, www.tillettgardens.com.

Kilnworks Pottery & Art Gallery is owned by artist Peggy Seiwert who turns out dozens of pottery designs, including ceramic fountains in tropical shapes. The gallery also exhibits works by other well-known local artists and sculptors, and has a working pottery studio is on-site. Call about special workshops and exhibits. The gallery is open Monday to Saturday, 9 am until 5 pm, at its location on Route 38/Smith Bay Road on the northeast shore near Grand Beach Palace Resort. Watch for the big green iguana holding the sign. ☎ 340-775-3979; www.kilnworkspotteryvi.com.

Mango Tango exhibits a large assortment of work by the most popular international artists. It also hosts a one-man show each month. Every artist represented at the spacious gallery spends at least some of their time in the Virgin Islands each year. The list includes such names as Don Dahlke, Max Johnson, Dana Wylder and Anne Miller. If you're looking for a specific Caribbean artist, chances are good that you'll find

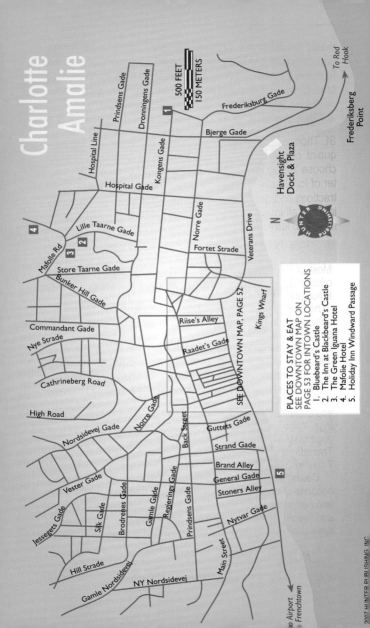

Charlotte Amalie

Prindsens Gade
Dronningens Gade
Hospital Line
Kongens Gade
Frederiksburg Gade
Bjerge Gade
Hospital Gade
Lille Taarne Gade
Norre Gade
Mafolie Rd
Store Taarne Gade
Fortet Strade
Bunker Hill Gade
Veterans Drive
Commandant Gade
Riise's Alley
Nye Strade
Raadet's Gade
Kings Wharf
Cathrineberg Road
High Road
Norre Gade
Nordsidevej Gade
Guttets Gade
Back Street
Strand Gade
Vester Gade
Brand Alley
Jessegers Gade
Silk Gade
Brodrehes Gade
Gamle Gade
Regjerings Gade
General Gade
Prindsens Gade
Stoners Alley
Hill Strade
Nytvar Gade
Gamle Nordsidevej
NY Nordsidevej
Main Street

500 FEET
150 METERS

Havensight Dock & Plaza

N

HUNTER PUBLISHING

To Red Hook

Frederiksberg Point

SEE DOWNTOWN MAP, PAGE 52

to Airport
to Frenchtown

2007 HUNTER PUBLISHING, INC

PLACES TO STAY & EAT
SEE DOWNTOWN MAP ON
PAGE 53 FOR INTOWN LOCATIONS
1. Bluebeard's Castle
2. The Inn at Blackbeard's Castle
3. The Green Iguana Hotel
4. Mafolie Hotel
5. Holiday Inn Windward Passage

them here. Selections include both originals and prints, most depicting island scenes. Find the colorful shop in the Al Cohen Mall at the top of Raphune Hill across from Havensight Mall. ☎ 340-777-3060.

◆ Where to Stay

St. Thomas has a complete range of accommodations from quaint city inns to luxurious ocean-side resorts. You may choose to stay in or near Charlotte Amalie and be in the center of local activity with easy access to shopping, tourist attractions and great restaurants. Or, you may prefer to check into an all-inclusive resort and be pampered without ever having to leave the property.

SPA SPECIFICS

Most of the top resorts offer guests massages, facials and other body-work services. Many now feature full-service spas. If you prefer an independent facility, try:

The Look Spa, at the marina in Frenchtown, is a welcoming oasis just outside the busy capital. Owner Bericia and her experienced staff offer a wide menu of individual nail, face and body treatments in addition to full- and half-day packages. Just drop in or call for an appointment. Open Monday-Friday 10 am-7 pm. ☎ 340-776-8672.

Zen Retreat Day Spa and Yoga Studio is just what you would expect at tranquil Tillett Gardens. The name alone tells you to expect Asian-inspired treatments and serene surroundings. Walk-ins are welcome, but call in advance to ask about yoga classes or specific therapeutic services. Open Monday-Thursday 8 am-8 pm, Friday 8 am-7 pm, and Saturday 9 am-7 pm. ☎ 340-774-8044.

Oasis Salon and Day Spa is popular with island residents because of the excellent massages and body wraps. All hair and nail services are offered, too, so call to book a few hours and live like a local. The serene oasis is open Monday-Saturday 9 am-6 pm in Red Hook Plaza, ☎ 340-774-4560.

NOTE: *The area code on St. Thomas is 340.*

ST THOMAS

Use the prices given for accommodations as a guide to the average high-season rate per standard double room. If the review is for an all-inclusive or all-suites resort, the listed price is the lowest available during high-season for two people sharing a room.

NOTE: *Hotel tax and service charge is 8% year-round.*

Rental Agencies

If you want to rent a condo, villa or private home, contact a couple of the following companies:

❖ **Paradise Properties** represents several villa complexes on the island. ☎ 340-779-1540 or 800-524-2038; fax 340-779-6109; www.st-thomas.com/paradiseproperties/.

❖ The president of **Calypso Realty**, Sharon Hupprich, has more than 20 years experience on St. Thomas. ☎ 800-747-4858; 340-774-1620; fax 340-774-1634; www.calypsorealty.com.

❖ **Beach Tops** is the rental agent for two- and three-bedroom villas at Tree Tops and Beach Top resort villages. ☎ 340-775-4110; fax 340-775-0377; www.beachtops.com.

SLEEPING WITH THE STARS

Our suggested list of lodging has reduced drastically for this Pocket Adventures book. You can browse the Internet as well as we can, and we encourage you to do so. Here you'll find possibilities to fit a variety of budgets. Properties marked with one star (☆) are highly recommended. When a single feature or the overall allure is particularly impressive, you'll find two stars (☆☆) beside the name. Three stars (☆☆☆) means, simply, WOW!

Charlotte Amalie & Vicinity

Bluebeard's Castle, PO Box 7480, Charlotte Amalie, St. Thomas, USVI 00801. ☎ 340-774-1600, 800-524-6599; fax 340-774-5134; www.bluebeards-castle.com. 160 rooms and suites. $180.

© Bluebeard's Castle

Sitting at the top of a hill overlooking the city and harbor, Bluebeard's Castle is part timeshare condos and part resort hotel, so rooms come in a variety of sizes. The grounds are lovely and the old tower that serves as the focal point for the resort adds a Pirates-of-the-Caribbean ambience. As one of the oldest structures on the island, Bluebeard's Tower is surrounded by tales of pirates, who are said to have used the lofty perch as a lookout and hideout between 1700 and 1718 – and may have buried discarded wives, slaughtered foes or captured booty under the stones (see below).

Despite the advanced age of the stone tower, the hotel is modern and in good-as-new condition. Each unit is furnished in rattan, decorated in bright island colors and outfitted with cable TV and refrigerators. The floors are cool ceramic tile and all rooms have ceiling fans as well as air conditioning. Suites are roomy and have well-equipped kitchens.

A complimentary shuttle transports guests over the hill to the beach on Magen's Bay, and the on-site pool has terrific views of Charlotte Amalie and the harbor. The resort is busy, even in low season, and there are plenty of activities to keep guests busy. Facilities include two tennis courts, a fitness center, gift shops, three restaurants and a bar with nightly entertainment. Golfers may arrange to play at nearby Mahogany Run. Ferries leave from town for St. John and Tortola.

ST THOMAS

PIRATE CASTLES

Bluebeard's and Blackbeard's castles dominate their own hills above Charlotte Amalie. Both are now luxurious hotels, but when they were built about 1680, they served as watchtowers for the island's natural harbor. There's no proof that pirates later used the towers for their personal business, and it's unlikely that any pirate actually lived in the castles. However, the thick-walled fortifications inspire all kinds of legends, and since secrecy surrounds the lives of these outlaws, some of the stories actually may be true. It is known that Blackbeard's was originally called Skytsborg (Danish for skyhill) and Bluebeard's was named Smitsberg (Smits' Hill) in honor of the island's governor when the tower was built.

The Green Iguana Hotel ☆, Mafolie Road, St. Thomas USVI 00802. ☎ 800-484-8825 or 340-776-7654, fax 340-777-4312; www.thegreeniguana.com. 9 rooms. $120.

© Green Iguana Hotel

Staying at this nine-room boutique hotel is more like staying in a private home, only better. The rooms are nicely laid out with a hilltop view toward Crown Bay; the bathrooms have roomy showers and dressing areas. The hotel is named for the green iguanas that live in the courtyard trees. Igor, the largest iguana, is more than two feet long, but quite harmless.

Best Western Emerald Beach Resort, 8070 Lindbergh Bay, St. Thomas, USVI 00802. ☎ 800-233-4936 or 340-777-8800; fax 340-776-3426; www.emeraldbeach.com. 90 rooms. $230.

© Best Western Hotels

If you want to stay near the airport, this Polynesian-like retreat is a good choice. It's right on the beach, has a waterfall swimming pool and a tennis court, and the seaside restaurant is open for every meal. All rooms are air-conditioned and have ceiling fans, refrigerators and coffee makers.

Hotel 1829, Government Hill, PO Box 1567, St. Thomas, USVI 00804. ☎ 800-524-2002 or 340-776-1829; fax 340-776-4313; www.hotel1829.com. 15 rooms and suites. $110.

This Spanish-style national historic site is named for the year it was completed by a French sea captain. Over the years, modern conveniences have been tucked into the old stone walls, and the multilevel inn is one of the leading small hotels in the Caribbean. It features high-ceilinged rooms with paddle fans, air conditioning, antique tiles, private baths, spectacular views and cable TV. Rooms surround a flower-filled courtyard that's been outfitted with a tiny swimming pool. A perfect blending of old and new. Even if you don't stay here, stop for a drink in the Dutch-kitchen bar or have dinner in the award-winning restaurant.

Mafolie Hotel, 7091 Estate Mafolie, St. Thomas, USVI 00802. ☎ 800-225-7035 or 340-774-2790; fax 340-774-4091; www.mafolie.com. 22 rooms. $155.

It's not fancy. In fact, the rooms and baths could be considered bare-bones basic, but the price is great and the views are spectacular. Mafolie sits 800 feet up in the hills above Charlotte Amalie with a dramatic panorama of the harbor. Stay here if you like small inns that are owned and operated by a family and have lots of personality. Guests gather poolside each morning for a light complimentary breakfast, then take the free shuttle to Magen's Bay Beach or hang around the pool enjoying

© Mafolie Hotel

ST THOMAS

snacks and drinks from the bar. Shoppers take a quick cab ride into town. The hotel's restaurant is an island favorite.

Marriott Morning Star Beach & Frenchman's Reef Resorts ☆☆, 5 Estate Bakkeroe, Flamboyant Point, PO Box 7100, St. Thomas, USVI 00801. ☎ 800-524-2000 or 340-776-8500; fax 340-715-6193; www.marriottfrenchmansreef. com. 504 units. $250.

These two resorts are located three miles east of Charlotte Amalie and can be reached by complimentary ferry service that runs hourly between the harbor and the Frenchman's Reef dock. Although Marriott owns the adjoining properties, each is unique.

Morning Star has 96 of the most luxurious room on the island in five three-story island-style buildings directly on the beach. Frenchman's Reef is a sprawling 406-room highrise perched dramatically on a cliff above the Caribbean across the bay from downtown Charlotte Amalie. All the rooms are typical of Marriott resorts in the states – nice, but no real surprises. The fantastic facilities and luxurious amenities are the attention-getters. Together, the two resorts have three pools, four tennis courts, five restaurants, six bars, a watersports center and a health club.

Holiday Inn Windward Passage, Veterans Drive (Rt. 30), Charlotte Amalie, St. Thomas USVI 00804. ☎ 800-524-7389 or 340-774-5200, fax 340-774-1231; www.holidayinn.st-thomas.com. 151 rooms and suites. $200.

© Holiday Inn Hotels

If you just want to shop, Windward Passage is a good hotel for you. All the rooms are air conditioned and outfitted with hair dryers, coffee makers, refrigerators, cable TVs and a safe for storing your jewelry purchases. When you need a break, jump into the hotel pool or take a free shuttle ride over to Magen's Beach.

East End

Bolongo Bay Beach Club & Villas ☆, 7150 Estate Bolongo, Route 30, St. Thomas, USVI 00802. ☎ 800-776-2840 or 340-775-1800; fax 340-775-3208; www.bolongobay.com. 75 rooms and 20 villas. $180 (room only), $500 (all-inclusive).

© Bolongo Bay Beach Club

The Doumeng family has owned and operated this informal resort on the south shore for more than 30 years. Repeat guests call it "Club Everything" because it packs two restaurants, three pools, a watersports center, health club, tennis courts, sand volleyball courts and a couple of basketball courts into eight acres set directly on a shady stretch of Caribbean beach. Guest choose between European and all-inclusive rates. Those who go for the top package get all meals, unlimited drinks and some water excursions. Don't come here expecting luxury. Bolongo's accommodations and facilities are geared toward the barefoot crowd who wants to lay back and have fun. If you can't vacation without checking your e-mail, WiFi hotspots are located around the pool

Ritz-Carlton ☆☆☆, 6900 Great Bay, St. Thomas, USVI 00802. ☎ 800-241-3333 or 340-775-3333; fax 775-4444; www.ritzcarlton.com. 200 rooms and suites. $500.

The name just about says it all. Elegance. Grandeur. Opulence. It looks like a palace in Venice, with 15 acres of lavish landscaping, a daydream swimming pool that seems to merge with the sea, and six three-story Renaissance-style buildings housing sumptuous guest rooms with marble

© Ritz-Carlton Co.

ST THOMAS

baths. The estate sits on a half-mile strand of white-sand beach that offers a variety of watersports. In addition, there are four lighted tennis courts and a full-service health club and spa. This splurge is definitely worth it.

Wyndham Sugar Bay Resort, 6500 Estate Smith Bay, Route 38, Smith Bay Road, St. Thomas, USVI 00802. ☎ 800-927-7100 or 340-777-7100; fax 340-777-7200; www. wyndham.com. 300 rooms. $400 (room only), $700 (all-inclusive).

The rates are high, but everything is included, so this newly-updated resort may fit into a moderate budget – especially if you bring the kids. Nicely appointed spacious rooms are in a two-tiered low-rise complex on a hill above the secluded beach that offers every type of water sport. On a typical day, you may drop the little ones at Kids Klub, workout in the fitness center, get a massage at Journey's Spa, then lounge by one of the three pools or get in a game of tennis before lunch. All meals and drinks are complimentary at the two restaurants and three bars.

The Anchorage, Route 317, Estate Nazareth, St. Thomas USVI 00802. ☎ 800-874-7897 or 340-775-2600, fax 340-775-5901; www.antillesresorts.com. 30 units. $375 (two-bedroom suite).

This upscale resort is part of a group of five St. Thomas properties run by Antilles Resorts. (Others in the group are Crystal Cove ☆, Point Pleasant, Sapphire Beach Resort and

Sapphire Village.) The Anchorage is similar to a private club with two- and three-bedroom units overlooking the beach at Cowpert Bay, about two miles from Red Hook. Each unit is a well-equipped condo with laundry facilities and cable TV. The palm-shaded grounds include two lighted tennis courts and a landscaped pool area.

Secret Harbour Beach Resort ☆, 6280 Estate Nazareth, St. Thomas USVI 00802. ☎ 800-524-2250 or 340-775-6550, fax 340-775-1501; www.secretharbourvi.com. 60 suites. $290 (studio).

This small, quiet resort is a cluster of low-rise buildings scattered in the hills and along the sand at Secret Harbor Beach, near Red Hook. Each spacious unit has a balcony looking out toward the calm water, a living/dining area, kitchen and one or two bedrooms. The resort's **Blue Moon**

Café is located on the water and serves good food all day at reasonable prices. On-site amenities include three tennis courts, a pool with hot tub, a beachside bar, dive center and gift shop.

© Secret Harbour Resort

ST THOMAS

◆ Where to Eat

You can eat extremely well in St. Thomas. Many great cooks choose to live on the island and create marvelous meals from the bounty of fresh seafood and local produce. However, you'll pay big-city prices for dinner at resort and upscale restaurants. Lunch is less expensive, and you can find excellent moderately-priced meals at casual cafés, bakeries and delis. (See page 33 for a listing of common West Indian specialties found at restaurants.)

> **TIP:** *Restaurants often change their hours during low season, so call to check.*

The following suggestions are a mix of restaurants in various price ranges. Most are located in or near Charlotte Amalie and neighboring Frenchtown, or in Red Hook. In addition, most resorts have at least one full-service restaurant and, usually, a beachside or poolside snack bar that serves sandwiches and light meals.

Use the prices given with each restaurant listing as a guide to the average price of a mid-range meal per person, excluding drinks and tip. There is no sales tax in the Virgin Islands, but restaurants may add a service charge, so check your bill before you figure your tip.

Charlotte Amalie

Virgilio's ☆☆☆, 18 Dronningens Gade/Main Street (enter on Store Tvaer between Main and Back Streets), ☎ 340-776-4920. Italian. Lunch $20, dinner $35. Open Monday-Sat-

© Virgilio's

urday, 11:30 am-10:30 pm. Credit cards accepted. Reservations recommended for dinner.

Stained glass set in exposed-brick walls. Cozy tables under crystal chandeliers. Soft music and rich aromas. If you're looking for an elegant and romantic dinner, this is the place. Patrons say owner Virgilio del Mare serves the best Northern Italian cuisine in the Virgin Islands.

Hervé ☆☆, Government Hill, ☎ 340-777-9703; www.herverestaurant.com. American/French. Lunch $15, dinner $30. Open Monday-Saturday, 11:30 am-3 pm and 5 pm-

10 pm; Sunday, 5 pm-10 pm. Credit cards accepted. Reservations recommended for dinner.

Hervé Chassin earns praise for his culinary skills, and his restaurant is considered one of the finest in the Virgin Islands. The recently remodeled hillside setting offers breathtaking views of the town. There's an excellent wine list and the bartender makes a fabulous Chambourd martini.

© Hervé's

Gladys' Café, Royal Dane Mall, ☎ 340-774-6604. Island specialties. Breakfast $8, lunch $10, dinner $18. Monday-Saturday, 6:30 am-3 pm; Sunday, 8 am-2 pm. Credit cards accepted.

Before you hit the shops, fortify yourself with Gladys' thick French toast or freshly baked bread with jam. Stop back for lunch to enjoy island specialties such as conch in butter sauce, or go American with a hamburger.

Lillian's Caribbean Grill ☆, 43-46 Norre Gade at the Grand Galleria across from Emancipation Garden. ☎ 340-774-7900. West Indian specialties. Breakfast $8, lunch $10, dinner $18. Monday-Saturday, 7:30 am-9:30 am and 11:30 am-5:30 pm. Credit cards accepted.

This is where locals come to enjoy a hearty breakfast or quick lunch of fish or chicken served with typical island side dishes. Lillian's also offers burgers and French fries, but the real delicacies are freshly made salads and West Indian cuisine.

Tickles Dockside Pub, Crown Bay Marina, West of Charlotte Amalie. ☎ 340-776-1595; www.ticklesdocksidepub.com. Breakfast $10, lunch $12, dinner $20. Open daily 7 am-10:30pm; bar stays open later. Credit cards accepted.

© Tickles Dockside Pub

Situated right on the dock at Crown Bay Marina, this local hangout is known for its great pancakes, burgers and seafood platters. Prices are low. Food is good. Bar chat is excellent. Sit outside on a nice evening, or dine indoors in the open-air dining room. You may have to wait for a table at peak dining times, but you almost always can get a spot at the long bar.

LUNCH SPOTS

For a lunch break in Charlotte Amalie, try **The Greenhouse** ($12), ☎ 340-774-7998, on Waterfront at Store Tvaer Gade near Chase Bank (also open for breakfast), or **Bumpa's** ($8), ☎ 340-776-5674, on Waterfront at Cardow's Walk near Diamonds International.

Cuzzins Restaurant & Bar (☆), 7 Back Street, ☎ 340-777-4711. West Indian. Lunch $15, dinner $25. Open Monday-Saturday, 11 am-9:30 pm. Credit cards accepted.

Local art and island recipes make this a must-stop. You'll be dining in a century-old building that originally served as a livery stable. Now the Back Street dining room is popular with hungry locals and tourists. We suggest you try the conch fritters and, if you've got a big appetite, order the *Cuzzin Nemo*, a mix of seafood in a Creole sauce served over pasta. Add a ginger beer or sea moss drink, and you've got a real Caribbean-style meal.

Frenchtown

Frenchtown, the close-in western suburb of Charlotte Amalie, has a selection of good restaurants and bars that are especially popular after dark. To reach the neighborhood by car, drive west on Waterfront Highway and turn left (south) at the first stop light past the pink-and-white post office.

Craig and Sally's (☆), 22 Honduras, Frenchtown, ☎ 340-777-9949. Eclectic/Gourmet. Lunch $15, dinner $40. Open Wednesday-Friday, 11:30 am-3 pm and Wednesday-Sunday, 5:30 pm-10 pm. Credit cards accepted. Reservations recommended for dinner.

A meal at this creative little restaurant is so much fun, you'll want to return again and again. Twenty types of wine are available by the glass; Craig, the connoisseur, will help you decide which of the more than 200 selections to try. Sally, the chef, concocts a different dinner menu each night based on the freshest available ingredients. You may want to make a meal of the appetizers and finish with a homemade dessert.

The Pointe Planet Villa Olga, 8 Honduras Frenchtown, ☎ 340-774-4262. Steaks and seafood. Dinner $40. Open daily, 5:30 pm-10 pm. Credit cards accepted. Reservations recommended.

Ask for a table right at the water's edge and plan to arrive when the bar opens at 5:30, so you can enjoy a drink while you watch the sun set. At dinner, order a gourmet specialty or try the 75-item buffet. Save room for the mud pie.

LUNCH SPOTS

For a quick lunch or snack, stop by the **Frenchtown Deli & Coffee Shop** (☎ 340-776-7211, lunch/snack $5-8) at the Frenchtown Mall for a cup of Green Mountain coffee and a bagel or sandwich. They make their own bread and you can take out or eat there. Open Monday-Friday, 6 am-8 pm; Saturday, 6:30 am-5 pm; and Sunday, 8 am-4 pm.

Red Hook

A string of fine restaurants and casual cafés line both sides of Route 32, which runs through Red Hook. The area bustles with activity because of the ferry dock and charter boat operations, and the little town really starts hopping after dark.

Café Wahoo, Piccola Marina/American Yacht Harbor, ☎ 340-776-6350. Dinner $25. This upscale Euro-Carib restaurant is open daily, 6-10 pm. Credit cards accepted. Reservations highly recommended.

Ultra-fresh fish is the catalyst that makes this split-personality restaurant so excellent. Owner Bruce McGiaty, a European-trained chef, proudly opens the door to his walk-in refrigerator to display glistening whole fish waiting to be cut into serving portions. At lunch time, the catch is used in sushi and tempura. In the evening, it becomes the focal point of creative gourmet dinners. Katja, Bruce's charming German wife, presides over the open-air dining room that's perched above Vessup Bay. Dinner patrons enjoy a splendid selection of entrées that include Caribbean wahoo encrusted with island spices, sea prawns flambéed in gin cream sauce with fettuccine, and Caribbean lobster teamed with filet of Black Angus beef. In addition, there are pastas, chicken and lamb. At lunch, the menu includes vegetarian and seafood rolls, tempura, sushi and salads.

Molly Malone's Irish pub (downstairs) and **Whale of a Tale**, a seafood restaurant (upstairs), are in one waterfront location at American Yacht Harbor, ☎ 340-775-1270. Molly's (breakfast $8, lunch $12, dinner $20) is open daily, 7 am-1 am. Whale of a Tale (dinner $30) is open Thursday-Sunday, 6 pm to 10 pm. Credit cards accepted. Reservations are accepted only at Whale of a Tale.

Owner Frank Brittingham is the Irish connection on St. Thomas. A board set up beside the bar at Molly Malone's keeps track of the number of days until St. Patrick's Day, and such things as shepherd's pie and ham 'n cabbage are featured on the menu. Upstairs, the new Whale of a Tale restaurant serves seafood, steaks and pasta.

Duffy's Love Shack ☆, Red Hook Plaza, Route 32 ☎ 340-779-2080. Eclectic. Lunch/snack $5-$10, dinner $20. Open daily, 11:30 am-2 am. No credit cards.

You won't have a problem finding this rocking, bubbling, green-shuttered island hut. It sits in the parking lot diagonally across from the ferry dock, and if the blaring music doesn't get your attention, the crowd will. The bartenders create exotic concoctions such as "Lime in Dee Coconut" and "Love

Potion Number 9" and serve them up in wacky containers that you take home. Food selections include steaks, ribs, burgers and tacos. Patrons often linger well into the early morning hours dancing on table tops, entering contests to win prizes, and just hangin'.

Off the Hook ☆, Route 32 next to the ferry dock in Red Hook. ☎ 340-775-6350. Seafood and Caribbean. Dinner $20. Open daily 6 pm-10 pm. Credit cards accepted. Reservations recommended.

If you want your seafood fresh off the boat, this is the place for dinner. Pasta, chicken and steaks are on the menu, but fish is the best choice. All entrées come with West Indian side dishes. Tables are outside with views of the harbor.

LUNCH SPOTS

Grateful Deli (☎ 340-775-5160, breakfast $5, lunch/snack $8), in the same parking lot as Duffy's, is the place for vegetarian meals, outstanding sandwiches, made-to-order omelettes and fresh salads. Open Monday-Friday, 7 am-6 pm; Saturday, 7 am-5 pm; Sunday, 7 am-3 pm.

Around the Island

The Agavé Terrace ☆☆☆, Point Pleasant Resort, #4 Smith Bay (Route 38), ☎ 340-775-4142, www.agaveterrace. com. Seafood. Dinner $30. Open nightly, 6 pm-10 pm. Credit cards accepted. Reservations recommended.

Greg Miller owns this elegant award-winning restaurant tucked into a lush hillside garden with breathtaking views of St. John. Arrive early to enjoy a drink on the terrace that offers a panoramic view of the

© Agavé Terrace

ocean. Then check out the catch-of-the-day choices written on a blackboard at the entrance. A steel pan band plays on

Tuesdays and Thursdays beginning at 7 pm. Other live music is presented on Mondays and Fridays.

Fungi's on the Beach, Point Pleasant Resort, Route 38, ☎ 775-4142. Lunch $12, dinner $20. This is Agavé's casual waterfront sibling. Head here after a hot afternoon in the sun for a local microbrew or one of their signature tropical drinks. The open-air café serves burgers, sandwiches and salads between 11 am and 10 pm.

The Old Stone Farm House ☆, Route 42 near the Mahogany Run Golf Course, ☎ 340-777-6277; www.oldstone farmhouse.com. Continental. Dinner $40. Open 5:30-9:30 pm, Tuesday-Sunday. Credit cards accepted. Reservations recommended.

© Old Stone Farmhouse

Chef Brian Katz has been voted the best chef on St. Thomas, and the Old Stone Farm House has been voted the top gourmet restaurant on the island, so set your expectations high. You won't be disappointed. The food is fantastic, and the ambiance of the 200-year-old stone building is superb. The menu features sushi, filet mignon, snapper and duck. Side dishes fall into the fantasy category with highlights such as truffle egg white salad and eel mango sushi roll.

◆ Nightlife

Unfortunately, St. Thomas has some problems with crime. It's a good idea to take a cab, rather than walk, when you go out in the evening, and many visitors prefer to bypass Charlotte Amalie after dark. Don't hesitate to go directly to a restaurant or club in town, but avoid strolling along the narrow, poorly-lighted streets.

Frenchtown is somewhat safer, but be cautious about walking along dark or isolated roads. Red Hook tends to be jumping every night, especially during high season. Pick up a free copy of *St. Thomas This Week* and check out the list of current entertainment and events.

You will always find a crowd and, usually, live music at the following popular nightspots:

Duffy's Love Shack ☆, Red Hook Shopping Plaza, Rte 2. ☎ 340-779-2080; www.duffysloveshack.com. Open daily 11:30 am-2 am with music and dancing starting around 9:30 pm. This place is an island legend. Locals know, and visitors soon learn, that it is the hotspot for tropical drinks and heavy partying. Bring cash – they don't take credit cards.

The Greenhouse, Veterans Drive, across from the waterfront in Charlotte Amalie. ☎ 340-774-7998. Open Sunday-Thursday, 10:30 am-2 am. If you want to find a party in the capital, head for this spot on the main road of the shopping district. Most nights, a local DJ emcees the music, and you can enjoy some type of drink special beginning about 9 pm.

Caribbean Saloon at the American Yacht Club in Red Hook, ☎ 340-775-7060, www.caribbeansaloon.com. The big screen is always tuned to sports events, and Happy Hour is Monday-Friday, 4 pm-7 pm and Monday-Thursday, 10 pm-1 am. Food and drinks are served until four in the morning, and a DJ plays music on Wednesday, Friday and Saturday nights.

Iggie's at Bolongo Bay Beach Resort, Route 30, ☎ 340-775-1800. Live music, fire eaters and *mocko jumbies* (stilt walkers) entertain on Wednesdays from 8 to 10 pm.

Epernay, Route 3016 in Frenchtown. ☎ 340-774-5348. Open Monday-Wednesday, 11:30 am-11:30 pm, Thursday-Saturday, 11:30 am-midnight. This wine and champagne bar isn't a late-night party-hardy type place. Here you'll enjoy a great dinner accompanied. A great variety of international wines are offered by the glass or bottle. You can stop in for hors d'oeuvres at the bar or reserve a table for dinner.

Tickles Dockside Pub, Crown Bay Marina. ☎ 340-776-1595; www.ticklesdocksidepub.com. Open daily 7 am-10:30pm. More a hangout than a restaurant, this popular open-air hotspot is known for daylong fun. There's live music at the bar several days a week.

Pistarkle Theater, Route 38, in Tillett Gardens on Smith Bay Road. ☎ 340-775-7877; www.pistarkletheater.com. Check St. Thomas This Week or call the theater to find out what's on stage.

Reichhold Center, Route 30, on the campus of The University of the Virgin Islands. ☎ 340-693-1559; www.reichholdcenter.com. Many performances are by visiting choirs and symphonies, but local groups also put on shows at this open-air theater. Call ahead for tickets, and ask for seats under the roof, if you suspect there's a chance of rain.

◆ Island Facts & Numbers

AIRPORT: Cyril E. King International Airport, ☎ 340-774-5100. STT is the airport code.

AREA CODE: The area code for all US Virgin Islands is 340. You may dial direct from the States. No area code is needed when dialing within St. Thomas.

BANKS, ATMs: Most banks are open Monday-Thursday, 9 am-2:30 pm and Friday from 9:30 am-2 pm and 3:30 pm-5 pm. ATMs are located throughout the island, including at the airport and both cruise-ship docks.

DRIVING: Traffic stays to the left. The speed limit is 20 mph in towns and 35 mph in the countryside.

ELECTRICITY: 110 volts, 60 cycles, as on the US mainland.

EMERGENCIES: Ambulance, ☎ 911; Fire Department, ☎ 911; Police, ☎ 911; Police Non-Emergency, ☎ 340-774-2211; St. Thomas Hospital, ☎ 340-776-8311; US Coast Guard Rescue, ☎ 340-714-2851; hyperbaric chamber for divers, ☎ 340-776-2686 or 787-865-5818.

GOVERNMENT: The US Virgin Islands are an unincorporated territory with a non-voting delegate elected to the US House of Representatives. Anyone born on the islands is a US citizen.

HOSPITAL: Roy L Schneider Hospital, ☎ 340-776-8311.

INTERNET ACCESS: Little Switzerland Internet Café, upstairs at their store on Main Street. ☎ 340-776-2010. **WiFi** access is popping up all over the island, with availability at Havensight Mall, several areas of downtown Charlotte Amalie and at the American Yacht Harbor in Red Hook. Resorts with hotspots (but not in all rooms) include Bolongo Bay, Holiday Inn, Marriott Frenchman's Reef, Ritz Carlton, Wyndham Sugar Bay and Secret Harbour.

LAUNDROMAT: La Providence behind Tutu Park Mall is open daily, 6 am-11 pm. ☎ 340-777-3747.

LIQUOR LAWS: The legal drinking age is 21, as on the US mainland. Minors may not enter bars or purchase liquor.

MONEY: The US dollar is the legal currency throughout the Virgin Islands. Travelers' checks and major credit cards are acceptable at most locations, but always carry some cash for smaller establishments.

NEWSPAPERS, MAGAZINES: The *St. Thomas Daily News* publishes an entertainment section each Friday. *St. Thomas This Week, USVI Playground* and *What To Do* are free publications that are available at hotels and other tourist-oriented locations throughout the island. Local news is published in *The Virgin Islands Daily News*, ☎ 340-774-8772, available at newsstands. US mainland newspapers are sold at major resorts.

POST OFFICE: US post offices are located on Main Street in Charlotte Amalie, and in Frenchtown, Havensight Mall, Sugar Estate and Tutu Mall. Stamps are priced the same as on the US mainland.

TAXES: There is no sales tax or departure tax. An 8% surcharge is added to all hotel bills.

TELEPHONE DIRECTORY INFORMATION: ☎ 913.

TOURIST INFORMATION: In the US, information is available from **The US Virgin Islands Division of Tourism**, 1270 Avenue of the Americas, New York, NY 10020 ☎ 800-372-USVI (8784); www.usvitourism.vi.

You can also get information from **The Caribbean Information Office**, ☎ 800-621-1270 (in the US); ☎ 847-699-7570 (outside the US); fax 847-699-7583, www.caribbeans.com, or from **The St. Thomas/St. John Hotel & Tourism Association**, PO Box 2300, Veterans Drive Station, St. Thomas, USVI 00803. ☎ 340-774-6835; www.sttstjhta.com.

In Canada, information is available from **The US Virgin Islands Tourism Department**, 703 Evans Avenue, Suite 106, Toronto, Ontario M9C 5E9, ☎ 416-622-7600.

In the UK, contact **The US Virgin Islands Tourism Department**, 2 Cinnamon Row, Plantation Wharf, York Place, London, England SW11 3TW, ☎ 0207-9785262.

On St. Thomas, stop by the **Hospitality Lounge** in the Grand Hotel, across from Emancipation Park on Tolbod Gade. It's open Monday-Friday, 8 am-5 pm. ☎ 340-777-8827.

WEBSITES: www.usvitourism.vi; www.st-thomas.com.

WEDDINGS: It's easy to get married in the USVI. For full details about the various requirements, call the Department of Tourism for a brochure called *Getting Married in the United States Virgin Islands*, ☎ 800-372-USVI. To apply for a license, write to the Territorial Court of the Virgin Islands, Box 70, St. Thomas, USVI 00804, ☎ 340-774-6680. You can also download a marriage application and a "Wedding & Honeymoon" brochure at www.usvitourism.vi.

Water Island

Water Island can be seen from the harbor in Charlotte Amalie. It's less than half a mile from shore, and you get there by taking the **Water Island Ferry** (☎ 340-690-4159/ 4446 or 340-775-5770), which leaves from the pier outside Tickles Dockside Pub at Crown Bay Marina west of the city. One-way daytime tickets cost $5 for adults (round-trip fare is $9); nighttime rates are a bit more, and kids pay half the adult fare. Check the timetable posted outside the pub, or call to make arrangements with the captain for a private run at an unscheduled time.

Charlotte Amalie with Water Island in the background.

Once you're on the island, take some time to explore its un-developed 500 acres, which stretch 2½ miles from tip to tip. You can walk among the ruins of long-abandoned planta-tions, dilapidated slave cabins, an old fort and empty ammu-nition bunkers, but the more interesting sites are the tranquil beaches and green rolling hills that top out at 300 feet. Except for the hour or so when passengers of the *Kon Tiki* party boat come loudly ashore at Honeymoon Beach each after-noon, the island is delightfully quiet. You'll understand why the 160 residents refer to it as "the last virgin."

◆ Sightseeing

Roads and paths lead to all the beaches and historical sites on the island, and since the land is only a mile wide and 2½ miles long, everything is within walking distance. You can sign up for a bike tour with **Water Island Bike Tours** (☎ 340-

ST THOMAS

714-2183 or 340-775-5770), which lasts about three hours and costs $50 per person, including the ferry ride over from St. Thomas, use of an 18-speed mountain bike, helmet, water, and guide.

Fort Segarra, built to protect the submarine base on St. Thomas during World War II, is at Flamingo Point, about 1½ miles southwest of the ferry dock at Phillips Landing. It has a rooftop observation deck that offers a superb 360-degree view of the Caribbean and surrounding islands. Most of the fort is underground, and you'll need a flashlight to explore its rooms and tunnels.

Carolina Point, north of the ferry dock, has a long history. It's listed on maps and historical papers from the 1700s as Carolina Lyst, and an archeological dig in 1998 unearthed cisterns, ovens and masonry foundations from that era. For more than a century, the Carolina Plantation and one other, La Providence, produced cotton, sugar and other crops with the labor of as many as 100 slaves. After emancipation in 1848, the plantations declined and their owners sold the land to the Danish East Asiatic Company.

Honeymoon Beach.

◆ Adventures on Water

Beaches

Palm-shaded **Honeymoon Beach** has fine white sand for lounging and calm water for swimming or snorkeling. You have a good chance of finding perfect solitude here, especially on a weekday. The *Kon Tiki* party boat may dock there around two in the afternoon, but the passengers don't stay long and there's plenty of beach for everyone. On weekends, residents use this beach for picnicking, swimming and volleyball games, and vendors come out to sell drinks, sandwiches and barbecue. You can walk to Honeymoon from the ferry dock at Phillips Landing in about 10 minutes. Follow the main road uphill to an intersection; take a right, and go downhill to the beach.

Limestone Beach.

Limestone Beach is directly across the island from Phillips Landing, and it will take you about 25 minutes to walk over the hill and back down to the beach. Since the water is rougher and deeper than at Honeymoon, don't plan to swim, but explore the tide pools and walk along the deserted rocky shore. Take the main road from the ferry dock, up the hill, as if you were going to Honeymoon Beach. When you get to the intersection, continue straight for a quarter-mile to Limestone Road, which is on the left, over a low rise. At the next intersection, turn left and walk toward a house, which has a narrow dirt road running along its left side that leads to the beach.

Sprat Bay is technically a public beach, but access to it is through a gated neighborhood and it's probably not worth the hassle to get there. If you decide to give it a try, plan to go by boat. The sand-and-pebble beach has calm water and is located off the main road northeast of Limestone Beach.

◆ Where to Stay

Flamingo Point Estate, ☎ 813-933-4132, www.greatrentals .com or www.flamingopointusvi.com, near Fort Segarra, is a cliff-top private home available for weekly rental. The four-bedroom, two-bath house has a great room (living, kitchen, and din-

© Flamingo Point

ing area) that opens onto a wide, wrap-around covered porch. Expect to pay about $1,600 per week for the house. If you need more room, there are two one-bedroom suites with full kitchens, private baths and living areas that can be rented along with the house for an additional $400 per unit per week.

© Providence Point
Aerial view of Providence Point.

Waterfront Cottage and Apartments, ☎ 340-774-6929 or 340-774-2635, www. water-island.com, at Providence Point, near Phillips Landing and Honeymoon Beach, are actually three two-bedroom houses owned by Alex Randall and his family. All the cottages are quite spacious and have a kitchen, living area and use of the boat dock and dinghy. Guests also have unlimited use of a spectacular multi-level pool and deck that sit at the tip of Providence Point, surrounded by the sea. Each cottage rents for $1,000 to $1,200 per week. Check out the pictures online or call Alex for more information.

Flamingo Bay Villas, ☎ 786-201-3733, www.water-is-land-villas.com, is a new group of duplex apartments with air-conditioned bedrooms, living areas with a queen-size sofa-sleeper and kitchenettes. Covered verandas offer terrific views of the harbor and St. Thomas. Maggie and Geoff Morrison rent the villas for $900 per week, which includes the use of a golf cart for sightseeing and transportation around the island.

Mi Casa, ☎ 340-775-5274, www.micasa-de-water-island.com, is a cozy cottage for two owned by veteran fisherman Steve Malpere, who runs Peanut Gallery Fishing Charters (www.fishingstthomas.com). A golf cart is included in the rental price, but you'll be tempted to spend most of your time sitting on the deck that overlooks the sea. Weekly rates are $1,200 per couple. Call Steve for information and available rental dates.

Turtle Hill, ☎ 215-641-1888, 215-990-4372, www.turtle hillwaterisland. com, is a two-bedroom, two-bath apartment located on the upper level of a hillside home overlooking Flamingo Bay. The living and dining area open onto a small kitchen, the covered veranda provides views of the sea, and a patio is furnished with an umbrella table for outdoor meals. Guests can use the downstairs laundry room and

© Turtle Hill

ST THOMAS

ride a golf cart to get around the island. A one-week rental runs $1,400. Contact Pam Callanan for details and reservation.

◆ Where to Eat

Pirate's Ridge Deli and Convenience Store is a small, well-stocked store, deli and open-air bar just up the hill from Honeymoon Beach. The daily lunch menu includes sandwiches, burgers and pizza, and you can choose to eat inside the air-conditioned restaurant or on the patio. On Friday, Saturday and Sunday evenings, the kitchen turns out steaks, ribs and fish for dinner. ☎ 340-774-9422. Lunch/snacks $8-$10, dinner $20.

    Heidi's Honeymoon Grill is a popular weekends-only eatery run by a local resident from her mobile restaurant parked on Honeymoon Beach. There's no phone, but you can check the dinner menu, which is posted weekly on the bulletin board at the ferry dock. Lunch/snacks $5-$8, dinner $15.

St. John

◆ Overview

St. John is the most "virgin" of the US Virgin Islands. Almost two-thirds of the 20-square-mile island is protected as a national park, which makes it a true paradise for nature lovers and outdoor adventurers.

The 108,000 people who live permanently on the island are united in their commitment to preserving St. John's unspoiled beauty and West Indian charm while offering tourists plenty of creature comforts. Eighteenth-century ruins and underwater coral gardens are rigorously safeguarded, and almost the entire shoreline is protected by the US Park Service. Yet, careful developers have managed to provide a wide selection of accommodations, restaurants and shops on the west end.

Cruz Bay is a small village that serves as the administrative capital and only real town on the island. The rest of St. John is made up of dense forests, steep hills and white-sand beaches bordering clear-to-the-bottom turquoise seas. Well-maintained roads run along most of the coast and cut through the interior to provide easy access to miles of hiking trails, excellent snorkeling and diving spots, and interesting historical sites.

Divers rate the underwater wrecks, reefs, caves and wildlife off St. John's shores among the best in the Caribbean. Visibility is normally good enough to allow snorkelers to view much of it from the surface, and the 225-foot underwater trail at **Trunk Bay** has signs identifying a variety of formations, fish and other sights. It's not unusual to spot sea turtles, rays and large schools of colorful fish near the shore.

◆ Getting There

Visitors to St. John arrive by boat, since there is no airport. Unless you have a private boat, the simplest way to reach St. John is to fly to St. Thomas then take a ferry from either the Charlotte Amalie harbor or Red Hook.

NOTE: *The area code on St. John is 340.*

By Ferry

FROM ST. THOMAS

Cruz Bay on St. John is only three miles across Pillsbury Sound from **Red Hook**, and ferries make the 20-minute trip every hour from 6 am until midnight. Schedules change, but normally the first ferry leaves Cruz Bay for St. Thomas at 6 am, and two early-morning ferries leave Red Hook for St. John at 6:30 am and 7:30 am, then hourly from 8 am until midnight. At night, the last ferry leaves Cruz Bay at 11 pm, and the last ferry leaves Red Hook at midnight. One-way tickets cost $5 for adults, $1 for children under 12, $1.25 for seniors. Contact Transportation Services for information and schedule changes, ☎ 340-776-6282.

Cruz Bay ferry dock.

Ferries leave the harbor in **Charlotte Amalie** for Cruz Bay every two hours between 9 am and 4 pm, with an additional ferry departing at 5:30 pm. Ferries from Cruz Bay back to Charlotte Amalie leave every two hours between 7:15 am and 2:15, with an additional ferry departing at 3:45 pm. One-way tickets for the 45-minute trip cost $10 for adults and $3 for children. Schedules may change, so contact Transportation Services to verify the timetable, ☎ 340-776-6282.

FROM THE BVI

If you're coming from the British Virgin Islands, Inter-Island Boat Services provides daily service between Cruz Bay and Tortola's West End. The crossing takes about 30 minutes and the round-trip fare is $35. In addition, the ferry from St. Thomas to Jost Van Dyke stops to pick up and drop off passengers on St. John on Fridays, Saturdays and Sundays. Service to Virgin Gorda is provided on Thursdays and Sundays. Call **Inter-Island Boat Services** for the exact schedule and fares, ☎ 340-776-6597.

◆ Getting Around

By Car

To see all of St. John it is a good idea to rent a four-wheel-drive vehicle. Good roads reach most of the island, but some of the best views and scenery are along dirt tracks. Representatives of car rental companies meet visitors at the ferry dock, so it's not hard to find wheels. However, in high season you should make a reservation, especially if you want to rent from a well-known company.

RENTAL CAR AGENCIES	
C & C	☎ 340-693-8164
L&L Jeep Rental	☎ 340-776-1120; www.bookajeep.com
St. John Car Rental ☆	☎/fax 340-776-6103 www.stjohncarrental.com
Varlack	☎ 340-776-6412; www.varlack-ventures.com

ST JOHN

Most companies have weekly and daily rates that range from $50 to $90 per day during the winter. Most companies require renters to be at least 25 years of age, with a valid drivers license and major credit card.

> **NOTE:** *Remember that driving is on the left side of the road.*

By Bus

Vitran buses leave from the ferry dock at **Cruz Bay** on the west end for **Coral Bay** on the east end every hour at 25 minutes past the hour. The cross-island trip takes about 45 minutes, and the buses return along the same route after they drop off riders. A one-way ticket is $1 for adults, 75¢ for children, 55¢ for seniors. ☎ 340-776-6346 or 340-774-5678.

By Taxi

Taxi drivers meet passengers as they get off the ferry in Cruz Bay. In addition, you'll find cabs along the streets in town and at the hotels, restaurants and main attractions throughout the island.

The fare from Cruz Bay to Coral Bay, at the opposite end of the island, is $16 for one passenger, $9 each for two or more passengers. Other fares vary but are regulated by the St. John Taxi Commission. You can always ask to see a rate card and agree on a fare before you enter the cab.

◆ Touring the Island

Guided Tours

You can get an overview of the entire island on a two-hour guided tour. Driver/guides are easy to find near the ferry dock, and you can also request a guide from **St. John Taxi Services**, ☎ 340-693-7530. Expect to pay about $30 for up to two people or $12 per passenger for three or more in one cab.

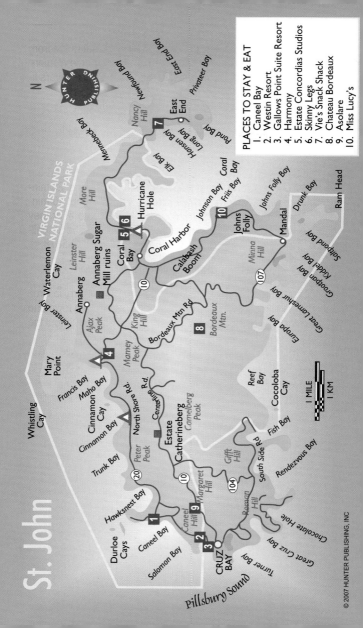

St. John

PLACES TO STAY & EAT
1. Caneel Bay
2. Westin Resort
3. Gallows Point Suite Resort
4. Harmony
5. Estate Concordias Studios
6. Skinny Legs
7. Vie's Snack Shack
8. Chateau Bordeaux
9. Asolare
10. Miss Lucy's

VIRGIN ISLANDS NATIONAL PARK

© 2007 HUNTER PUBLISHING, INC

Island tours also are offered by: **Varlack Ventures** ☆, ☎ 340-776-6412, www.varlack-ventures.com; **Wesley Easley Tour Bus** ☆, ☎ 340-693-8177; **C&C Taxi Service**, ☎ 340-693-8164.

STAR ATTRACTIONS

The following sites and attractions are recommended. Those with one star (☆) are worthy of a detour, and you should consider allowing extra time for those marked with two stars (☆☆).

Independent Four-Wheel-Drive Tour

The best way to explore St. John on your own is in an open-air four-wheel-drive vehicle that allows maximum visibility as you navigate back roads and steep hills. Although the island is only nine miles long, allow an entire day to cover the most interesting sites. You'll need several more days to hike in the **Virgin Islands National Park** and snorkel or dive the many extraordinary underwater sites.

Cruz Bay, on the west end of the island, is the logical starting point for any tour. Ferry boats from St. Thomas arrive at the dock here, and you can walk through the charming little town before you pick up your rental car. There are unique shops, funky bars and quirky restaurants along the main streets.

INFORMATION SOURCES

Pick up maps and island information at the **Tourist Center** between the clinic and the post office just north of the park across from the ferry dock in Cruz Bay, ☎ 340-776-6450. The **Virgin Islands National Park Service Visitor Center** is across from Mongoose Junction off North Shore Road in the northern section of the bay known as **The Creek**. Here you'll find a variety of information about park activities including ranger-led hikes and tours. The center is open daily, 8 am-4:30 pm. ☎ 340-776-6201; www.nps.gov/viis.

Cruz Bay.

The **Elaine Ione Sprauve Library and Museum of Cultural Arts** is located in the restored greathouse of Estate Enighed (EN-ee-high), which was established about 1750 and became a major source of sugar production on St. John. In 1976, the site was admitted to the National Register of Historic Places and refurbished as a library and museum. If history interests you, stop in to see the permanent collection of historical artifacts and rotating exhibits of local art. It's located on the east end of the business center in Cruz Bay, on Route 104, and is free. Monday-Friday, 9 am-5 pm. ☎ 340-776-6359; www.library.gov.vi/sprauve.

The **Ivan Jadan (Zhadan) Museum** pays tribute to the greatest Russian tenor of the 20th century. Jadan was the premier lyric tenor of the Bolshoi Theater from 1928 until 1941, when he became the first major artist dissident to escape Stalin's reign of

Jadan, 1937.

terror. He spent his last 40 years on St. John. Find the museum south of the ferry dock off Bay Street on Genip/Frangipani Lane. It's open Monday-Saturday, 9 am-11 am and 4-6 pm. ☎ 340-776-6423; www.ijadan.vi.

When you're ready to leave Cruz Bay, take **Route 10** (Centerline Road) heading east into the national park. You'll have fabulous views as you drive along the mountain ridge that runs east/west through the island. A couple of miles outside of town, just past the Community Health Center, watch for a newly paved road called John's Head Road (Route 206) that leads to the beaches along North Shore Road. Turn left to the partially restored ruins of **Estate Catherineberg** (also known as Hammer Farms).

Estate Cathrineberg was one of the first thriving sugar plantations on St. John. Ruins of the rectangular-shaped factory lie near the intersection of Route 10 and John's Head Road. Evidence of a rum distillery are a short distance away. Across the road, you'll find a restored windmill that is in excellent condition and has intriguing tunnels. Nearby, there are ruins of a warehouse with lovely stone archways.

Return to Centerline Road and continue to **Coral Bay** ☆, a sleepy little village favored by the yachting crowd for its protective harbor. Coral Bay was the first spot on St. John to be settled by the Danes in the 17th century, and several ruins in the area are left over from pre-emancipation days.

The yellow building with the red roof sitting on a hill is the **Emmaus Moravian Church**. You probably won't be able to get inside, but local legend says the site is haunted by a spirit that appears as a ram on nights with a full moon. The story stems from accounts that John Reimert Sodtmann and his stepdaughter were murdered on this spot during the first day of the slave rebellion in 1733. The ruins of **Fort Berg**, which the slaves captured after murdering Sodtmann, are on Fortsberg Hill, which juts out into Coral Bay above Harbor Point.

After Coral Bay, Route 10 continues as **East End Road** and becomes dramatic with steep climbs and sharp turns. The views are spectacular, but the road is rough and leads to the sparsely populated arid tip of the island. Unless you have several days on the island, your time will be better spent turning back west and following Route 10 to Route 20 and **The Annaberg Ruins**.

Annaberg Ruins.

The Annaberg Plantation ☆☆ is the best-preserved estate on St. John, and a stroll through the grounds will give you a good grasp of what it was like to live on the island as a master or a slave before emancipation. The National Park Service has outlined a 30-minute self-guided walking tour of the property and tagged each building with a descriptive plaque to make your visit more enlightening.

Annaberg was established in 1718, and run by overseers who reported to the absentee owner, Christopher William Gottschalk. Since the landholder didn't live on the island, there is no "greathouse," but you can inspect the remains of the 16-structure wattle-and-daub slaves' quarters. The dirt-floor hovels were topped with a thatch roof made from sugar cane leaves.

Elsewhere on the estate, you'll see a cookhouse, jail, sugar factory and windmill made of native stones, imported bricks (brought over as ballast used to stabilize slave ships) and island coral. The 40-foot windmill was built in the early 1800s to supplement the power generated by the horsemill. Both mills at Annaberg ran full speed all day and night during harvest, since juice had to be extracted from the cane within 24 hours of cutting to prevent spoilage.

> **FACT:** *A wind-driven mill could crush up to 100 cart loads of sugar cane per day, while the less efficient animal-driven mill could crush only half that amount.*

Looking up at an old arch.

Adults visitor (age 16 or older) to the plantation are charged a $4 per person admission fee; kids are free. There are no official visiting hours for the ruins, but the National Park Service conducts tours and gives living-history demonstrations at various times. Contact the NPS Visitors Center in Cruz Bay for information, ☎ 340-776-6201; www.nps.gov/viis.

As you walk around the plantation, you'll have excellent views of the British Virgin Islands and **Leinster Bay**. A map near the windmill identifies the distant islands, and a trail beginning at the picnic area runs along the shoreline to a beach at the eastern end of **Waterlemon Bay**. This path is part of an old Danish road that allows unobstructed views across the Sir Francis Drake Channel, and there is great snorkeling between the beach and tiny **Waterlemon Cay**.

Back on Route 20, it's a short drive west to **Maho Bay** ☆ and one of the Caribbean's most lavish eco-minded campgrounds. (See *Where to Stay*, page 180, for camping information.) From this point to Cruz Bay, Route 20 (North Shore Road)

Leinster Bay.

passes a series of clear-water bays bordered by long stretches of sandy, palm-shaded beach. **Cinnamon Bay** has the longest beach as well as campsites, **Trunk Bay** ☆ features an underwater snorkel trail, and **Hawksnest Bay** has three close-in reefs that harbor abundant sea creatures. Visitors to Trunk Bay are charged a $4 per person per day user fee.

◆ Adventures on Water

Best Beaches

St. John's coast is lined with more than 35 marvelous beaches, so it's difficult to assemble a concise group of "bests." **Trunk Bay** ☆ tops most lists, and you'll want to spend some time there, but plan to visit a few of the other beaches as well. The sweeping white sands of the northern beaches tend to be the most crowded, but the National Park Service keeps them in good condition. Many south-shore beaches are tricky to access from land, so they are more private, but lack facilities.

If you have only a day on the island, head directly to Trunk Bay. You won't be disappointed. If you have more time, try several beaches, including the more remote ones. Each offers incredible views and most provide passage to excellent underwater scenery along offshore reefs. Unlike other islands, where developers claim the best oceanfront property, most of St. John's beaches are within the national park, so you won't find fast-food joints and high-rise condos messing up the landscape.

Trunk Bay.

PUBLIC OR PRIVATE?

All beaches in the Virgin Islands are public from the water to the line of vegetation growth. However, land abutting the beach may be privately owned, and owners may restrict access to the beach through their property. Presently, there are very few restrictions, but this could change at any time. When you approach a beach by land through private property or a neighborhood, ask permission. Hotels and campgrounds usually request that guests register at their office. Individuals simply appreciate the courtesy of being asked.

NORTH SHORE BEACHES

The following beaches, listed west to east from the town of Cruz Bay, are some of the best on St. John's northern coast.

Solomon Bay and **Honeymoon Bay** are between Cruz Bay and the Caneel Bay Resort off Route 20 (North Shore Road). You can walk there along the Lind Point Trail that begins at the National Park Visitor Center in town (1.1 miles with a .4-mile ascent), but you'll probably want to drive or take a cab to the parking area at the top of the hill just past Mongoose Junction. The path that connects to the Lind Point Trail is on the right at the end of the paved road. After walking about 50 yards, you'll come to the main trail, where you'll turn right and continue another 50 yards to the Solomon Bay Spur Trail on the left. If you want to go to Honeymoon Bay, simply bypass the spur trail and continue on along the Lind Point Trail.

At the end of either trail, you'll be rewarded with a breathtaking view of distant islands across Pillsbury Sound from a shaded white sand beach. The fringing reef between the two bays provides some of the best snorkeling off the north shore, but since it lies in shallow water, novice snorkelers may have trouble avoiding contact. Swimmers will appreciate the feet-friendly soft-sand bottom at both beaches.

> **TIP:** *Park rangers don't approve, but it's well known that skinny dipping and nude sunning takes place at Solomon Bay.*

Caneel Bay ☆ is home to the well-known Caneel Bay Resort that Laurance Rockefeller developed in the early 1950s. You are required to register as a day guest if you're not staying at the re-

Caneel Bay Beach.

sort. Ask the security guard at the entrance where to park. Check in, then head for the ocean. The bay called Caneel is actually a series of beaches, but unless you arrive by boat or stay at the resort, you can visit only one, Caneel Beach. And that's ok, because it's stunning. If you don't want to hassle with the restrictions, go a couple of miles farther east to Hawksnest Bay or Trunk Bay.

Hawksnest, the next beach east on Route 20, is popular with locals and may be crowded on weekends. White sand stretches from the beach into the water for easy access, cov-

ered picnic tables are scattered around the area, and trees between the parking lot and water provide shade. You'll find lovely elkhorn coral on the reef straight out from the middle of the beach.

Hawksnest Bay.

Trunk Bay ☆, just over a mile east of Hawksnest, has the best facilities on the island, and is perhaps the most gorgeous beach in the Virgin Island chain. Shaded white sand, clear turquoise-blue water, stunning views and a 200-yard labeled snorkeling trail draw crowds of tourists. Try to arrive early in the morning or just before sunset to enjoy the beach at its uncrowded best. The $4-per-person admission fee buys you access to the picnic area, snack bar, equipment-rental stand, showers and shops.

Cinnamon Bay ☆☆ is the longest beach on St. John. Over a half-mile of soft white sand stretches along this north-shore bay and extends into the water. Facilities include a restaurant, snack bar, restrooms, picnic tables and telephones. Lifeguards are on duty during the day, and **Cinnamon Bay Watersports Center**, ☎ 340-776-6330. Beach Shop rents snorkeling equipment, lounge chairs, kayaks, bikes and windsurfing boards. You can also arrange for scuba tours or sailing trips right on the beach. Windsurfing is good here, especially in the afternoon, when the wind picks up. During the winter months, the waves are big enough for surfing and boogie boarding. Tiny

Cinnamon Bay.

Cinnamon Cay is just offshore, a hiking trail starts across the road from the parking lot, and Cinnamon Bay Campground offers overnight facilities. (See *Hiking* and *Where to Stay* for more information.)

Maho Bay ☆, right beside Route 20 just over a mile from Cinnamon Bay, is especially popular with children because of the calm, shallow water. Sea grass provides a home for fish, rays and turtles, so snorkeling is good. Maho Bay Campground extends up the nearby forested hillside with access off a secondary road about 1½ miles east from where Route

Maho Bay.

20 curves inland from the beach. **Little Maho Bay**, at the campground, is small, but offers soft white sand and gentle waters for swimming. Day visitors can register to use the facilities here, which include a restaurant, restrooms, general store and an activities desk. **Maho Bay Watersports Center**, ☎ 800-392-9004, 340-776-6240, offers kayaking, windsurfing, scuba and snorkeling.

ST JOHN

Waterlemon Bay, off a dirt road just past the parking lot for the Annaberg Plantation, is at the eastern end of Leinster Bay. The beach is rocky, but the water is excellent for snorkeling, especially around Waterlemon Cay, just offshore. A hiking trail at the far eastern end of Waterlemon Bay Beach leads to an area where you can enter the water and snorkel

out to the cay. Between the main island and cay, the water is shallow, the bottom is sandy, and you may spot turtles, rays and starfish. A reef surrounds three sides of the cay. The current can be strong at

Waterlemon Bay.

times, so be cautious, and don't try it at all if you're a weak swimmer. There are no facilities here, so bring snacks, drinks and snorkeling equipment.

SOUTH SHORE BEACHES

During the winter, the surf on north shore beaches can be too rough for comfortable swimming and snorkeling. When that occurs, the south shore beaches are a fine alternative. They are less crowded year-round, and many offer excellent snorkeling along the rocky shores and nearby reefs. The following, listed west to east from the town of Cruz Bay, are some of the best on the south coast.

Frank Bay is on the southern edge of Cruz Bay, and you easily can walk there from town. From the ferry dock, go south on Strand Street, past Wharfside Village, to Bay Street. Follow Bay past Gallows Point Resort to the beach at Frank Bay. You'll have fantastic views of offshore islands from the shaded rock-and-sand beach, but getting into the water can be tricky because of coral and sea urchins near the shore.

Chocolate Hole, about a mile east of town off Route 104 (South Side Road) on blacktopped Chocolate Hole East Road, is usually quiet, but you'll have to work your way around moored boats to get to a clear swimming spot. Once you're in the water, you'll find good snorkeling around the reef off the eastern end of the beach. Homeowners in the area currently allow access through the neighborhood.

Klein Bay is great for snorkeling. Get there by going east on Route 104 until the paved road turns left and heads north up Gift Hill and a dirt road forks off to the right and continues east toward Fish Bay. Take the dirt road to the right and drive about a half-mile to a cement road. Turn right onto the paved road, then right again on a little road that dead-ends at a trail leading to the water.

> **NOTE:** *If you see homeowners about, ask permission to take the path across private land down to the beach. Usually, no one minds.*

Klein Bay Beach is on the eastern side of the larger **Rendezvous Bay**, and on the western side of a spit of land called Dittlif Point. (Fish Bay is on the eastern side.) The beach at Klein is made up of pebbles, but you won't have much trouble walking on them as you enter the water. Once the pebbles turn to rock and coral, watch out for spiky sea urchins. The water is calm on this western side of Dittlif Point, and you often can spot turtles, rays and other interesting creatures, along with abundant fish.

Genti Bay is at the end of the popular **Reef Bay Trail**, and hikers often swim and picnic there. The National Park Service leads scheduled group hikes, but if you want to do it on your own, pick up the trail on Route 10 (Centerline Road) about five miles east of Cruz Bay. The trail is 2.2 miles long and the one-way hike takes about two hours. Along the way you pass interesting ruins. At the end, you will be rewarded with the sandy beach at Genti Bay, which is part of the larger Reef Bay. (See page 166 for more information on the Reef Bay Trail.)

ST JOHN

Salt Pond Bay lies at the end of Route 107, which branches off Route 10 at Coral Bay. A downhill trail to the beach begins at a parking area about four miles south of the 107/10 intersection.

> **TIP:** *This end of the island is arid, so the quarter-mile trail passes through cactus scrub with no shade. Plan to go early in the day, bring plenty of water and wear sunscreen and a hat.*

When you reach the water, you'll find a secluded white sand beach, picnic tables and a chemical-toilet outhouse. The sea is usually calm here and snorkeling is excellent. The left side of the bay has large rocks and a reef. The right side is also rocky with some coral, but the area off mid-beach is covered with seagrass.

If you want to see the salt pond, follow the **Drunk Bay Trail**, which starts at the south end of the beach. Evaporated ocean water leaves crystalized salt in the pond, and you can

sometimes find interesting things living in shallow pools. Consider making the two-mile trek out to **Ram's Head Point** at the far tip of the peninsula. The point itself is on top of a 200-

Drunk Bay & Ram's Head.

foot sheer cliff that plunges straight into the ocean. The hike is demanding, but you'll enjoy dramatic views from this mystical spot.

Little Lameshur Bay and **Great Lameshur Bay** are difficult to access, but worth the trouble. Many adventurous hikers trek to the beach along a steep and rugged road at the western end of Route 107, past Salt Pond. Rental companies hate to hear that you attempted this road in one of their vehicles, but if you have a robust four-wheel-drive and off-road experience, go for it!

You'll come to Great Lameshur Bay first. The beach is made up of cobblestones and rocks extend into the water. Little Lameshur, to the west, is a white-sand beach with picnic tables and toilets. A narrow stretch of land called **Yawzi Point** separates the two. Both usually are deserted and you can spend an entire afternoon exploring the trails, ruins and coves along the two bays. Remember to bring plenty of water and snacks.

Scuba Diving & Snorkeling

More than 5,000 acres of the Virgin Islands National Park lie underwater. Perfect, clear, calm water makes snorkeling and scuba diving excellent ways to explore these pristine regions, and **Trunk Bay's** labeled **snorkeling trail** is a good place to start. Blue and white plaques along the 200-yard trail identify the types of coral and sea life common in the Virgin Islands. You're likely to see parrotfish, angelfish, sergeant majors, blue tang and butterfly fish among the coral. Entrance fee at Trunk Bay is $4 per person for anyone over 16 years of age, and snorkel equipment is available for an additional $4 plus a $25 refundable deposit. Contact the National Park Service for information about scheduled snorkeling tours, ☎ 340-776-6201, www.nps.gov/viis.

Cinnamon Bay Watersports rents snorkeling equipment on the beach at Cinnamon Bay for $4 plus a $25 refundable deposit. The best snorkeling is around the offshore island of **Cinnamon Cay**, and the best way to get out there is by kayak, which you also can rent at Watersports for $10 an hour. ☎ 340-776-6330.

Other spots with excellent snorkeling include:

Waterlemon Cay off the eastern end of Leinster Bay. Here you'll find starfish, yellowtail snapper and jawfish. Currents can be strong, so only strong swimmers should attempt to swim from the beach to the cay. The surf may be too rough for snorkeling during winter.

Salt Pond Bay, on the far southern tip of the island, has coral reefs on each end of the bay which attract abundant fish and sea creatures. You may spot an octopus, turtle, or eel among the rocks.

Chocolate Hole, on the southwestern coast, has interesting rocks jutting from the water just offshore. A shallow reef on the west side of the rocks attracts parrotfish, rays, squirrelfish, and turtles. Even novice snorkelers can navigate this area since the water is usually calm on the south side of the island.

Rent snorkeling equipment in Cruz Bay from **Cruz Bay Watersports** (☎ 340-776-6234) for $10 per day. Most dive operators will allow snorkelers to go along on scuba trips and **Cruz Bay Watersports** runs a daily snorkeling trip from the Westin Resort dock each afternoon. The cost, including equipment, is $55. Make reservations in advance.

Certified divers will want to explore some of the 30 sites within a 20-minute boat ride of St. John. Many of the sites are off the northwestern coast, and favorites include the tunnels at **Thatch Cay**, the rocky ledges at **Congo Cay** and the submerged areas of **Carvel Rock**. Visibility usually is excellent, and the craggy islets and colorful coral mounds draw crowds of large fish, rays and eels. **Eagle Shoals**, a large reef plateau with a hollow center off Coral Bay on the southeastern coast, is more remote and less visited. Experienced divers will want to explore the caves and swim-through tunnels here.

DIVE OPERATORS

The following dive shops offer first-class PADI instruction, multi-level certification, guided dive trips and equipment rental. Most operators schedule two boat trips daily and arrange instruction courses to meet visitors' vacation plans.

Expect to pay $60 for a one-tank dive, $25 for a two-tank dive, about $100 for an introductory resort-course dive and $385 for an open water certification course. Snorkelers can often go along for $20 on half-day trips and $30 on full-day trips. Divers with their own equipment can expect a 10% discount.

Cruz Bay Watersports, with locations at Cruz Bay in the Lumberyard Complex south of Mongoose Junction, and at the Westin Resort, has three custom dive boats and features wreck, reef, drift and night dives. Introductory and refresher classes are held daily at the Westin Resort pool. ☎ 340-776-6234: fax 340-693-8720; www.divestjohn.com.

Low Key Watersports ☆, on the water at Wharfside Village in Cruz Bay, leads dive tours and snorkeling expeditions. Owners Bob and Ann Marie also run a retail shop with resort clothing and sports equipment. Other services include tank fills, day sails to the nearby British Virgin Islands, kayak tours and parasailing. ☎ 800-835-7718 or 340-693-8999; fax 340-693-8987; www.divelowkey.com.

6-Paq Scuba is an unusual name for an unusual dive operation. PAQ stands for "Pretty Awesome Quality" and sums up owner Colette Diede's goal of providing customer-tailored fun and high-end service. The NAUI/PADI shop specializes in guided tours for small groups to out-of-the-way spots. You can book a private or semi-private charter dive. ☎ 340-776-1057; www.6paqscuba.com.

Maho Bay Watersports books scuba trips through the activities desk at Maho Bay Camps. The PADI shop offers full service from certified-diver trips to beginning instruction. Lo-

ST JOHN

cated on the beach at the eco-camp, ☎ 340-776-6240; www.
maho.org/scubadiving.

Snuba

Snuba ☆ is an alternative to snorkeling and diving, and a
combination of both. Using a special dive system that floats
so you don't have to wear a tank, you can dive up to 20 feet.
No experience is necessary and anyone over the age of eight
can do it. The $65 price includes a guided underwater tour
and all equipment. Give it a try at Trunk Bay with **Snuba of
St. John**. ☎ 340-693-8063; www.visnuba.com.

Boating & Sailing

The Virgin Islands are a legendary cruising area and all visitors to St. John should plan to spend some time on the water.
Day sails including lunch and drinks range from $90 to $100;
half-day excursions with snorkeling stops are priced around
$60.

SCHEDULED CRUISES

Gypsy Spirit II, a 35-foot DuFour yacht captained by Doug
and first mate Teka, specializes in weddings and vow renew-
als, but also offers day sails, champagne sunset cruises and
longer charters. ☎ 340-344-2211.

Wayward Sailor ☆ is owned by Philip Chalker, a master licensed captain with more than 25 years of Caribbean sailing
experience. He runs full-day trips with two snorkel stops and
lunch, half-day trips with one snorkel stop and snacks, and a
champagne-and-hors d'oeuvres sunset trip. Since Captain
Philip is a minister, he is authorized to officiate at on-board
marriage ceremonies. ☎ 340-473-9705; www.wayward
sailor.net.

Breath ☆ was built as a small tall ship by her owner and
captain Peter Muilenburg and has been featured in several
magazines. Peter and his wife, Dorothy, have snorkeled every reef and visited every cove of every Virgin Island since
they arrived in 1968. They enjoy showing *their* islands to up

Opposite: Sailboat © Dean Perrus/Dreamstime

to 12 guests in scheduled and customized sailing trips. ☎ 800-655-7630 or 340-776-6922.

© Adventurer

Catamaran Adventurer.

Adventurer, a 50-foot catamaran, has a large deck and sunning nets for relaxing during the full-day sail to Jost Van Dyke, the half-day snorkeling sail or the champagne sunset sail. It leaves from the Westin Resort, ☎ 340-693-8000, extension 1832, or 340-693-7328; www.adventurervi.com.

Sea Gypsy Charters, run by Captain Catherine Packo, specializes in full-day snorkeling trips around the US and British Virgin Islands. She supplies the powerboat, *Lucky Dog*; you bring money for lunch, snorkel gear and a passport, if you want to go to stop in BVI. ☎ 340-693-8020; www.cathypacko.com.

CHARTER BOATS

Expect to pay about $1,250 per person per week for a crewed charter. Bare-boat rates with no provisioning average $2,000 per boat, per week for a vessel that sleeps up to four passengers.

Adventures in Paradise will help you select a boat to suit your needs and make all the arrangements for your vacation charter. The office is located across from the post office in Cruz Bay, ☎ 340-779-4527.

Powerboats can be booked through ***Ocean Runner*** on the waterfront at Wharfside Village in Cruz Bay, ☎ 340-693-8809, www.oceanrunner.vi, or ***Nauti Nymph*** at the Westin Resort in Cruz Bay, ☎ 340-775-5066. For something more modest, stop by **Noah's Little Arks** at Wharfside Village. They rent fully-equipped dinghies for island-hopping for $130 per day. ☎ 340-693-9030.

NOTE: *US Citizens will need to show a valid passport on all visits to the British Virgin Islands.*

Fishing

Charter boats leave St. John for the same sportfishing spots frequented by St. Thomas fishermen. Boats from **American Yacht Harbor** (☎ 340-775-6454) in Red Hook will stop at Cruz Bay to pick up passengers before heading for the north drop or close-in reefs.

FISHING OPERATORS

The following companies book excursions out of St. John:

Adventures in Paradise, next to the post office in Cruz Bay, arranges all types of watersports adventures, including fishing. ☎ 340-779-4527.

St. John Adventures, at Gallows Point in Cruz Bay, will book a variety of excursions, including sport fishing. ☎ 800-323-7229 or 340-693-7730.

Gone Ketchin' ☆, a 31-foot Rampage Sportsfisher, is available for fishing charters from Cruz Bay. ☎ 340-714-1175; www.goneketchin.com.

Parasailing, Windsurfing & Kayaking

Arawak Expeditions ☆, based at Cruz Bay, rents kayaks and runs guided full-day, half-day and multi-day kayaking/camping trips. Contact them for details and reservations, ☎ 800-238-8687 or 340-693-8312; www.arawakexp.com.

Low Key Watersports, at Wharfside Village in Cruz Bay, schedules parasailing and sea kayaking excursions. ☎ 800-835-7718 or 340-693-8999; www.divelowkey.com.

Wind N Surfing Adventures in Cinammon Bay rents kayaks and windsurfing boards. ☎ 340-693-5902.

Crabby's Watersports ☆, next to Voyages at Coral Bay, rents sea kayaks, snorkel gear and dinghies. They can also arrange other activities with various operators. ☎ 340-714-2415; www.crabbyswatersports.com.

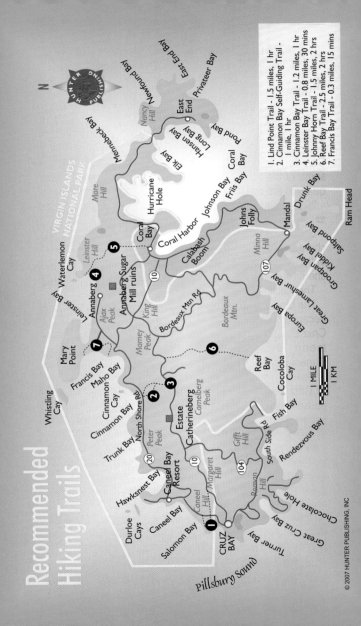

Recommended Hiking Trails

1. Lind Point Trail - 1.5 miles, 1 hr
2. Cinnamon Bay Self-Guiding Trail - 1 mile, 1 hr
3. Cinnamon Bay Trail - 1.2 miles, 30 mins
4. Leinster Bay Trail - 0.8 miles, 2 hrs
5. Johnny Horn Trail - 1.5 miles, 2 hrs
6. Reef Bay Trail - 2.5 miles, 2 hrs
7. Francis Bay Trail - 0.3 miles, 15 mins

VIRGIN ISLANDS NATIONAL PARK

N
HUNTER PUBLISHING

© 2007 HUNTER PUBLISHING, INC.

1 MILE
1 KM

Pillsbury Sound

Whistling Cay
Durloe Cays
Hawksnest Bay
Caneel Bay
Salomon Bay
CRUZ BAY
Turner Bay
Great Cruz Bay
Chocolate Hole
Rendezvous Bay
Fish Bay
South Side Rd
Reason Hill
Gifft Hill
Margaret Hill
Caneel Hill
Caneel Bay Resort
Peter Peak
North Shore Rd
Trunk Bay
Cinnamon Bay
Cinnamon Cay
Maho Bay
Francis Bay
Mary Point
Waterlemon Cay
Leinster Bay
Annaberg
Ajax Peak
Annaberg Sugar Mill ruins
Mamey Peak
King Hill
Bordeaux Mtn Rd
Estate Catherineberg
Camelberg Peak
Bordeaux Mtn.
Reef Bay
Cocoloba Cay
Europa Bay
Great Lameshur Bay
Groopan Bay
Kiddel Bay
Saltpond Bay
Ram Head
Drunk Bay
Mandal
Minna Hill
Johns Folly
Calabash Boom
Friis Bay
Johnson Bay
Coral Bay
Coral Harbor
Hurricane Hole
More Hill
Leinster Hill
Elk Bay
Hansen Bay
Long Bay
Pond Bay
East End
Privateer Bay
Essex End Bay
Newfound Bay
Nancy Hill
Memebeck Bay

20
10
104
107
10

◆ Adventures on Foot

Hiking

Hiking trails in St. John's national park are as fantastic as the beaches and underwater treasures. Pick up a map and trail-guide brochure at the Virgin Islands National Park Headquarters on North Shore Road a block north of the ferry dock in Cruz Bay. Park rangers conduct guided hikes and tours of some of the most popular trails and historical sites. Headquarters are open every day except Christmas from 8 am to 4:30 pm, and all trails are open daily during daylight hours. ☎ 340-776-6201; www.virgin.islands.national-park.com.

Choose one of the 22 trails outlines in the trail-guide brochure available from the park department to hike independently. All trails are marked and well maintained, but you should always walk with another person on self-guided hikes.

The following are *Adventure Guide* favorites:

The **Lind Point Trail** (1.1 miles, 1 hour, one way) is popular because it starts near the National Park Headquarters in Cruz Bay and is relatively easy, ending at beautiful Honeymoon Beach on Caneel Bay.

Heading north out of Cruz Bay, the trail passes through cactus scrub for about 0.2 miles, then forks, with the path straight on leading to the Solomon Bay spur (see *Best Beaches*), and the main trail to the right ascending to the north. Take the uphill route to the right another 0.2 miles to the **Lind Point Battery**

Early part of the Lind Point Trail.

Overlook (160-foot elevation). English cannons once stood on the point to defend the harbor from possible takeover by French troops, and now you can sit and observe modern-day activity in the town and bay. As you walk around the point and gaze in all directions, you will see offshore cays and islands and the northern coast of St. John.

Leave the overlook and hike east through dry forest and past intriguing rock formations. Continue past two spur trails (the first goes to the Virgin Islands Biosphere Reserve and the second to Solomon Bay) to a third spur that leads uphill to the Caneel Hill Trail across North Shore Road. From here the Lind Point Trail continues downhill to Honeymoon Beach.

> **TIP:** *Always tell someone where you plan to hike and when you plan to return. The activities director or receptionist at your hotel can keep track of this information if you don't know anyone else on the island.*

The **Cinnamon Bay Self-Guiding Trail** (0.5 miles, 1 hour, round trip) is an easy loop hike past the ruins of a 19th-century sugar plantation. Pick up the trail across North Shore Road from the entrance to Cinnamon Bay campground. Signs identifying sections of the historic plantation and surrounding vegetation mark the shaded trail that passes by the grave sites of Danish settlers. Walls from the sugar factory sit at the beginning of the trail, and a distillery to the southwest was used to produce bay rum oil after the sugar market collapsed. From the distillery, the trail passes through a tropical forest where bay rum trees grow. The cemetery is down a short spur trail. As you hike back toward the road, you will pass some of the oldest and largest fruit trees on the island. The estate house, west of the factory, was built early in the 20th century out of galvanized steel to replace the original home that was destroyed by a hurricane.

Don't confuse the self-guiding loop trail with the **Cinnamon Bay Trail** ☆ (1.1 miles, 1 hour, one way), which is longer and more difficult. The marker for this trail is east of the ruins of Cinnamon Bay plantation's storage house. The trail follows an old Danish road and ascends about 700 feet, with the steepest part at the beginning. Most of the hike is through forest and takes you to an overlook with a fantastic view.

The **Francis Bay Trail** (0.3 miles, 15 minutes, one way) is easy to hike. Pick up the trail at the Park Service storage building near the intersection of Leinster Bay Road and the road that leads to Maho Bay Campground. You will pass the ruins of the Francis Bay Estate, which are in shaky condition and shouldn't be explored. Vegetation along the path is dry scrub that has not recuperated from years of cattle grazing, and you'll wonder why you're bothering with this trail... until you come to ponds that harbor an abundance of birds, including herons, kingfishers, sandpipers and egrets. Past the ponds, you can head downhill toward the beach at Francis Bay or take the trail to the left to benches and a boardwalk along the salt pond.

> **TIP:** *Always carry plenty of water when hiking on St. John. Clean drinking water is not available within the park, and hiking in the heat causes quick dehydration.*

The **Leinster Bay Trail** ☆ (0.8 miles, 30 minutes, one way) offers gorgeous views of Leinster Bay and the Sir Frances Drake Channel, which divides the USVI from the BVI. The trail begins near the picnic area at the Annaberg Plantation on the paved Leinster Bay Road. It is part of an old Danish road that runs along the water's edge, and you can cool off with a  swim at the beach about halfway down the trail. Ruins of the Leinster Bay Estate are at the end of the trail.

NOTE: *Keep a little way back from the ruins and don't climb on them; they are fragile and may collapse.*

At the east end of the bay, the **Johnny Horn Trail** (1.8 miles, 2 hours, one way) connects with the Leinster Bay Trail and a spur path leads north to Waterlemon Bay. Tiny Waterlemon Cay lies just offshore. Excellent snorkeling exists between the main island and the cay. (See *Scuba Diving & Snorkeling*, page 153.)

The **Reef Bay Trail** ☆☆ (2.2 miles, 2 hours, one way) is considered one of the best hikes in the Caribbean, and the National Park Service (☎ 340-776-6201 for reservations) offers guided outings that include return by boat from the beach at the end of the trail. While the trail is downhill, rangers warn that the hike can be difficult due to its length and rocky terrain. If you go on your own, remember that the return hike will be uphill and quite strenuous.

The trail begins at stone steps across from the parking area 4.9 miles east of Cruz Bay on Centerline Road, and descends through subtropical forest that was never cleared for sugar cane fields. After a rain, the trail in this area can be slippery. As you hike down the valley, the vegetation turns to dry forest then scrub, and you may spot wild donkeys and hogs nearby.

About a half-hour into the hike, you'll come to the ruins of the 18th-century Jossie Gut Sugar Estate. (The word *gut* describes low spots where rainwater collects and flows towards the ocean. The bottom of a *gut* generally is washed down to bare rock, while the sides nourish abundant vegetation.) Farther down the trail, you'll pass the ruins of a house that was part of Estate Par Force. A few minutes later, you will come to the turn off to the **Lameshur Bay Trail** (1.5 miles, 1½ hours, round trip) on the left. This trail leads to a path to the Reef Bay Greathouse and connnects to the beach at Lameshur Bay.

Continue until you come to the marked **Petroglyph Trail** ☆ (0.2 miles, 15 minutes, round trip) on the right. The trail is flat and ends at a waterfall and freshwater pool. The pictures and symbols carved into the rocks around the pool have not been scientifically dated and many theories surround their origin. Most people think the carvings were made by pre-Columbian Indians, probably the Tainos, and there are some similarities with aboriginal markings found on other islands. Another explanation is that the carvings were made by runaway slaves who hid out in the area.

Back on the Reef Bay Trail, you will go along level ground to the partially restored Reef Bay sugar factory. See the horsemill that used animal power to crush sugar cane, and the boiling room where crushed cane was dried before it was burned. The boiling bench and copper boiling pots were once used to cook the cane juice into sugar. Behind the horsemill you will find above-ground graves of the former owner of the estate and his two daughters.

Just beyond the ruins is your reward – the beach at **Genti Bay**. See *Best Beaches*, page 153.

Tennis

Tennis players may use the public courts near the fire station in Cruz Bay on a first-come, first-serve basis. The courts are lighted until 10 pm. Guests at the **Westin Resort** have complimentary use of six lighted courts. Others may reserve a court by paying a $15-per-hour fee. Call for reservations, ☎ 340-693-8000. **Caneel Bay Resort** has 11 courts managed by Peter Burwash International under the direction of pro Patrick Alle. Call about lessons or matches and events, ☎ 340-776-6111.

Golf

St. John isn't known for its golf courses, but a new entertainment park now offers miniature and reality golfing. **Pastory Gardens** ☆ is off Centerline Road, about a mile from the ferry dock in Cruz Bay. The miniature course has 18 holes with 40- to 60-foot putting greens set among garden-like landscaping. A more challenging game is offered by **Virtual Reality Golf**. This simulator allows you a chance to play a

ST JOHN

round on one of 38 top PGA courses. Clubs are available, or you can bring your own.

Even if you're not a golfer, stop by the Gardens to see the butterfly conservatory. As many as 500 butterflies live in the indoor habitat, and you' be surrounded by them as you walk among the plants and trees.

Pastory Gardens entrance.

During your visit, have lunch or dinner at **Compass Rose Restaurant and Bar,** which serves dinner from 4 pm until 10 pm (the bar stays open until midnight). ☎ 340-777-3147; www.pastorygardens.com.

◆ Adventures on Wheels

Biking

Arawak Mountain Biking offers guided tours of the national park on front-suspension mountain bikes. Routes are designed for both novice and experienced bikers, and you can choose either a half-day ($50) or full-day ($90) tour. Be sure to bring a camera. ☎ 800-655-7630 or 340-693-8312; www. arawakexp.com.

◆ Adventures on Horseback

You'll experience a whole different type of sightseeing when you travel on the back of a donkey or horse. **The Carolina Corral** ☆ in Coral Bay offers a wide choice of adventures that take riders along the coast and into the mountains. Full-day, half-day, sunset, full-moon and hourly rides are available. Call owners Jeff and Dana for details and prices, ☎ 693-5778; www.st-john.com/trailrides.

◆ Shopping

Many visitors enjoy shopping on St. John more than on St. Thomas because, although the choices aren't as extensive, the pace is more relaxed and the majority of shops offer unique goods. The island's charm and serenity draw artists and craftsmen who take great pride in the quality of their work. Many have their own stores and others sell exclusively through local retailers. Shoppers who take the time to browse through a variety of shops will be rewarded with some excellent discoveries.

> **DECODING THE STARS**
>
> This *Pocket Adventures* guidebook trims the list of shops on St. John to a manageable roster of those with special features, outstanding service or superior products. All are recommended , but those with one star (☆) deserve particular notice, and a two-star award (☆☆) means "you just gotta browse there."

Cruz Bay

The main town has several shopping areas. **Wharfside Village** is to the right (south) as you step off the ferry dock. **Mongoose Junction**, a larger complex, is a couple of blocks to the left (north) and about five minutes on foot from the dock. Between these two commercial centers, souvenir shops and upscale boutiques are scattered along the streets in the **downtown** area. A multi-level shopping

Mongoose Junction.

center, **The Marketplace**, is located on Southside Road, which leads to the Westin Resort.

MONGOOSE JUNCTION ☆☆

Mongoose Junction is a lively modern complex designed in Caribbean style and constructed of stone and wood. It covers most of the block across from the National Park Headquarters on Route 20 (North Shore Road), and includes restaurants and bars that often feature live entertainment. Some of the most interesting stores are described below.

Mongoose Junction offers shaded shopping.

WHARFSIDE VILLAGE

Right on the water, just to the right (south) of the dock as you exit the ferry from St. Thomas, you will find Wharfside Village. It's an attractive, multi-level complex of restaurants, bars and shops, and a great place to pass the time while you wait to board the ferry. Some of the most interesting shops are described below.

Galeria del Mar ☆ is a colorful little shop full of local art and crafts. Some of the best offerings are the canvas and paper reproductions of original oil paintings and digital watercolor reproductions. The pottery and handblown glass pieces are equally outstanding. Everything is hand selected by owners Alex and Rachelle. ☎ 340-693-9399; www. galeriadelmar.com.

Freebird Creations features eclectic modern-design jewelry, wearable art, tribal masks, ethnic beads and waterproof watches. There are also more than a hundred types of gemstones. On a recent visit, we couldn't resist the petrographic jewelry. ☎ 340-693-8625; www.freebirdcreations.com.

DOCKSIDE BUILDING

St. John Spice is about what you'd expect, and more. Browse. Sniff. Enjoy. Before you leave, pick up the popular Cruz Bay Grill Rub, their best-selling item. Look for owners Ruth and Ron if you have questions. The shop is above Columbian Emeralds. ☎ 877-693-7046 or 340-693-7046; www. stjohnspice.com.

ELSEWHERE IN CRUZ BAY

Pink Papaya ☆ is in the Lemon Tree Mall behind Chase Manhattan Bank. Owner and artist Lisa Etre stocks the store with original gifts, home accessories, paintings, sculpture and jewelry. Bright island colors jump out at you in this shop. ☎ 340-693-8535; www.pinkpapaya.com.

Deborah Designs, also at Lemon Tree Mall, displays original hand-painted clothing and accessories by St. John artist Deborah Willard. The shop is open 10 am until 9 pm Monday through Saturday, and sometimes on Sunday if customers call ahead to let her know they're coming. ☎ 340-693-7533.

Coconut Coast Studios ☆ is an art gallery and gift shop housed in a West Indian cottage on the waterfront at Frank Bay, a five-minute walk south of the ferry dock, just past Gallows Point Resort on Bay Street. The studio features the work of well-known Caribbean artist Elaine Estern. Check the website for examples of her work, and call ahead if you're interested in meeting the artist at her studio. ☎ 800-887-3798 or 340-776-6944; www.coconutcoaststudios.com.

Sparky's, behind the park pavilion across from the ferry dock, has great prices on souvenir T-shirts and stocks current newspapers and magazines from the states. This is also the place to pick up film, sunglasses, snacks and duty-free liquor. ☎ 340-776-6284.

Starfish Market, a full-service grocery and deli is on the lower level of The Marketplace on Southside Road. Stock up on rotisserie chicken, sandwiches, drinks, fresh meats and seafood, plus all the supplies you need for your condo or live-aboard boat. The market is open 7:30 am until 8:30 pm daily. ☎ 340-779-4949.

Coral Bay Jewelers, across from the town park, near the ferry dock in Cruz Bay, is known for attention-grabbing one-of-a-kind pieces. Start a collection of "St. John Bay Bracelets," which represent the island's magnificent coves. You can order online, but you'll be tempted to buy everything if you're in the store. ☎ 340-776-6167; www.stjohnjewelers.com.

Coral Bay Area

Jolly Dog ☆ is in the Shipwreck Landing complex. Here you'll find people clothes and doggie wear baring the Jolly Dog logo. There's also a selection of "Stuff You Want," which includes island souvenirs, gifts and jewelry. Store number two is **Jolly Dog Trading Co**, across the harbor at Skinny Legs Restaurant. Good buys here include island-made clothes, and jewelry. On the nearby deck, **The Doghouse** stocks St. John logo T-shirts and Caribbean-style clothing.

Take time to browse through all three stores. Each is different, but all heel to the same master. ☎ 340-693-5900; www.thejollydog.com.

> **TIP:** *Check out the handmade leather goods at* ***AWL Made Here****, ☎ 340-777-5757.*

Syzygy Gallery, on the Skinny Legs dock, exhibits the one-of-a-kind glass mosaics by Lisa Crumrine, watercolors by Vicki Rogers, paintings by Lori Donerty and monoprints by Alyson Benford. The shop is open daily from 11:30 am until 6 pm. ☎ 340-693-0084.

> **SHOPPING** *TIP: **3 Virgins**, Coccolobo Mall, ☎ 340-344-3263, is said to sell the best bikinis int he Caribbean.*

◆ Where to Stay

Although most of St. John is sheltered by the national park and undeveloped, the island has a diverse list of places to stay. Visitors may choose from high-priced resorts, economical villas or guesthouses, and budget-range campgrounds. Unlike most islands in the Caribbean, St. John's beaches are not lined with high-rise hotels and many fine accommodations are not on the water. However, you're never far from the ocean, no matter where you stay, and if you want to be directly on the beach, you'll find both expensive resorts and economical campgrounds situated on stunning stretches of white sand.

Rental Agencies

To rent a cottage, villa or private home, contact several of the companies listed below and compare the offerings and rates.

- ❖ **Catered to Vacation Property Management**, PO Box 704, Cruz Bay, St. John, USVI 00831, ☎ 800-424-6641 or 340-776-6641; www.cateredto.com.
- ❖ **VIVA! Villas**, PO Box 1747, St. John, VI 00831, ☎ 888-856-4601 or 340-779-4250; www.vivacations.com.
- ❖ **Caribbean Villas and Resorts**, PO Box 458, Lumberyard Mall, Cruz Bay, St. John, USVI 00831, ☎ 340-776-6152 or 800-338-0987; www.caribbeanvilla.com.
- ❖ **On Line Vacations Inc.**, 9901 Connections East, Coral Bay, St. John, USVI 00830, ☎ 888-842-6632 or 340-776-6036; fax 693-5357; www.onlinevacations.com.
- ❖ **Destination St. John**, PO Box 8306, Cruz Bay, St. John, USVI 00831, ☎ 800-562-1901 or 340-779-4647 (phone/fax); www.destinationstjohn.com.
- ❖ **Book-It V.I.**, PO Box 1552, St. John, USVI 00831, ☎ 800-416-1205 or 340-693-8555; fax 693-8480; www.bookitvi.com.
- ❖ **Vacation Vistas**, PO Box 476, Cruz Bay, St. John, USVI 00831, ☎ 340-776-6462; www.vacationvistas.com.

Prices

Use the prices given for accommodations as a guide to the average high-season rate per standard double room. If the review is for an all-inclusive or all-suites resort, the listed price is the lowest available during high-season for two people sharing a room. Expect to pay an additional 8% tax year-round.

SLEEPING WITH THE STARS

Our suggested list of lodging has been very selective for this pocket guidebook. You can browse the Internet as well as we can, and we encourage you to do so. Here you'll find only the most recommended possibilities to fit a variety of budgets. Properties marked with one star (☆) are highly recommended. When a single feature or the overall allure is particularly impressive, you'll find two stars (☆☆) beside the name. Three stars (☆☆☆) means, simply, WOW!

Resorts

Caneel Bay ☆, PO Box 720, Cruz Bay, St. John, USVI 00831. ☎ 888-767-3966 or 340-776-6111; fax 693-8280; www.caneelbay.com. 166 rooms and suites. $450.

The resort has changed a bit since Rosewood Hotels took over as property managers a few years ago, but Caneel Bay still sets the standard for laid-back, understated, totally indulgent opulence. Since its beginning almost 50 years ago, the 170-acre resort has repeatedly been recognized for its compatibility with nature, and Rosewood appears dedicated to preserving that reputation.

Air conditioning has been added. Dabs of color have popped up in the traditionally tasteful taupe decor. But, change has come slowly and discreetly, so as not to startle or offend long-time devotees who return year after year and stay weeks at a time. Seclusion, privacy and tranquility are still the resort's best features.

When you check into Caneel Bay Resort, you have exclusive access to seven postcard-perfect beaches and a vast expanse of beautifully landscaped lawn criss-crossed by paths lined with almost 2,000 varieties of plants. The Beach Hut offers all types of watersports equipment and arranges for snorkeling, scuba and fishing excursions. A freshwater swimming pool, 11 all-weather tennis courts, an activities pa-

ST JOHN

vilion, a fully-equipped fitness center and three restaurants are tucked here and there among the fragrant gardens.

All rooms offer views of either the tropical gardens or the ocean, and premium rooms feature balconies that open directly onto one of the white-sand beaches. If you want to really splurge, check into Cottage 7, which was Laurance Rockefeller's private estate house. It now houses a secluded collection of mini-suites with dramatic ocean views. Casual upscale wicker furniture, handwoven fabrics and plantation ceiling fans provide luxurious comfort in all rooms, but don't expect in-room TVs or whirlpool bathtubs.

> **TIP:** *Children under eight years old are not allowed to visit Caneel Bay Resort from early-January to mid-March. However, at other times, families with children are lodged in a special section of rooms, and the kids are entertained in the Turtle Town Activities Room.*

Westin Resort, St. John ☆☆, PO Box 8310, Route 104, Great Cruz Bay, St. John, USVI 00831. ☎ 800-808-5020 or 693-8000; fax 340-779-4985; www.westinresortstjohn.com. 285 rooms and suites, plus 96 Westin Vacation Club villas. $410.

© Image courtesy Starwood Resorts

Architecture buffs and gardeners will want to visit the Westin, even if they don't stay overnight. The sharp angles, oversized windows and steep roof lines of 13 low-rise buildings contrast pleasingly with the gentle slope of lushly landscaped grounds toward a soft, palm-lined beach bordering the calm, turquoise-blue waters of Great Cruz Bay.

The focal point of the resort is the vast freshwater swimming pool. It covers a quarter-acre and features a waterfall and two jacuzzis. Other amenities include a well-equipped fitness center and a spa offering massage therapy and facials. In addition, there are six tennis courts, a Kid's Club Activity Center, a gift shop, liquor store and hair salon.

All rooms are air conditioned and feature cable TVs, VCRs, minibars, coffee makers, direct-dial telephones with computer ports and voice mail, in-room safes and hair dryers. Out on the beach, guests enjoy snorkeling, windsurfing and boating. Cruz Bay Watersports arranges scuba training and trips.

Gallows Point Suite Resort, PO Box 58, Cruz Bay, St. John, USVI 00831. ☎ 800-323-7229 or 340-776-6434; fax 340-776-6520; www.gallowspointresort.com. 60 suites. $435.

You'll see Gallows Point to your right as you approach St. John by ferry. The resort consists of 14 two-level buildings clustered near the beach on a landscaped peninsula that juts out into the bay. It makes an ideal location for visitors who want to be near the shops and restaurants in Cruz Bay.

Each suite includes a full kitchen and a living area with a sleeper-sofa and louvered doors that open onto a patio with views of either the ocean or harbor. Garden suites have air-conditioned bedrooms and oversized showers. Upper-level suites have a loft bedroom and an extra half-bath. All are decorated in pastel island-style fabrics and have tile floors and wicker furniture. Amenities include a small beach with outstanding snorkeling, a small pool, a gift shop and an activities center. The bar, located on the third level, is an excellent

© Gallows Bay Resort

place for sunset drinks. Zozo's Ristorante has great views and outstanding Northern Italian cuisine. ☎ 340-693-9200.

Harmony ☆, PO Box 310, Cruz Bay, St. John, USVI 00830. ☎ 800-392-9004 or 340-715-0501; fax 340-776-6504; www.maho.org. $200.

Harmony is one of four award-winning eco-resorts on St. John. It sits on a shady hill above the tent-cottages at Maho Bay Camps on the island's north shore. Each two-story building runs on solar and wind power and is built of recycled materials. Beams are composted wood scraps. Floor decking and walls were recently newspapers. Bathroom tiles are made of ground glass bottles and rugs come from old rubber tires. But, you'd never know it. The spacious contemporary units look very much like those at a typical island hotel, and are just as clean, comfortable and attractively furnished.

Estate Concordia Studios, Coral Bay, St. John, USVI 00830. ☎ 800-392-9004 or 340-715-0501; fax 340-776-6504; www.maho.org. $140.

These spacious studios, set on 51 oceanfront acres above Salt Pond Bay, are an excellent choice if you plan to explore this remote area of the national park on the island's southeastern coast. Each open-air unit has a breathtaking view of the ocean and Ram Head peninsula. Great hiking trails and outstanding snorkeling spots are nearby, and there is an on-site swimming pool. You'll need a car to get around. Cruz Bay is about a 40-minute drive from the resort, and the north-shore beaches are 20 to 30 minutes away. The nearby village of Coral Bay has limited shopping, a few restaurants and a watersports center. All studios have tile floors, comfortable furniture and ceiling fans. Each building is elevated above lush natural vegetation and constructed around pre-existing trees.

Campgrounds

Maho Bay Camps ☆☆, PO Box 310, Cruz Bay, St. John, USVI 00830. ☎ 800-392-9004 or 340-715-0501; fax 340-776-6504; www.maho.org. 114 tent-cottages. $115 (cottage).

Maho Bay has 114 camping accommodations. The units are 16-foot-square wooden platforms covered with canvas and screens and outfitted with two twin beds, a couch, table and chairs, cooking utensils, electric lamps and a propane stove. All tent-cottages are connected by elevated wooden walkways and many have stunning ocean views from their private decks.

Relax on Maho Beach.

ST JOHN

Hillside amenities include a rustic dining pavilion where guests congregate for meals and programs, as well as a supply store. Bathhouses have low-flow flush toilets and pull-chain showers. An excellent watersports center on the white-sand beach offers snorkeling, diving, kayaking and windsurfing.

> **TIP:** *Make your reservations for Maho Bay Camps well in advance. This is one of the most highly acclaimed eco-tourism destinations in the world, and many campers return year after year, so the best units are booked early.*

Concordia Eco-Tents ☆☆☆, Coral Bay, St. John, USVI 00830. ☎ 800-392-9004 or 340-715-0501; fax 340-776-6504; www.maho.org. 11 tent-cottages. $125 (cottage).

The high-tech lodging here exemplifies eco-tourism at its best. Each tent-cottage sits high up in the trees and has a private bath and a kitchen with running water, which makes life civilized without compromising the environment. Evidence of conservation is everywhere. All power comes from the sun and wind, shower stalls are tiny so you're not likely to linger, and the toilet is a composting type, which is an educational experience.

The compound is adjacent to Estate Concordia Studios overlooking Salt Pond Bay, and the views of the ocean are spectacular. Each unit can sleep up to six on twin beds, loft mattresses and a queen-size futon. Meal preparation is simplified by the running-water sink, propane stove and refrigerator. Large screened windows allow plenty of cool ventilation from constant trade winds.

Coral Bay shops and restaurants are about 10 minutes away by car. Guests can use the swimming pool and laundry facilities at Estate Concordia.

Cinnamon Bay Campground ☆, PO Box 720, Cruz Bay, St. John, USVI 00831. ☎ 800-539-9998 or 340-776-6330; fax 776-6458; www.cinnamonbay.com. 126 bare sites, tents and cottages. $80 (tent) - $110 (cottage).

If you plan to spend your vacation in your swimsuit, this is the place for you. Cinnamon Bay has the longest beach on St. John and as a guest at this National Park Service campground, you're never more than a two-minute walk from the water.

You can choose between three types of accommodations: bare sites, tents or cottages. Bathhouses with flush-toilets and cool-water showers are nearby, and you can store valuables in a safe or locker. Since the campground is located in the national park, rangers lead nature tours and give presentations in the amphitheater. The on-site Tree Lizards Restaurant serves island specialties, including vegetarian dishes, and there's a general store for groceries and supplies. Down on the beach, the watersports center rents surfboards, windsurfers, kayaks, sailboats and snorkeling equipment.

◆ Where to Eat

Don't plan to dress for dinner unless you've got reservations at one of the posh hotel restaurants. You'll be eating casually, most likely on a patio or in an open-air dining room.

Meals on St. John range from cheap, excellent island food served at roadside stands to expensive yet marvelous seafood. Be sure to try the *patés* (pronounced like the French, but not at all the same thing), which are bundles of deep-fried pastry filled with spice-laden meat or fish. These make a delicious inexpensive meal. Pick up picnic supplies at **Dolphin Gourmet Market**, near the ferry dock, ☎ 340-776-5322.

> **TIP:** *One way to dine less expensively is to have your main meal at lunchtime, when prices tend to be somewhat less.*

The following are a mix of restaurants chosen for their location, ambiance or particularly delicious food. For such a small island, St. John has a lot of places to eat. Most are in the town of Cruz Bay or the village of Coral Bay. In addition, every resort has at least one fine restaurant and a snack bar. Use the prices given as a guide to the average price of a mid-range meal per person, excluding drinks and tip. There is no sales tax in the Virgin Islands, but restaurants may add a service charge, so check your bill before you figure your tip.

> **TIP:** *Restaurants often change their hours during low season, and some close for several weeks during the summer, so call ahead to avoid disappointment.*

DINING WITH THE STARS

Every restaurant we review is carefully picked. Some are marked with stars. One star (☆) indicates that the restaurant is highly recommended, two stars (☆☆) mean you should make an extra effort to eat there, and three stars (☆☆☆) promise an experience to remember. The rating may be for super value or an amazing view or, perhaps, simply the best "cheeseburgers in paradise."

ST JOHN

Cruz Bay

Paradiso ☆☆, Mongoose Junction, ☎ 340-693-8899. Innovative American with an Italian twist. Lunch $20, dinner $30. Monday-Saturday, 11 am-3 pm and 5:30 pm-10 pm. Credit cards accepted. Reservations are a must in high season.

This is one of the most popular and attractive restaurants in the overwhelmingly popular and attractive Mongoose Junction complex. A crowd gathers at the long brass-and-hardwood bar most evenings, and many people stay on to enjoy a dinner of traditional fare infused accompanied by unique sauces and intriguing ingredients. The air-conditioned stone-walled dining room is especially popular on warm afternoons, but the outdoor balcony is the place to people-watch after the sun goes down.

Morgan's Mango, North Shore Road, Cruz Bay, ☎ 340-693-8141. Upscale Caribbean. Dinner $20. Daily, 5:30 pm-10:30 pm. Credit cards accepted. Reservations recommended.

More than 30 frozen drinks are made at the huge wrap-around bar that encloses a garden-like dining room. The dinner menu reflects the tastes of various cultures that make up the Caribbean and may include dishes from Cuba, Jamaica and Haiti. A couple of vegetarian choices are available and the seafood is dependably fresh. Look for this popular spot across from the national park office and the ferry dock.

Woody's Seafood Saloon, inland from the ferry dock, ☎ 340-779-4625; www.woodysseafood.com. Fish and traditional American. Lunch $12, dinner $16. Sunday-Thursday, 11 am-1 am; Friday-Saturday, 11 am-2 am. Credit cards accepted.

This popular hangout is just plain fun. Regulars say Woody's puts on the best happy hour in the Caribbean from 3 pm until 6 pm every afternoon, and it's the only place on the island where you can get a full meal late at night. There's an extensive list of frozen drinks and a good choice of beers. The menu is surprisingly varied for such a casual setting and features spicy food that tastes great with the icy drinks.

La Tapa, across from the Scotia Bank, ☎ 340-693-7755. Tapas and continental dishes. Dinner $25. Daily, 5:30 pm-10 pm. Credit cards accepted. Reservations recommended.

This is one of the most delightfully surprising little restaurants in the Virgin Islands. *Tapas* are to the Spanish what hor d'oeuvres are to the French – exquisite bite-sized snacks to enjoy with icy drinks and warm friends. Here in Cruz Bay, the tiny meat, fish and vegetable treats are served in this bistro filled with local art. The menu also includes full-course meals, featuring seafood and steaks flavored with exotic spices and served with island fruits and vegetables. Seating is limited, so call early for reservations.

The Lime Inn, Lemontree Mall, ☎ 340-779-4199. Seafood/Caribbean. Lunch $12, dinner $20. Monday-Friday, 11:30 am-3 pm, 5:30 pm-10 pm; Saturday, 5:30 pm-10:30 pm. Credit cards accepted. Reservations recommended.

If you ask a resident where to get good local cuisine, the answer will often be The Lime Inn. This tropical open-air restaurant features a long list of frozen drinks and non-alcoholic smoothies. The lunch menu offers salads that may be topped with chicken, shrimp or tenderloin. There's also a nice choice of sandwiches. For dinner, you might start with brie en croûte followed by coquille St. John or filet mignon stuffed with crab or blue cheese. Everything comes with potato, rice or pasta and fresh bread.

Fish Trap ☆, Cruz Bay/Rain Tree Inn, ☎ 340-693-9994; www.thefishtrap.com. Seafood/International. Dinner $25. Tuesday-Sunday, 4:30-9:30 pm. Credit cards accepted. Reservations recommended for dinner.

Fish nets and windsocks decorate this garden terrace restaurant at the Rain Tree Inn, which sits behind the Mount Carmel Church across from Wharfside Village in Cruz Bay. Owned and operated by the Willis family for more than 25 years; chef Aaron Willis is repeatedly voted "Best Chef on the Island." The kitchen specializes in fresh fish favorites such as conch fritters, grilled tuna and fried mahi-mahi and vegetarians have several choices. There's always a tempting selection of fresh-catch dishes. Regulars know to save room for the coconut cake topped with hot rum caramel sauce.

Stone Terrace, across from Wharfside Village, ☎ 340-693-9370, www.stoneterrace.com. Steak and seafood. Dinner $30. Tuesday-Sunday, 6 pm-10 pm. Reservations recommended. Credit cards accepted.

The eclectic international menu here changes frequently and features seasonal favorites such as stuffed mushrooms, garlic-and-brie-glazed breast of duck and filet mignon  topped with a spicy lobster sauce. The bar opens an hour earlier, closes an hour later, and offers an award-winning wine list.

Coral Bay

Skinny Legs ☆, Coral Bay/Route 107, ☎ 340-779-4982; www.skinnylegs.com. Light meals. Lunch/dinner $10-$12. Daily, 11 am-9 pm. No credit cards.

Yachties, hammock dwellers, beach bums and just plain folks hang out and hideout at this super casual joint on Coral Bay. The menu, like the restaurant, is full of comforts. There are terrific burgers, great chili dogs, fresh grilled fish, friendly games of horseshoes and live sports on the satellite TV. What more could you want on a St. John afternoon?

East End

Vie's Snack Shack ☆, Route 10/East End, ☎ 340-693-5033. West Indian snack food. Lunch/snacks $5-8. Tuesday-Saturday, 10 am-5 pm. No credit cards.

Try to stop at Vie's when no one else is around so you can chat with this delightfully friendly St. John native. She's full of information and doesn't mind telling a few local tales while she fries your johnnycakes and garlic-laced chicken. You'll eat your meal on a picnic table under the trees with roosters and kittens at your feet. This is St. John as it used to be, and you may be tempted to stay forever. Be sure to sample the *patés* (fried meat or fish pies) and the homemade coconut tarts. Vie is one of the best cooks on the island, turning out scrumptious down-home meals in her simple roadside shack.

Around the Island

Chateau Bordeaux ☆☆, Route 10-Centerline Rd, ☎ 340-776-6611. Mediterranean/ Caribbean. Dinner $30. Monday-Saturday, dinner seatings at 5:30 and 8:30 pm. Credit cards accepted. Dinner reservations required.

You'll be served a fantastic meal here atop Bordeaux mountain, the highest point on the island. The menu features a variety of meats and seafood with interesting sauces. Examples include herb-sauced lamb, fish poached in wine and stuffed pork tenderloin. The appetizers are especially creative, there's a good wine list, and you'll be tempted by cheesecake for dessert. Plan to arrive before dark so you can enjoy a fruit-flavored daiquiri while you watch the sun set.

Asolare ☆, Route 20-North Shore Rd, ☎ 340-779-4747; Gourmet French Asian. Dinner $40. Dinner, 5:30 pm-9:30 pm. Credit cards accepted. Reservations required.

The views from this elegant old stone house on Caneel Hill just outside Cruz Bay are stunning. If you arrive before dark, you can watch the sun slip into Pillsbury Sound and the lights start to glitter on St. Thomas. Your dinner will be no less dazzling. The chef creates entrées centered around a unique blend of Asian, Pacific Rim and European recipes which results in dishes such as fish sizzled in exotic spices and served with a fruity sauce, Peking duck sweetened with a nutty glaze and perfectly grilled steaks accompanied by ginger-spiked vegetables. After-dinner treats include palate-

ST JOHN

calming choices like tropical-fruit soufflés and homemade ice cream.

> **TIP:** *For a real island treat, stop at **Miss Lucy's** on Route 107 at Friis Bay, ☎ 340-693-5244. Miss Lucy herself recently celebrated her 90th birthday and is no longer a beloved fixture at the restaurant, but the food is better than ever. Overlook the lack of decor and dig into a platter of crabcakes with lobster sauce, served with side veggies for $25.*

◆ Nightlife

Anyone who says there's no nightlife on St. John simply isn't looking in the right place. While it's true that locals and visitors enjoy active days and tend to turn in early, that doesn't mean the island goes to sleep as soon as the sun sets. Check the listings in St. John publications (*This Week, St. John Times*) for current shows and events.

Cruz Bay

Cruz Bay is the liveliest spot on the island after sundown. Local singles and business people drift toward **Zozo's Ristorante** (☎ 340-693-9200) at Gallows Point Resort, up the hill from the ferry dock overlooking Cruz Bay. Those out for an elegant evening favor the bar at **Caneel Bay Resort**, where a band plays each night from 8-10:45 pm (☎ 340-776-6111). Up at the **Westin Resort** (☎ 340-693-8000), **Snorkels Bar and Grill** serves food and drinks until 11 pm every night and the **Beach Café and Bar** stays open until midnight.

If you're looking for something more casual, take to the streets. Start at **Mongoose Junction**, where the bar at **Paradiso's** (☎ 340-693-8899) is popular, but closes around 10 pm. Continue on to **Morgan's Mango** (☎ 340-693-8141) across from the national park office near the ferry dock. Thursday is Margarita Night, but you'll find a crowd around the bar most nights. Again, the action stops about 10 pm.

Woody's Seafood Saloon (☎ 340-779-4625) stays open until 1 am during the week and until 2 am on weekends. Happy Hour kicks things off from 3 pm until 5 pm each afternoon. While Woody's is casual, **JJ's Texas Coast Café**, (☎ 340-776-6908) is ultra casual. Some would call it a dive, but in a nice way. It's across the park from the ferry dock, and tourists follow the locals there every evening. **Duffy's Love Shack** (☎ 340-776-6065), like its well-known sister establishment in Red Hook, is a loud, wild, rum-soaked place to hang out. Many of the outlandish drinks are oversized and potent, and refills often come at a slashed price. The Shack occupies a downtown spot a block inland from the ferry dock and recognizable by the almond tree growing through the thatched roof. You can stay until 1 am during the week and until 2 am on Friday and Saturday nights.

Quiet Mon Pub ☆ (☎ 340-779-4799; www.QuietMon. com) is a rare find in Cruz Bay. It's a bit of an Irish Pub, it is. During the day, you can get a proper hot lunch, but hang around for nightfall, if you want a real treat. The place is open till the wee hours, about 4 am. The beer is super cold and on tap, and all holidays

are celebrated in true Irish style – especially St. Patrick's Day. You can check your e-mail at the computers in the cyber café.

Fred's on King Street (☎ 340-776-6363) has live music on Wednesday and Friday nights. It gets crowded, so show up early to claim your space.

Coral Bay

In the Coral Bay area, **Shipwreck Landing** (☎ 340-693-5640) is the place for live entertainment. A variety of bands play most Wednesday-Sunday evenings until 11 pm, and the

ST JOHN

music may be anything from cool jazz to steamy reggae. **Skinny Legs** (☎ 340-779-4982; www.skinnylegs.com) usually has a band on Friday nights during high season. At other times, the satellite TV shows live sporting events and customers challenge each other to a game of darts or horseshoes. It's impossible to be bored here, but the action ends at 9 pm.

◆ Island Facts & Numbers

AIRPORT: **Cyril E. King International Airport** on St. Thomas ☎ 340-774-5100. STT is the airport code.

AREA CODE: The area code for all US Virgin Islands is 340. You may dial direct from the States.

BANKS, ATMs: Most are open Monday-Thursday, 9 am-2:30 pm and Friday from 9:30 am-2 pm and 3:30 pm-5 pm. A 24-hour ATM is located at **Bank of Nova Scotia** at The Marketplace in Cruz Bay, ☎ 340-776-6552, and **First Bank** in Cruz Bay, ☎ 340-776-6881. Other ATMs are located in tourist areas throughout the island.

DRIVING: Traffic stays to the left. The speed limit is 20 mph in towns and 35 mph in the countryside.

ELECTRICITY: 110 volts, 60 cycles, as on the US mainland.

EMERGENCIES: Ambulance, ☎ 911; Fire Department, ☎ 911; Police, ☎ 911; Police non-emergency, ☎ 340-693-8880; **Myrah Keating Smith Community Health Clinic**, 28 Sussanaberg, Cruz Bay, ☎ 340-693-8900; **US Coast Guard Rescue**, ☎ 340-714-2851; hyperbaric chamber for divers, ☎ 340-776-3497 or 787-865-5818.

GOVERNMENT: The US Virgin Islands are an unincorporated territory with a non-voting delegate elected to the US House of Representatives. Anyone born on the islands is a US citizen.

HURRICANE INFORMATION: www.gopbi.com/weather/storm or www.nhc.noaa.gov.

INTERNET ACCESS: Connections, near the ferry dock at Cruz Bay (☎ 340-776-6922) and at the Tourist Information Office in Coral Bay (☎ 340-779-4994).

LIQUOR LAWS: The legal drinking age is 21, as on the US mainland. Minors may not enter bars or purchase liquor.

MONEY: The US dollar is the legal currency throughout the Virgin Islands. Travelers' checks and major credit cards are acceptable at most locations, but always carry some cash for smaller establishments.

NEWSPAPERS, MAGAZINES: *This Week in St. Thomas/St. John* and *What To Do: St. Thomas/St. John* are free publications that are available at hotels and other tourist-oriented locations throughout the island. Newspaper include *The Daily News*, ☎ 340-774-8772; www.virginislandsdailynews. com.

TAXES: There is no sales tax or departure tax. An 8% government tax is added to all hotel bills, and the St. John Accommodations Council collects a voluntary $1-per-day surcharge that is used to fund non-profit island projects.

TELEPHONE DIRECTORY INFORMATION: ☎ 913.

TOURIST INFORMATION: In the US, information is available from **The US Virgin Islands Division of Tourism**, 1270 Avenue of the Americas, New York, NY 10020, ☎ 800-372-USVI (800-372-8784) or 212-332-2222; fax 212-332-2223; www.usvitourism.vi.

You may also get information from **The Caribbean Information Office**, ☎ 800-621-1270 (in the US); 847-699-7570 (outside the US); fax 847-699-7583, or from **The St. Thomas/St. John Hotel & Tourism Association**, PO Box 2300, Veterans Drive Station, St. Thomas, USVI 00803, ☎ 340-774-6835; www.sttstjhta.com.

ST JOHN

In Canada, information is available from **The US Virgin Islands Tourism Department**, 703 Evans Avenue, Suite 106, Toronto, Ontario M9C 5E9, ☎ 416-622-7600.

In the UK, contact **The US Virgin Islands Tourism Department**, 2 Cinnamon Row, Plantation Wharf, York Place, London, England SW11 3TW, ☎ 0207-9785262.

On St. John, stop by the **Tourist Office** near the post office on the south side of the ferry dock in Cruz Bay to pick up information. It's open Monday-Friday, 8 am-noon and 1 pm-5 pm. ☎ 340-776-6450.

The **National Park Visitor Center** on the north side of the ferry dock is open daily 8 am-4:30 pm; ☎ 340-776-6201.

WEBSITES: www.usvitourism.vi.

WEDDINGS: It's easy to get married in the USVI. Call the Department of Tourism for a brochure called *Getting Married in the United States Virgin Islands*, ☎ 800-372-USVI. To apply for a license, write to the Territorial Court of the Virgin Islands, Box 70, St. Thomas, USVI 00804, ☎ 340-774-6680. Download documents at www.usvitourism.vi.

St. Croix

◆ Overview

Rolling hills, uncrowded beaches, vine-covered plantation ruins and charming Danish architecture make St. Croix (say *croy*) the most diversified of the three US Virgin Islands. **Point Udall**, the easternmost point of the United States, is arid and rocky. The island grows wetter and wider as it spreads westward, and a tropical forest covers the lush northwest side. Between the scrub land and the forest are 28 miles of northern hills and southern plains ringed by an array of beaches. **Buck Island**, off the northeast shore, is part of the US National Park system and is St. Croix's most popular watersports area.

Courtesy NASA

The island isn't as densely populated or commercial as St. Thomas. Nor is it as slow-paced and ecologically-preserved as St. John. With 84 square miles, St. Croix is larger than either of its sister Virgins. Its economy is bolstered by industry as well as tourism. The 55,000 residents, mostly native born Cruzans (or Crucians) or transplanted North American

"Continentals," welcome approximately two million visitors each year.

Christiansted, the capital, is built on the north shore around a coral bay that once served as a Danish port. Its historic streets are lined with colorful buildings and covered passageways that house duty-free shops and fine restaurants. **Frederiksted**, on the west coast, is a tiny town with a few quaint shops and some notable Victorian architecture. Nearby are well-preserved and renovated plantations that are open to the public.

St. Croix raised the American flag in 1917 when Denmark sold the western Virgin Islands to the **United States** for $25 million. At that time, the sugar boom was over, slaves had been freed and the island had suffered a series of hurricanes, earthquakes and fires. Tourism began to turn the economy around after World War II. Further prosperity developed when the Hess Oil refinery and the Harvey aluminum plant were opened in the 1960s.

1754 map of St Croix by Danish cartographer I.M. Beck.

◆ Getting There

By Air

Several international carriers fly from US gateways to **Henry E. Rohlson Airport** (STX) on the southern coast, about seven miles from the town of Christiansted. The Tourist Information Office has a well-stocked counter inside the modern terminal. Major rental-car companies are on site.

Airline service and schedules change frequently and new flights are being added as St. Croix becomes more popular. **American Airlines** (☎ 800-433-7300 or 340-778-2000; www.aa.com) and **US Airways** (☎ 800-428-4322; www. usairways.com) fly directly to the island. **American Eagle** (☎ 800-433-7300), **Cape Air** (☎ 800-352-0714), **Caribbean Sun** (☎ 866-864-6272, www.flycsa.com) and **Seaborne** (☎ 888-359-8687, www.seaborneairlines.com) offer inter-island connections.

Taxi vans meet all flights and carry up to eight passengers to various stops in one direction. Fares are regulated; expect to pay $9 per person for transportation to hotels near Christiansted and $6 per person for taxi service to locations near Frederiksted. In addition, drivers charge $1 per piece for luggage.

By Seaplane & Hydrofoil

Island Lynx Ferry (☎ 800-260-2603 or 340-773-9500; www.island lynx.com) zips passengers from St. Thomas to St. Croix in 75 minutes on a three-deck 100-foot catamaran. Round-trip tickets are $78 for adults and $68 for children. Check the website or call for schedules, which change frequently.

> **NOTE:** *The area code for St. Croix is 340.*

ST CROIX

◆ Getting Around

By Car

Primary roads on St. Croix are paved and well maintained, but secondary roads are often rough and poorly marked. Only one road (the Melvin H Evans Highway) on the island has four lanes and a 55-mph speed limit. The rest are two-lane roads with a speed limit of 35 mph in the countryside and 20 mph in town.

A variety of rental cars is available from agencies at the airport and in both of the main towns, and a valid driver's license, issued by the US, UK or Canada may be used for up to 90 days. Daily rental rates run between $45 and $55, and you should reserve a car in advance during high season. If you plan to explore along the scenic back roads – and you should – consider paying a little extra for a four-wheel-drive vehicle. Remember to drive on the left.

NOTE: *Street parking in Christiansted is limited to two hours.*

The following companies are recommended. Those with a star are notable for courtesy and dependability.

RENTAL CAR AGENCIES	
Avis	☎ 800-331-1084 or 340-778-9355 (airport); 340-713-1347 (Kings Alley/seaplane landing)
Budget	☎ 888-264-8894 or 340-778-4663 (airport) or 340-713-9289 (King Christian Hotel); www.budgetstcroix.com
Centerline ☆	☎ 888-288-8755 or 778-0450 (phone/fax)
Hertz	☎ 800-654-3131 or 340-778-1402
Olympic ☆	☎ 888-878-4227 or 340-773-8000; fax 773-6870; www.stcroixcarrentals.com
Thrifty	☎ 800-367-2277 or 340-773-7200; fax 773-7202

By Taxi

By law, all taxi drivers on St. Croix must carry an official taxi tariff list and present it when a prospective passenger asks about the fare from one point to another. It's always a good idea to do this before you climb into a cab, even though most drivers on the island are remarkably honest and friendly. Be aware that there are additional charges for radio-dispatched cabs and trips that take place between midnight and 6 am. If you request a private cab, the driver is allowed to charge up to four times the additional-passenger rate.

> **TIP:** Look for the official taxi tariff schedule in each free issue of **St. Croix This Week**, found at the airport, tourist offices and all hotels.

In addition to the taxi stands at the airport exit, you'll find drivers available in Christiansted on King Street near Government House and at Market Square. In Frederiksted, taxis sit at Fort Frederik. Contact the Taxi Commission (☎ 773-8294) if you have a problem with a driver or leave something in a cab.

TAXI COMPANIES	
St. Croix Taxi Association (airport)	☎ 340-778-1088
Antilles Taxi Service (Christiansted)	☎ 340-773-5020
Caribbean Taxi and Tours (Christiansted)	☎ 340-773-9799
Cruzan Taxi Association (Christiansted)	☎ 340-773-6388
Frederiksted Taxi Service (Frederiksted)	☎ 340-772-4775

By Bus

Public transportation is limited, slow and not recommended, but you can go through mostly residential areas to Christiansted and Frederiksted on an air-conditioned **VITRAN** bus. Buses run Monday-Saturday, 5:30 am-9:30 pm. The fare is $1 (55¢ for anyone 55 years of age or older) each way, and you must have the exact change. For information and schedules, call the VITRAN office, ☎ 340-773-1290.

St. Croix

Point Udall

Buck Island

East End Bay

Teague Bay

82

60

Grass Point

Coakley Bay

East End Road

South Shore Road

60

Great Pond Bay

82

62

62

Caribbean Sea

Christiansted Harbor

Christiansted

83

62

Canegarden Bay

75

74

62

Salt River Bay

75

N Side Rd

80

66

73

Krause Point

73

Cane Bay

N Shore Road

Davis Bay

Scenic Road

69

70

Melvin H Evans Hwy

64

Airport

Hams Bluff

76

Mahogany Road

Queen Mary Hwy

Long Point

78

58

Frederiksted

63

66

Long Point Bay

63

70

Sandy Point

N

© 2007 HUNTER PUBLISHING, INC

4 MILES

6 KM

◆ Touring the Island

Guided Tours

St. Croix Heritage Tours ☆ conducts walking tours of Christiansted ($21) and Frederiksted ($10). They include visits to historic buildings, courtyards and market places. Ask about their safari bus trips to lesser-known plantations and nature tours to ecological sites. Contact them for information about scheduled and private tours. ☎ 340-778-6997.

St. Croix Safari Tours takes visitors on a three-hour island tour in an open-air safari bus Monday-Saturday. The tour leaves from Carambola Beach. Call for information and reservations, ☎ 340-772-3333.

Sweeny's St. Croix Safari Tours ☆ leaves from the Old Scale House near the wharf in Christiansted Monday-Friday at 10 am and returns at 3:30 pm. The $45 tour includes stops at historical spots and guide Sweeny Toussaint offers abundant information about the island's culture, history and vegetation. Call for information and reservations, ☎ 800-524-2026 or 340-773-6700.

Caribbean Adventure Tours offers a variety of kayaking, hiking, photography and ecological tours to off-the-beaten-track locations. Guides are knowledgeable, entertaining and experienced. Call for a schedule of destinations, ☎ 800-532-3483 or 340-778-1522; www.stcroix kayak.com.

© St Croix Kayak

Self-Guided Tours

The following sites and attractions are recommended. Those with one star (☆) are worthy of a detour, and you should consider allowing extra time for those marked with two stars (☆☆).

A colorful Christiansted street.

A WALKING TOUR OF CHRISTIANSTED ☆☆

Driving Christiansted's narrow one-way streets and finding a parking spot near the center of town can be a problem, so it's best to park on the outskirts of town and tour the city on foot.

This is the most picturesque and interesting town in the Virgin Islands, and a large part of it is recognized as a National Historic Site. Founded in 1734, soon after the Danish West India and Guinea Company bought St. Croix from France, Christiansted served as the capital of the Danish West Indies from 1755 until 1871. The narrow streets were designed for mule-driven carts, and the colorful buildings were built to survive hurricanes and take advantage of cool ocean breezes. Today, chic boutiques, trendy restaurants and intimate hotels occupy the former homes and businesses of the wealthy Danes.

Begin your walking tour at **Fort Christiansvaern** ☆☆, a yellow-brick bastion that stands watch over the town's harbor. It was completed in 1749 in a star-shaped design and partially rebuilt in 1771 after it was damaged by a hurricane. Despite several additions and alterations, the fort is an excellent example of colonial military architecture and is maintained as a historic monument by the US National Park Service. Take time to explore the barracks, kitchen and dungeons. The fort is open weekdays, 8 am-4:45 pm, and week-

Fort Christiansvaern.

ends, 9 am-4:45 pm. There is a $3 admission fee, which also includes admittance to the Steeple Building. ☎ 340-773-1460; fax 773-5995.

A **Visitor's Center** is located at the fort, and you can stop in to pick up informational brochures and maps before continuing your walking tour. The office is open weekdays, 8 am-5 pm, ☎ 340-773-0495.

TIP: *There's a parking lot adjacent to the fort, but be sure to get your car out before the 5 pm closing time.*

DID YOU KNOW?

The mother of Alexander Hamilton, the first United States Secretary of the Treasury (1789-1795), Rachel Fawcett Lavien, was imprisoned for several months at Fort Christiansvaern for fighting with her first husband. After her release, she moved to the island of Nevis, where she met and married James Hamilton, a Scottish aristocrat, who became Alexander's father. Alexander Hamilton was born on Nevis but lived on St. Croix during his teenage years.

Leaving the fort, walk along Hospital Street or across the grassy lawn of the D. Hamilton Jackson Park to the **Old Danish Customs House**. The park is named for a labor leader and judge who started the first independent newspaper on the island. The structure was built by the Danes in 1751, and the sweeping staircase was added in 1829.

Christiansted

SIGHTS & ATTRACTIONS

1. Fort Christiansvaern,
   Visitor's Center
2. Old Danish Customs House
3. The Scale House
4. Government House
5. Old Market Place
6. Steeple Building
7. Apothecary Hall
8. National Park Service
   Headquarters

PLACES TO STAY & EAT

9. Hotel Caravelle
10. Hotel on the Cay
11. King Christian
12. King's Alley
13. Tutto Bene
14. Bacchus
15. RumRunners
16. Avacado Pitt
17. Fort Christian Brew Pub
18. Pink Fancy

NOT TO SCALE

Anchor Way

Flag Drive

East End Road

Palm Avenue

Fort Street

Chandlers Wharf

Gallows Bay P.O.

Dock

Gallows Bay

Protestant Cay

Christiansted Harbor

Hospital Street (Hospital Gade)

Lobster Street

Green Street

Church Street (Kirke Gade)

East Street

Fisher Street

New Street

Little Hospital Street

Queen Cross Street (Dronningens Tvaergade)

Hill Street

King Cross Street

Post Office

Boardwalk

Kings Alley

Comanche Walk

Pan Am Pav.

Caravelle Arc.

Library

Strand Street

King Street (Kongens Gade)

Company Street

Queen Street

Prince Street

Market Street

Watergut

© 2007 HUNTER PUBLISHING, INC

Cross King Street and continue walking toward the water to **The Old Scale House**, a yellow building near the wharf that was built in 1856. The building once served as a weighing and inspection site for goods passing through the port and now houses the headquarters of The National Park Service, ☎ 340-773-1460. Before you look around, stop at the small shop run by the NPS to pick up free information about the island's parks and browse through books on Caribbean history, plants and ecology. The Old Scale House is open daily, 8 am-4:45 pm.

When you leave the Old Scale House, follow King Street away from the harbor until you see **Government House** on the left, just before the intersection of Queen Cross Street. This elegant building is actually two houses that were built in the 1700s and joined in 1830 to accommodate the offices of the Danish government. Today it is used by the US Virgin Islands as administrative offices. If the gate is open, go into the inner courtyard to see the gardens and small pools. A majestic staircase leads to a ballroom that is used for official government gatherings. ☎ 340-773-1404.

Lord of Saboth Lutheran Church.

Across Queen Cross Street you'll see **Lord God of Saboth Lutheran Church**, which was built around 1740 by members of the Dutch Reformed Church. The Lutheran congregation that originally met in the Steeple Building, moved to this structure in 1831 and added the Gothic Revival-style tower over the front entrance in 1834.

Turn back along King Street to Queen Cross Street and take a right to get to Company Street, where you'll find **Old Market Place** a block down on the right. The open-air building that now serves as a farmer's market stands on the site used by slave traders in the 1700s. Shop here for the island's freshest fruits and vegetables, on sale Monday-Saturday, 7 am-6 pm. For the best selection, arrive early on Saturday morning.

Walking back along Company Street toward Fort Christiansvaern until you reach **Christiansted Apothecary Hall**. A drugstore was founded here in 1828 by a Danish pharmacist, and continued to operate as a dispensary until 1970. Recently, the property was reopened by the St. Croix Landmarks Society (www.stcroixlandmarks.com)as a museum, featuring more than 600 of the original pharmaceutical wares and equipment. Inside the courtyard, look for a display of island archeology. You can visit here free of charge, Monday-Saturday, 10 am-2 pm. ☎ 340-772-0598.

Just before you arrive back at the fort, you'll see the white **Steeple Building** ☆ with a red-topped belfry on the right side of Company Street. It was the first church constructed by the Danes after their colonization of the island and is now a museum displaying archeological artifacts from Carib and Arawak Indian settlements as well as relics from colonial-era sugar plantations. Admission is $3, and the same ticket allows you admission into Fort Christiansvaern. The museum is

The Steeple Building.

open Monday-Friday, 8 am-4:45 pm and Saturday, 9 am-noon.

OFFSHORE TRIP

Hop aboard a ferry at Christiansted Harbor for a quick $3 ride over to nearby **Protestant Cay**. The little dab of land got its name in the 17th century when French protestant refugees from the predominantly-Catholic island of St. Christopher (now St. Kitts) settled among the Dutch in the area that is now Christiansted.

These exiles were denied gravesites on the main island, and were forced to take their loved ones out to the cay (pronounced like "key") for burial. Today, the little islet is a refuge for the St. Croix ground lizard and home to **Hotel on the Cay**, where you can indulge in watersports or have lunch while enjoying a wonderful view of Christiansted. ☎ 800-524-2035 or 340-773-2035; fax 773-7046; www.hotelonthecay.com.

TIP: *Take time to stroll along the Christiansted waterfront. The boardwalk offers restaurants, shops and views.*

A WALKING TOUR OF FREDERIKSTED

St. Croix's *other* town might be considered a work in progress. It isn't as pretty or lively as Christiansted, but there have

been great improvements in recent years, and its west-end location puts it close to many of the island's best attractions.

Don't plan to spend a lot of time here, unless a special event is scheduled. Then the lethargic little village stirs itself into a frenzy of activity often featuring bands, mocko jumbies

Frederiksted

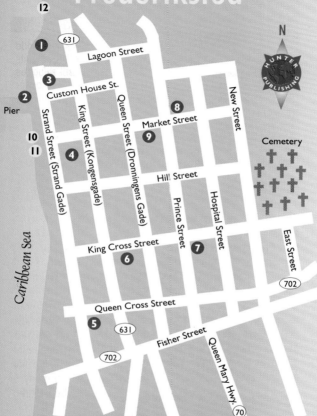

SIGHTS & ATTRACTIONS
1. Fort Frederik
2. Visitor's Center
3. Old Customs House
4. Victoria House
5. Old Public Library
6. Apothecary Hall
7. St. Pauls' Anglican Church
8. St. Patrick's Catholic Church
9. Public Market Place

PLACES TO STAY & EAT
10. The Frederiksted Hotel
11. Blue Moon
12. Changes in Latitude

© 2007 HUNTER PUBLISHING, INC

NOT TO SCALE

and an arts and crafts market. Check the current edition of *St. Croix This Week* or call the Visitor Center, ☎ 340-772-0357, for a listing of events.

MOCKO JUMBIES

Mocko jumbies are stilt-walkers dressed in colorful costumes who perform at festivals, march in parades and entertain at special events. Many islanders of African descent love traditional stories of jumbies, or ghosts, who appear mysteriously to take the blame for bad luck or the credit for good fortune. Slaves told children stories of jumbies to coax children into good behavior. In some tales, jumbies appear in threatening situations to conquer bad guys and rescue the righteous. These stories are still popular today, and modern Caribbean and African writers often use jumbie-like characters in their stories.

Do see the fort. It sits beside the cruise-ship pier and is every bit as fascinating as Fort Christiansvaern. The Danes built **Fort Frederik** ☆ in the mid-1700s to deter smugglers. They named it for their monarch, King Frederik V. The date 1760 is inscribed over the entrance and signifies the year that the fort was completed. The bronze bust on the lawn outside the fort is of Moses "Buddhoe" Gottlieb, who led 8,000 slaves on a rebellious march on the fort July 3, 1848. In response, Governor General Peter Von Scholten stood up in his carriage parked outside the fort and announced the emancipation of all slaves in the Danish West Indies. Today, you can tour the restored courtyard, stables, officers' kitchen, detention cells,

a small art gallery and a museum with interesting historical relics and police memorabilia. Commandant's quarters are on the second floor. The fort was recently declared a National Historic

Landmark. There's no admission fee. Open Monday-Friday, 8:30 am-4 pm; Saturday, 1 am-4 pm. ☎ 340-772-2021.

> **TIP:** *A **Visitor's Center** is located at the pier adjacent to the fort. Stop in for maps and brochures on weekdays between 8 am and 5 pm. ☎ 340-772-0357.*

The Old Customs House is across Lagoon Street from the fort. It was built in the late 1800s and renovated after Hurricane Hugo in 1989. The outdoor fountain was added in 1998 to celebrate the 150th anniversary of emancipation.

Much of Frederiksted was destroyed by fire in 1878, so the predominant architecture of the oldest buildings is Victorian. An excellent example is **Victoria House**, a block south of the Old Customs House on Strand Street. Since this is a private home, you can't tour the interior, but architecture buffs will be interested in the elaborate gingerbread trim.

Other sites with interesting architecture line the main road. From Victoria House, stroll up Strand Street and notice the old archways and buildings that face the waterfront. The **Caribbean Museum Center for the Arts** at #10 has special and permanent collections of local art. It's open Tuesday-Saturday, 10 am-5 pm, ☎ 340-772-2622. Just past Queen Cross Street, you'll find the still-operative **Old Public Library** (☎ 340-772-0315).

At the corner of King Cross and Prince Streets, is **St. Paul's Anglican Church**, which is a recently restored early 19th-century mix of Georgian and Gothic Revival architecture with a lovely sandstone tower (☎ 340-772-0818). Back toward the north on Prince Street is **St. Patrick's Roman Catholic Church** (☎ 340-772-5052), built in 1843 with three spires. Diagonally across Market Street, you may find locals passing the time among vendors selling fresh produce on the spot that has been the **Public Market Place** since 1751.

The Western Countryside by Car

Beginning at the western end near Frederiksted, take Route 76 (Mahogany Road) east through the towering trees of the

Rain Forest. This northwest section of the island receives only about 40 inches of rain each year, so technically it's a *tropical forest*, since a true rain forest gets at least 80 inches of precipitation each year. However, the area is a lovely tropical woodland with centuries-old mahogany, silk-cotton, samaan and turpentine trees mixed with tangled vines and thick ferns.

© Lawrence Sawyer/iStockPhoto

As you drive slowly through the forest, watch for hummingbirds, yellow warblers and bananaquits (the national bird). Well-worn paths lead off road, and you may want to stop and explore for a short distance. The best hikes are along unpaved roads and trails found north of Route 76. (See *Hiking*, page 238, for more information.)

The Carl and Marie Lawaetz Museum ✩ is located at Estate Little La Grange just over a mile east of Frederiksted. The former sugar plantation became a museum under the direction of the St. Croix Landmarks Society and conduct tours for visitors. The experience is somewhat like visiting distant cousins while passing through town. You'll be shown the dining room that is furnished with items bought second-hand by Danish farmer Carl Lawaetz in 1896, and the kitchen that was added in 1909. You even get to peek into the upstairs bedrooms to admire the original mahogany four-poster beds with mosquito netting. Open Wednesday-Saturday, 10 am-

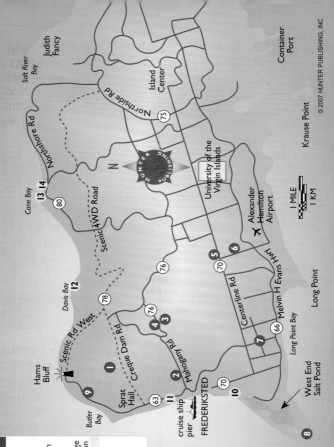

Western St. Croix

SIGHTS & ATTRACTIONS
1. Rainforest
2. Carl & Marie Lawaetz Museum
3. St. Croiz Leap
4. Mount Pellier Hut Domino Club
5. St. Geroge Village Botanical Garden
6. Cruzan Rum Factory
7. Estate Whim Plantation Museum
8. Sandy Point National Wildlife Refuge
9. Estate Mount Washington Plantation

PLACES TO STAY & EAT
10. Cottages by the Sea
11. Sandcastle on the Beach
12. Carambola
13. The Waves at Cane Bay
14. Off the Wall

© 2007 HUNTER PUBLISHING, INC

HUNTER PUBLISHING

N

Judith Fancy

Salt River Bay

Island Center

Container Port

Krause Point

Northside Rd

75

Cane Bay

80

13 14

Northshore Rd

Scenic 4WD Road

University of the Virgin Islands

Alexander Hamilton Airport

Davis Bay

12

78

76

Scenic Rd West

Creque Dam Rd

Hams Bluff

9

1

Sprat Hall

Butler Bay

63

11

Mahogany Rd

2

4

76

3

5

70

6

Centerline Rd

66

Melvin H Evans Hwy

7

FREDERIKSTED

cruise ship pier

70

10

West End Salt Pond

Long Point Bay

Long Point

8

1 MILE
1 KM

4 pm. Admission is $8 for adults and $4 for children. ☎ 340-772-0598; www.stcroixlandmarks.com.

> **TIP:** *Take time to visit the lush gardens and ruins.*

St. Croix Leap Project, two miles from Frederiksted on Route 76, is an open-air workshop for artisans who craft tables, mirror frames, carving boards, statuettes and other items from local fallen wood – no trees are cut down. Their works are for sale, and the shop is open Monday-Friday, 9 am-5 pm; Saturday, 10 am-5 pm. ☎ 340-772-0421.

Nearby, **Mt. Pellier Hut Domino Club** looks like a rundown shack, but actually offers a unique attraction – beer-drinking pigs. Stop at the bar to buy a can of non-alcoholic beer from Norma the bartender. Take your room-temperature beer out to the tidy enclosed pens where five hogs wait for their treat. Hand the unopened can to Oreo, Tony, J.J., Shily or Toni and stand back while the beast opens the can and gulps the beer. If this spectacle stirs up your own thirst, head back to the bar and order a MammaWanna, a tasty drink reported to be a medicinal aphrodisiac. The Domino Club is open daily from 8 am "till the last customer leaves." ☎ 340-772-9914.

At the intersection of Route 76 and Route 705, turn right and drive south, then take another right onto Route 70 (Centerline Road or Queen Mary Highway) to head back west. A sign marking the palm-shaded lane that leads to **St. George Village Botanical Garden** ☆☆ is on the right side soon after you turn onto Centerline Road. Be sure to have plenty of film in your camera, because you'll want pictures of this lush 16-acre oasis built around the ruins of an 18th-century sugar plantation that is registered as a National His-

Great Hall at the Botanical Garden.

© St. George Botanical Garden

toric Site. Pick up a self-guiding tour map at the visitors' center in the Great Hall that was built to join two original workers' houses. This will guide you through the grounds, which include examples of the dry-to-wet ecosystems on St. Croix. An old Danish cemetery is across from the Great Hall with graves dating from 1733 to 1917. The grounds themselves were once the site of an Arawak Indian Village from 100 to 900 AD. The Botanical Gardens are open daily, 9 am-5 pm. Admission is $6 for adults and $1 for children. ☎ 340-692-2874; www.sgvbg.org.

Leaving the Botanical Gardens, turn right then immediately left to go south on Route 64 (West Airport Road) to visit the **Cruzan Rum Factory**. St. Croix's Cruzan rum is distilled by the Virgin Islands Rum Industries among the ruins of Estate Diamond Plantation. The half-hour guided tour ends with a complimentary rum drink at a bar and you can purchase bottles to take home (remember that US citizens are allowed to return with five liters of duty-free liquor, plus an extra bottle if it is produced in the Virgin Islands). Tours are given Monday-Friday, 9 am-11:30 am and 1 pm-4:15 pm. The charge is $4. ☎ 340-692-2280; www. cruzanrum.com.

The distillery.

Return to Route 70/Centerline Road and drive west, a left turn. **Estate Whim Plantation Museum** ☆☆ is on the left, about two miles before you reach Frederiksted. Allow plenty of time at this well-preserved estate that brings to life the historical time when slave labor provided great wealth to Danish plantation owners. There's an exquisite neo-classical-style Greathouse that was built in the 1700s with three-foot-thick stone walls and only three rooms. The grounds contain buildings designed for living and producing sugar in the 18th and early 19th centuries. Admission is $8 for adults, $5 for seniors and $4 for children. The plantation is open Monday-Saturday, 10 am-4 pm, November-April, and Monday, Wednesday, Friday and Saturday, 10 am-3pm, May-October. Tours are given every half-hour. ☎ 340-772-0598; www. stcroixlandmarks.com.

Old windmill at Estate Whim.

Sandy Point National Wildlife Refuge ☆ is about three miles from Frederiksted on the peninsula that juts out into the Caribbean at the far southwestern end of the island. At the intersection of Route 661 and Route 66, turn onto a dirt road and drive west for just less than a mile to the refuge gate. You'll go along the **Westend Salt Pond** to another dirt road that leads to a parking area. Leave your car in the lot and walk out to the beach that is surrounded on three sides by the Caribbean Sea. Shorebirds and migratory birds feed in this protected area and sea turtles dig nests in the sand to lay their eggs. Be careful not to disturb a nest since harming or removing turtle eggs is illegal.

The refuge is usually open only on the weekend from sunrise until sunset and is periodically closed from April to August to protect nesting birds or turtles. Check the schedule with the refuge office in Christiansted (☎ 340-773-4554) before you plan a visit.

North of Frederiksted, Route 63 follows the coast past several sandy beaches hidden by profuse vegetation and brings you **Estate Mount Washington Plantation**. Until 1984, no one realized this 1750-era Danish plantation was buried under thick greenery on the far northwest end of the island. Now, the trees have been cut back and the underbrush cleared away to reveal an attractive three-story rum factory, an intriguing dungeon and one of the few water mills on the island. It's interesting to stroll the flower-filled grounds and poke among the vine-covered ruins. A shop on the property displays West Indian antiques and takes custom orders for handcrafted mahogany reproductions. These unmanned plantation ruins are open daily from roughly 9 am-5 pm, but if you want to visit the antique shop, call to verify hours. ☎ 340-772-1026.

About a mile farther north, stop at the isolated beach at **Ham's Bay** to gather shells and wander among the tidal pools. **Scenic Road West** (Route 78), a rugged dirt road that leads east through the forest, can be explored on foot or in a four-wheel-drive vehicle. A lighthouse sits on **Ham's Bluff**, northeast of the bay, and you can hike to it, if you're in good condition. (See *Hiking* for more information about exploring the Scenic Road.)

Driving East & West from Christiansted

Driving west along Route 75 (Northside Road), watch for Route 751, which leads to **Estate Judith Fancy**. This modern-day neighborhood is built on the site of a 1750s Danish plantation, and the ruins of the greathouse and tower remain. Judith herself is said to be buried on the property. Follow Hamilton Drive into the development and turn east onto Caribe Road to see the plantation's ruins. You can drive around and view the attractive homes, then go to the end of Hamilton Drive and look down on **Salt River Bay**, where Columbus anchored on November 14, 1493, during his second voyage. You may wonder if the Carib Indians were watching from this overlook as Columbus's ships approached the island.

ST CROIX

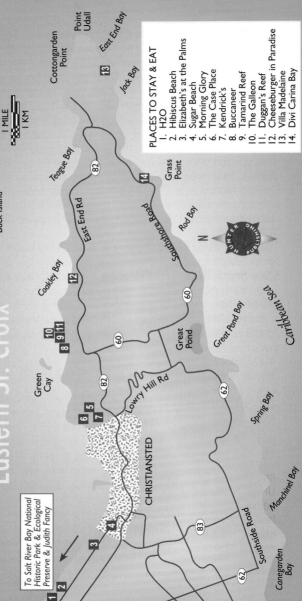

Eastern St. Croix

PLACES TO STAY & EAT

1. H2O
2. Hibiscus Beach
3. Elizabeth's at the Palms
4. Sugar Beach
5. Morning Glory
6. The Case Place
7. Kendrick's
8. Buccaneer
9. Tamarind Reef
10. The Galleon
11. Duggan's Reef
12. Cheeseburger in Paradise
13. Villa Madelaine
14. Divi Carina Bay

To Salt River Bay National Historic Park & Ecological Preserve & Judith Fancy

Buck Island

Point Udall

Cottongarden Point

East End Bay

Jack Bay

Teague Bay

East End Rd

Coakley Bay

Green Cay

Southshore Road

Grass Point

Rod Bay

Great Pond Bay

Great Pond

Great Pond Bay

Caribbean Sea

Christiansted

Lowry Hill Rd

Spring Bay

Manchinel Bay

Southside Road

Canegarden Bay

N

HUNTER PUBLISHING

1 MILE
1 KM

© 2007 HUNTER PUBLISHING, INC.

Get to **Salt River Bay National Historical Park and Ecological Preserve** ☆ by driving west on Route 75, then north on Route 80. The park was established in 1993 to celebrate the 500th anniversary of Columbus' discovery. In addition to being the only known US site that Columbus' crew actually visited, archeologists have found relics of human settlements dating from the second century AD and the park contains the only discovered prehistoric ceremonial ball court in the lesser Antilles. Furthermore, the largest remaining mangrove forest in the US Virgin Islands surrounds this estuary where the Caribbean Sea meets the Salt River, and several endangered species nest here. You don't have to be a biologist or historian to appreciate the multiple significance of the place. Plans are in the works to build a museum and develop interpretive trails through the area.

Call the **St. Croix Environmental Association** about guided tours of the park and preserve. ☎ 340-773-1989. (See *Hiking* and *Diving* for information about trails and the underwater canyon in the preserve.) Information is available from the National Park Service, ☎ 340-773-1460.

East of Christiansted, Route 75 (East End Road) becomes Route 82 and leads to **Green Cay Marina** (☎ 340-773-1453; fax 773-9651), where impressive yachts tie up across from the **National Wildlife Reserve** on **Green Cay**. The forest on the small nearby island provides nesting sites for endangered brown pelicans and several species of herons and egrets. The last significant population of the St. Croix ground lizard also lives on the island, so the reserve is closed to visitors, but bird watchers will want to aim their binoculars at the cay for interesting sightings.

Continue along Route 82 until it becomes a rough dirt road and ends at **Point Udall** ☆, the easternmost spot in the United States. Many visitors make their way out to the point before dawn to witness the first rays of sun as they touch US land on a new day. Anytime you visit the cliff top, you'll be granted a great view of distant islands and the turquoise Caribbean Sea.

ST CROIX

Take Route 60 off Route 82 at Knight Bay to cut across the narrow east end of the island to the south shore. This striking coastline is rolling and grassy, quite different from the north and west shores. **Grass Point** juts out into the sea and provides a captivating view. Many types of birds live and nest in the area, especially around **Great Pond Bay**, and paths lead from the road down to the shore. This is a great place to stretch your legs before taking Route 62 back to Christiansted.

A Day on Buck Island

Buck Island Reef National Monument ☆☆ is a US National Park located off St. Croix's northeast coast 4½ miles from Christiansted's harbor. The island itself is only half a mile wide and a mile long, but the protected area includes 704 acres of water and an extraordinary coral reef system that features the most superb marine garden in the Caribbean. *National Geographic* magazine calls it one of the 10 best beaches in the world, and sunbathers, swimmers, snorkelers and sailors call it paradise.

Plan to spend an entire day exploring the island, sunning on the wide sandy beach and snorkeling the underwater nature trail. Several companies operate guided boat trips from

Christiansted and Green Cay Marina, and you can rent your own boat from concessioners in town. Almost all provide snorkeling equipment and guided tours give a short lesson before they set you free to explore the marked underwater trail.

Family on the beach at Buck Island.

© Linda Morland/Dreamstime

ST CROIX

Maximum water depth is about 12 feet and visibility is routinely excellent. If you feel unsure about your swimming or snorkeling abilities, go with a guide who will outfit you with an inflatable vest and lead you along the trail. If you take your own boat, check with the National Park Service (☎ 340-773-1460) about maneuvering through and anchoring in protected waters.

Guided tours usually include a beach picnic, and you can also bring your own lunch or use the grills located at **West Beach** and **Diedrich's Point**. There are tables and pit toilets at both locations. Marked hiking trails begin in each area. You can hike up to an observation point on the island's ridge in 30 to 45 minutes, and walk completely around the shore in about two hours. Be sure to wear shoes (not flip-flops) and carry plenty of water.

Hawksbill turtles, green sea turtles, frigate birds, least terns and brown pelicans nest on the island, and several species of tropical birds perch in the trees. The elkhorn coral barrier reef stretches 2,000 yards around two-thirds of the coast and shelters a wide variety of colorful fish, including angels, blue tangs and parrotfish. Expect to pay $60-$85 per adult for full-day trips and $40-$50 for half-day trips.

© Big Beard Adventures

Renegade, *run by Big Beard Adventures, takes visitors to secluded areas such as Turtle Beach, shown here.*

DAY-TRIP OPERATORS

❖ **Big Beard Adventures** offers full-day trips to Buck Island on *Renegade*, a 42-foot catamaran with a glass bottom. Lunch and rum punch on a secluded St. Croix island is included. Half-day trips are available on the *Buck Island Flyer*, a 40-foot catamaran. Both boats leave from the wharf in Christiansted. ☎ 800-773-4482 or 340-773-4482; www.bigbeards.com.

❖ *Diva* takes only six passengers on a 35-foot Beneteau sailboat, so you feel as though you're out sailing with friends. Call Captain Francis Waters for reservations and information about trips leaving from Christiansted. ☎ 340-778-4675; www.buckisland-diva.com.

❖ **Caribbean Sea Adventures** runs full- and half-day tours in glass-bottom power or sail boats. All trips include snorkeling gear and a guided tour of the reefs, and a box lunch can be ordered at an additional charge. Call the office in Christiansted, ☎ 340-773-2628; www.caribbean seaadventures.com.

❖ **Captain Heinz's** *Teroro II* takes passengers to Buck Island from Green Cay Marina aboard the 42-foot trimaran. Call for information on the tours, which leave at 9 am and 2 pm. ☎ 340-773-3161.

◆ Adventures on Water

Best Beaches

Splendid white-sand beaches are St. Croix's most popular tourist attractions. All are open to the public, but some beach-front hotels may charge a small fee for use of their amenities. Most of the island's beaches have sandy-bottom areas for swimming, and many offer outstanding snorkeling around rocky outcroppings or coral reefs. Some of the island's most stunning beaches are in their natural state; their lack of facilities is offset by their wild beauty.

While every one of St. Croix's beaches is someone's favorite, the following are listed as a guide to those most often mentioned by residents or frequent visitors as something special.

Cane Bay ☆ is probably the best everything-to-everybody beach on the island. Get there by taking Route 80 along the scenic north coast. Look for the beach across from the Cane

ST CROIX

Cane Bay Beach.

Bay Plantation. The water can get rough here, and the beach is narrow, but the sand is white and shaded, and the close-in snorkeling and scuba diving is terrific. The renowned Cane Bay Wall drops more than 120 feet less than 150 yards off-shore, so divers enter from the beach and swim out to the drop. Snorkelers can see fabulous reef formations and fish near the surface. Restaurants and bars are nearby, and Cane Bay Dive Shop rents snorkeling and scuba equipment.

Davis Bay, just west of Cane Bay at the junction of Route 80 and Route 69, is another long, palm-shaded white-sand beach where swimming is good. The Sunterra Carambola Resort has a restaurant and dive shop right on the beach. Public access is through a pathway from a parking lot on Route 80, and the guard at the resort's entrance shack will give you directions, if necessary. The water can have rolling surf at times.

> **TIP:** *Part of the beach is rocky, so enter the sea from the smooth-bottomed west end.*

Protestant Cay is the beach closest to Christiansted, but visitors must take a $4 round-trip ferry ride from the wharf across to the cay. Hotel on the Cay offers watersports, lounge-chair rentals and the services of their restaurant and bar. Beach-bumming, swimming and snorkeling are all great. A steel band plays on the beach each Sunday.

Protestant Cay Beach.

Cramer Park recently underwent a renovation, so restrooms and changing areas are nice. You can bring a picnic and use the tables provided or visit the restaurant nearby. The beach here is popular with locals and can be crowded on weekends. Water is usually calm, offering good swimming conditions. Seagrape trees provide shade. Get there by taking Route 82 east along the north shore, almost to Point Udall, and take a left at the fork in the road near the St. Croix Yacht Club.

Grapetree Bay is home to the new Divi Carina Bay Resort, and the long sugar-white beach is a favorite with snorkelers. Watersports equipment is available for rent and a beachside snack bar provides drinks and light meals. Find the resort and beach by following Route 82 east from Christiansted, then turning right at the fork in the road near the St. Croix Yacht Club and continuing to the south shore.

Grapetree Bay.

Isaac Bay ☆ and **Jack Bay** ☆ have the two most isolated and pristine beaches on the island. You have to hike down

Isaac Bay.

from Point Udall at the end of Route 82 by taking a dirt path to East End Bay, then walking back west along a trail that takes you up and over a headland to Isaac Bay. From there you can take a path over the hill on Isaac Point to Jack Bay. You'll rarely have company, and visitors regularly swim and sunbathe in the nude (although it's illegal). The water is calm and snorkeling is terrific along the close-in barrier reef.

Shoy Beach ☆ is also secluded, but not nearly as difficult to reach as Isaac/Jack Bay. It's located in an exclusive area known as Estate Shoy (aka Buccaneer Estates), just east of the Buccaneer Resort. Take Route 82 east from Christiansted and turn into the Buccaneer Resort grounds. At the hotel's guard shack, turn right and continue on to another shack, where you'll have to check in with the guard who monitors the upscale neighborhood. He'll direct you to park at the end of the dirt road that runs beside the golf course. Follow a path about 150 yards to the powdery white-sand beach. Palms provide shade and the water is crystal-clear and calm. Private homes surround the beach. There is no food service or other facilities. Go to the east end of the beach for swimming and the west end for snorkeling.

Buccaneer Beach borders the Buccaneer Resort and, if you're not a guest of the hotel, you'll be charged $4 for use of the lounge chairs, restrooms, and changing facilities. You can rent watersports equipment from the beach center and order lunch from the Mermaid Restaurant. Watch for resort signs on Route 82, two miles east of Christiansted.

Chenay Bay Beach ☆ is excellent for swimming, snorkeling and windsurfing. Chenay Bay Beach Resort, on the beach, allows non-guests to use the lounge chairs if they purchase food or drinks from the snack pavilion. Hammocks, kayaks, snorkel gear, windsurfers and Sunfish may be rented. The beach is three miles east of Christiansted on Route 82.

Reef Beach on Tague Bay off Route 82 is a popular wind-surfing spot. Watersports equipment and lounge chairs can be rented, and Duggan's Restaurant is a favorite for lunch. Seagrape trees provide shade for lounging and picnicking.

Sprat Hall Beach is on the west coast, a mile north of Frederiksted on Route 63. The Sprat Hall Plantation Hotel sits on a hill above the beach and charges non-guests a $2 day-use fee. You can rent lounge chairs and have lunch at the Beach Restaurant. Snorkeling is good. The long beach is excellent for leisurely walks.

Rainbow Beach is one of the favorites along a stretch of western coast just north of Frederiksted off Route 63. It is hidden from the road by dense vegetation and has calm water and soft white sand. It's popular with swimmers, snorkelers and beachcombers. A restaurant and bar are close by.

Rainbow Beach.

ST CROIX

TURTLE WATCHES

Environmental groups and hotel owners regularly patrol the beaches for signs of turtle nests. They attempt to protect these area or move the eggs to a safe place. If you are lucky enough to see a nest just under the surface of the sand, report its location to the nearest hotel or the St. Croix Environmental Association, ☎ 340-773-1989. Do not disturb the nest.

Scuba Diving & Snorkeling

St. Croix is essentially surrounded by an extensive, well-developed barrier reef and has the largest living reef of any Caribbean island. In an attempt to protect the reef from anchor damage, a non-profit organization called The **Island Conservation Effort** oversees 22 moored dive sites along the coast. Conscientious dive operators regularly anchor at more than 20 additional prominent sites, and seasoned divers claim the island actually offers hundreds of excellent scuba locations. Moreover, a portion of the coral reef that encircles **Buck Island National Park** is maintained as a marked underwater trail for snorkelers.

A snorkeler swims above coral.

A vibrant **wall** runs the length of the northern coast and begins near the shore in about 30 feet of water. This allows novice divers and snorkelers to see plenty of spectacular formations and marine life. Since the wall plummets to more than 13,000 feet, experienced divers enjoy the thrill of descending down one of the steepest drops in the world. Many of the best sites are accessible from the beach, and many more can be reached by a short boat ride.

Snorkelers at Buck Island.

While you certainly must go to **Buck Island,** the reef and underwater trail have become a bit haggard due to storm damage and the constant assault of adoring visitors. Ordinarily, Mother Nature would have healed the reef's hurricane wounds quickly, but careless and uninformed snorkelers kick, touch and stand on new growth so that it is destroyed as quickly as it forms. Nonetheless, the tiny island and its underwater treasures are unique and captivating, so go, follow the markers along the ocean floor, swim with the parrotfish, feed the grouper and please, please don't stand on anything except sand.

Scuba divers have an abundant choice of excellent dive sites, including **Frederiksted Pier**. For years, the sponges and corals that developed on the support pillars of the town's dock created a diver's paradise. Then, in 1989, Hurricane Hugo raged across the island and wrecked Frederiksted's harbor, including the pier. A new pier was inaugurated

Diver, Frederiksted Pier.

in 1994, and the pilings of the old pier were dumped in Butler Bay beside some sunken ships.

The new pier has some interesting fresh growth on its support columns, and many claim this is the best night dive in the Caribbean. Divers routinely spot seahorses, lobster and eels among the colorful sponges. If you don't go with a dive operator, check with the Harbor Master at the pier before you enter the water. (Be prepared to show your certification card.)

At the western end of the north-shore reef is **Northstar**, one of the steepest walls in the world. You can swim out to the drop by entering from the beach at Davis Bay, but most divers find it easier go out by boat, since there is often a moderate current and the area has a lot of rocks. Expect to see an amazing wall with plunging shafts full of staghorn and brain corals, tube sponges and sea fans. Many types of tropical fish, turtles and eels live along the reef.

East of Northstar, you'll find a couple of different dive sites at **Salt River**. Dolphins and sharks often hang out along the east and west walls that border the 300-foot **Salt River Canyon**. The east wall features **Russ Rock** and **Barracuda Bank**, which are loaded with corals and sponges. Look for black and gorgonian coral, barracuda and stingrays. The west wall is covered with brilliant purple sponges and has little swim-through canyons along its slope. Like the east wall, it hosts an extraordinary variety of marine life.

Long Reef offers a shallow dive (50 to 80 feet) and an abundance of brilliantly colored fish. As you gradually descend along the reef and a series of shallow caves, watch for turtles, octopi, lobsters and rays. If you see a shark, it's most likely an agreeable nurse shark, so admire it and move on. The elkhorn corals are fantastic.

Four wrecks are sunk in **Butler Bay** off the western coast. While the wrecks themselves are nothing special, they do make a remarkable artificial reef. The 170-foot container ship named *Rosa Maria,* sank when her crew unloaded her heavy cargo from only one side and flipped her over. She was towed out to Butler Bay and sunk in 100 feet of water. South of *Rosa Maria* are the 140-foot fishing boat, *Suffolk Maid*, a

60-foot tug boat, *Northwind*, and a 300-foot barge, *Virgin Island.* These three wrecks are in more shallow water and make ideal second dives after the *Rosa Maria.*

DIVE OPERATORS

Because St. Croix dive sites are so diverse, it's possible, in one day, to explore one of five wrecks, slowly drift down a steep coral-studded wall, check out one of the largest living reefs in the Caribbean, and still have time to do a pier dive after dark.

To make all of this possible, some of the dive shops on the island have banded together to offer a **Dive the Island Passport**, a pre-paid pass good for two-tank dive sets with different operators. For a complete description of this program, take a look at the Diverse Virgin website, www.diversevirgin. com.

If you decide not to purchase the Passport, you still can arrange individual dives with any of the following shops. Expect to pay $65 for a one-tank dive, $85 for a two-tank dive, $20 for an introductory resort-course dive that requires no experience, and around $300 for a certification course.

ST CROIX

St. Croix Ultimate Bluewater Adventures is a PADI Gold Palm operator and has been rated one of the best dive shops in the Caribbean by readers of *Rodale's Scuba Diving Magazine.* Several factors figure into their popularity. The staff is super-friendly, the shop is well stocked and conveniently located just steps from Christiansted Harbor, and the dive boat is outfitted with lots of creature comforts and never goes out overcrowded. For a real treat, book a night dive, which leaves early enough to watch the sunset. Owners Ed and Molly Buckley oversee a truly first-class operation, and all the instructors and dive masters strive to make your diving experience the highlight of your vacation. Look for the "SCUBA" sign above the shop's entrance next to the St. Croix Aquarium at 14 Caravelle Arcade in Christiansted. ☎ 877-567-1367 or 340-773-5994; fax 773-5910; www.stcroixscuba.com.

Cane Bay Dive Shop is on the north shore across from the renowned Wall. Their one- , two- and six-tank beach-dive packages include visits to several sites along the drop-off within easy reach of the shore. The one- and two-tank boat dives are tailored to meet the skills, interests and schedules of their divers. Non-divers often tag along to snorkel above their scuba-certified friends, and all levels of instruction are available, including resort course. Find this five-star PADI fa-

© Cane Bay Dive Shop

cility on Route 80 (North Shore Road) at Cane Bay. ☎ 800-338-3843 or 340-773-9913; fax 778-5442; www.canebay scuba.com. Satellite stores are located on Strand Street in Frederiksted (☎ 340-772-0715), in the Pan Am Pavilion in Christiansted (☎ 340-773-4663), in DIVI Resort (☎ 340-713-1519) and at Carambola Beach Resort (☎ 340-773-3800).

© Cane Bay Dive Shop

Diver at Cane Bay Wall.

Dive Experience is a five-star PADI facility and National Geographic Dive Center owned by Michelle Pugh, an amazing Hall of Fame diver and underwater photographer with over 30 years experience. She oversees a friendly, professional staff that enjoys showing off their favorite dive sites. Every afternoon the shop runs a one-tank Fish Feed Dive that allows participants to get familiar with moray eels, barracudas and other congenial critters. Additional dives are scheduled to sites along the walls and canyons of the coral reefs. The shop is at 1111 Strand Street in Christiansted. ☎ 800-235-9047 or 340-773-3307; www.divexp.com.

Anchor Dive Center is a PADI five-star facility located five- to 15-minutes by boat from dive sites in the Salt River National Park and Ecological Preserve. Because of their extensive experience in the park area, the staff has discovered many secluded spots that they enjoy sharing with visitors. Instructors take one to six divers per boat to sites within the park and elsewhere around the island. Find the dive center at the Salt River Marina. ☎ 800-532-3483 or 340-778-1522; www.anchordivestcroix.com. Anchor Dive Center also runs

ST CROIX

diving operations from Divi Carina Bay Resort and Carambola Beach Resort.

N2 The Blue Diving Adventures ☆ is perfect if you're new to diving or like a lot of attention. Owners Derrick and Anne Hill and their friendly crew take no more than six divers at a time, whether they are guiding you from their boat or from the beach. If you're an experienced diver and just need equipment or an air fill, their well-stocked shop is conveniently located near Cane Bay, on the way out to the West End. Look for the blue-trimmed yellow building on North Shore Road, about a mile east of Cane Bay. ☎ 866-712-2583 or 340-713-1475; www.n2blue.com.

The Scuba Shack ☆ in Frederiksted is owned by David and Sue Ward, both avid divers, devoted ecologists and enthusiastic students of life underwater. David has years of experience with the some of the world's top marine scientists and, thus, a huge knowledge of the underwater ecosystem, which he eagerly shares with his staff. "The Shack" is known for its NAUI and PADI instruction, specialty courses (including Nitrox), gear rental, retail equipment sales and kayak rentals. Look for them on the water north of the Frederiksted Pier, across from Changes in L'Attitudes Beach Bar, ☎ 888-789-3483 or 340-772-3483; www.stcroixscubashack.com.

Scuba West, run by Californians Chris and Laura, specializes in guided day or night dives from the Frederiksted pier. You may want to try one of each to compare the differences. In addition, the crew leads boat dives in the calm waters off the west end and at the wall in Cane Bay. This full-service PADI center offers all types of certification programs and advanced training. The shop is at 330 Strand Street in Frederiksted. ☎ 800-352-0107 or 340-772-3701; www.divescubawest.com.

Boating & Sailing

SCHEDULED CRUISES

Buck Island is by far the most popular day-trip by boat. Only a few companies are licensed to take visitors to the national park, so boats are often booked full during high season or when cruise ships are docked in town. Make your reservation early. If you want the option of snorkeling and picnicking at more isolated spots or prefer a sunset sail along the coast, you'll have several choices of scheduled cruises and custom-designed trips.

> **TIP:** *From February through April, you are likely to spot humpback whales in the waters around St. Croix.*

Rates for a full-day excursion with lunch run about $75 for adults and $55 for kids. Prices for half-day and sunset sails vary widely depending on the types of refreshments served and the length of the trip, so shop around before you make a reservation. The operators listed below have a reputation for excellence.

Big Beard's Renegade.

© Big Beard Adventures

Big Beard's Adventure Tours ☆ offers visitors a choice of full-day or half-day sailing trips from Christiansted to Buck Island. The full-day excursion aboard *Renegade*, a 42-foot glass-bottom catamaran, is the most popular choice. A half-day sail aboard the 40-foot *Buck Island Flyer* leaves at noon and doesn't include lunch. *Big Beard* himself (aka John

Macy) is an ordained minister and performs weddings dressed in his white captain's uniform. Look for the bearded captain on the wharf in Christiansted. ☎ 340-773-4482; www.bigbeards.com.

DIVA is a 35-foot Beneteau sailboat captained by Francis Waters. No more than six passengers take each of the personalized tours, so you feel as though you're an invited guest on a private yacht. ☎ 778-4675; www.buckisland-diva.com.

Teroro II is a 42-foot trimaran operated by captains Carl and Heinz from Green Cay Marina. They have many years of sailing experience and are excellent snorkeling guides. ☎ 340-773-3161.

Caribbean Sea Adventures ☆ runs full- and half-day tours in glass-bottom, power- or sailboats. The sunset sail, which cruises along St. Croix's north coast, includes snacks and rum punch. Contact the office at 59 King's Wharf in Christiansted for information and reservations. ☎ 340-773-2628; www.caribbeanseaadventures.com.

© Bilinda Charters

Bilinda Charters.

Bilinda Charters sails a 37-foot Albin Stratus from Green Cay Marina to secluded reefs for snorkeling. Half-day trips leave at 9 am and 2 pm. The sunset cruise departs at 4 pm. Contact the crew at the marina for information on private two- and three-hour sail-and-snorkel outings. ☎ 340-773-1641; www.sailbilinda.com.

If you want to watch a sailing regatta, contact the St. Croix Yacht Club at Teague Bay for information on regattas held on the island. ☎ 340-773-9531; www.stcroixyc.com.

Fishing

Since the world famous six-mile-deep **North Drop** extends from Puerto Rico to the waters around St. Croix, sportfishing is popular with many visitors. At least 20 world records have been set here, and fishermen often land blue marlin, sailfish, kingfish, wahoo and yellowfin tuna. The following captains welcome guests aboard their boats for full- and half-day charters.

Expect to pay Rates are around $100 per hour. Bait and tackle usually are included, and snacks may be offered, but don't expect a catered buffet lunch. On occasion, the captain will cook the catch for a chartered party.

Fish with Carl and you'll definitely hook some big ones. Captain Carl Holley takes you out to the deep end of the ocean in his 36-foot Hatteras, called *The Mocko Jumbie*. Check the website for photos of record catches and awesome good times. ☎ 340-277-4042; www.fishwithcarl.com.

Fantasy Sportfishing, booked through Caribbean Sea Adventuress in Christiansted, offers four- , six- and eight-hour excursions on a fully outfitted 38-foot Bertram Special Edition. View photos and make reservations online, or call when you get to the island. ☎ 340-773-2628; www.caribbeanseaadventures.com.

Stress Buster Fishing Charters is run by the laid-back but experienced and licensed Brailey family. They aim for a good time and big catches on their 28-foot seriously-rigged super-powered fishing boat. ☎ 340-713-5317 or 863-698-2701 (cell); www.stressbusterfishing charters.com.

MARINA UPDATES

Contact the following marinas for updated information about charter operators and private boats for rent: **St. Croix Marina** at Gallows Bay, ☎ 340-773-0421; **Salt River Marina**, ☎ 340-778-9650; **Green Cay Marina**, ☎ 340-773-1453.

ST CROIX

Kayaking ☆

Caribbean Adventure Tours ☆ leads three-hour kayak expeditions through the historic Salt River National Park and Ecological Preserve and along the north shore. This is an ideal way to explore the hidden inlets and scout for wildlife among the mangroves. The $45 trip includes time to hike and swim on a secluded beach and paddle to the spot where Columbus came ashore in 1493. ☎ 800-532-3483, 340-778-1522; www.stcroixkayak.com.

Other Watersports

St. Croix Watersports, across the harbor from Christiansted on Protestant Cay, rents all types of watersports equipment, including Waverunners, Sea-Doos, windsurfing boards and snorkeling gear. They offer parasailing through **Paradise Parasailing**. If you want to explore without getting wet, ask about a stay-dry underwater tour in the semi-submersible Oceanique. Make reservations with one phone call at ☎ 340-773-7060; www.stcroixwatersports.com.

© Jim Selmor

Kitesurfer.

ST CROIX

Kite St. Croix is a certified kite board rental shop and school with the latest equipment. You can sign up to learn or participate in this hot new sport under the Caribbean's best condi-

Opposite: Kayaks on beach © Stacey Lynn Brown/iStockPhoto

tions on either calm or rolling seas. Contact Bill Kraft or Isabelle Picard to reserve equipment or arrange for lessons. ☎ 340-773-9890; www.kitestcroix.com.

◆ Adventures on Foot

Hiking

Some parts of St. Croix simply must be seen on foot. You can't fully enjoy the beauty of the rain forest, Salt River Bay National Historic Park or the bays below Point Udall unless you walk the rugged paths that lead to the most remote and stunning sites.

Olasee Davis is a native of St. Thomas, author of two ecology books and a specialist in the natural resources department at the University of the Virgin Islands. He is one of St. Croix's best-kept secrets. He leads group hikes through the rain forest and to off-the-tourist-track destinations in the hills and along the coast. Contact him at ☎ 340-643-3179.

GROUP & PRIVATE GUIDED HIKES

Group and private guided hikes of various difficulty can be arranged with herbalist and naturalist Ras Lumumba at **Ay-Ay Eco Hike and Tours**, ☎ 340-772-4079, or with club members through the **St. Croix Hiking Association**, ☎ 340-692-9984.

RAIN FOREST TREKS

If you want to strike out on your own, try the dirt roads and paths off **Route 76** that lead through the **Caledonia rain forest** in the island's northwest. No organization or governmental department maintains marked trails here, but several routes are suggested below, and it's easy to find your own interesting off-road paths on this mostly-rural island. Be sure to ask permission if you want to trek across private property.

St. Croix's **rain forest** is actually a tropical woodland because it gets too little precipitation to be the genuine thing. However, it's close enough to be an excellent place for hiking. You can drive this route in a four-wheel-drive vehicle, but you'll enjoy it more if you explore on foot.

Take Route 63 north from Frederiksted along the west coast to Creque (say *creeky*) Dam Road (Route 58), a narrow recently paved lane that runs east from Sprat Hall Estate. Park and continue on Creque Dam Road until you reach the 150-foot dam, a distance of about a mile. You can turn around here and return to your car, or continue through the forest of terpentine and mahogany trees to open fields that allow you good views. Eventually, Creque Dam Road intersects Route 763, which is sometimes called the Western Scenic Road. This is another ideal turnaround point, and you will have about a three-mile hike back to your car. If you continue south on 763, you'll reach Mahogany Road (Route 76) near St. Croix Leap woodworking shop (see page 247).

Route 78, known as **Scenic Road**, meanders through the forest north of Creque Dam Road. Park your car at the end of Route 63 where concrete pillars mark the beginning of Scenic Road. Walk along the dirt road as it ascends gently into the forest. After about a mile, you'll come to a panoramic view of the countryside below. In another 1½ miles you'll come to a gate across a path to your left that leads down a steep hill to the ruins of a sugar mill. Additional trails from the mill lead down to isolated beaches on **Annaly Bay**.

Two picturesque hikes begin at the intersection of Scenic Route 78 and Route 69, which is known as **The Beast** because bikers must tackle this monster hill during the annual Beast of the Americas Paradise Triathlon. Notice the enormous cartoon-like paw prints painted at the bottom of the steep grade near the junction of Route 80 as a year-long memento of the triathlon.

Contestant of St. Croix's triathlon climbing The Beast.

© Rich Cruse/St Croix Triathlon

ST CROIX

The first hike goes west on Route 78 from Route 69 and passes below Carambola Golf Course with excellent views to the south. The second hike heads east on Route 78 from Route 69 and goes up and down hills past lush foliage. You'll have occasional views across the countryside as you walk toward Mount Eagle, the island's highest point at 1,165 feet, and Blue Mountain, which is 1,096 feet high. Turn around after 1½ miles, just as you reach the paved road that leads to private homes.

Salt River is historically significant because it is the only documented landing of a Columbus expedition on territory now owned by the United States. Ecologically, the area is important because of its mangrove thicket which provides a habitat for baby fish as well as endangered and migrating birds. You can explore the park and preserve by parking in the paved lot on the west side of the bay on Route 801 off Route 80. Walk north along the beach to the tidal pools.

Overview of Salt River Bay.

Another possibility is to leave your car at the end of Route 751 off Route 75 in the neighborhood called **Judith Fancy**. Look for a trail leading up to an old dirt road that goes to the east side of the bay. This area is known as Cabo de las Flechas, or Cape of the Arrows, because of the conflict between Columbus' men and Carib Indians when the Europeans came ashore looking for water in 1493. The multicolored rocks along this section of coast are called Easter Rocks. The mangroves are best explored by kayak, but you can get muddy exploring in drier sections on foot.

Tennis

St. Croix has three lighted public tennis courts at **DC Canegata Ballpark** on East End Road (Route 75) at the intersection of Spring Gut Road (Route 85) on the east side of Christiansted. Call ☎ 340-773-3850. One public court is located near **Fort Frederik** in Frederiksted (call the Frederiksted Tourist Bureau for information, ☎ 340-772-0357).

Several resorts provide complimentary use of courts to guests and allow non-guests to play for a fee. The **Buccaneer Hotel** charges guests $16 per hour for daytime play. Advance reservations are required. ☎ 340-773-2100, extension 736.

Chenay Bay Beach Resort has two courts and charges $5 per person per hour for play by those not registered at the hotel, ☎ 340-773-2918. **Tamarind Reef Hotel** features two lighted Cal Grass courts. Non-guests may play for $8 per person per hour by reserving at ☎ 340-773-4455.

Golf

St. Croix offers spectacular golf. Concierges on other islands often arrange for golfer-guests to fly here for the day to enjoy the excellent courses and striking views.

The Buccaneer has a sprawling 18-hole course with lovely ocean views. Play is near the water in several spots and the fairways roll over gentle hills. The course is on the grounds of the Buccaneer Hotel off Route 82 at Gallows Bay. Non-guests should call for rates and availability. ☎ 340-712-2144; www.thebuccaneer.com/golf.htm.

The Buccaneer's course offers sea views.

Carambola Golf Course was designed by Robert Trent Jones, Sr., who considered it one of his top achievements. Many believe it to be the most beautiful course in the world.

It's made up of 18 well-groomed holes laid out in a garden-like setting with hilltop vistas. Golf pro Greg McCulloch oversees the par three course. The course is on Route 69, above Carambola Beach Resort. Consider stopping by the restaurant for lunch and views, even if you're not playing golf. Call in advance for a tee time. ☎ 340-778-5638; www.golfcarambola.com.

The Reef has a 3,100-yard nine-hole executive course and driving range. Many say this course is a real challenge and a lot of fun. The course is across from Tague Bay on Route 82 at the east end of the island. ☎ 340-773-8844.

> **TIP:** *Greens fees vary with season and time of day.*

◆ Adventures on Horseback

Seeing the rain forest or coastline from atop a horse will give you a whole different view of St. Croix. Two outfitters give guided rides, and if you enjoy horseback riding, you should book a trip with both.

© Paul and Jill's

Paul and Jill's Equestrian Stables will arrange a ride through the rain forest near Frederiksted. The stable is owned by Paul Wojciechowski and Jill Hurd, who know where to find plantation ruins and panoramic overlooks concealed in the forest. Bring your camera. Jill and Paul have a large number of horses trained to carry beginners as well as experienced riders, and novices will be taught basic skills during the ride. Find the stables near Sprat Hall on Creque Dam Road (Route 58) off Route 63 north of Frederiksted. Two-hour rides cost about $75 and reservations should be

made a day in advance by calling ☎ 340-772-2880; www.
paulandjills.com.

Equus Rides offers sunset and night rides on horseback.
Their mountain-and-sea tours leave from Off the Wall Restaurant near Cane Bay on North Shore Road. You don't have
to know how to ride to enjoy the trip. Call for exact times and
reservations. ☎ 340-778-0933.

◆ Adventures on Wheels

St. Croix is an excellent island to explore by bike. You don't
have to be an experienced rider to give it a try; many roads
have light traffic and beaches offer wide-open space for
cruising. Hardy riders may want to tackle the rugged, hilly
tracks in the rain forest. (See *Hiking* for trail suggestions.)

Mountain Biking

Endurance Sports rents three types of Trek bikes for $40
per day and $25 per half-day. If you're a serious biker, they
have super rugged bikes that can be rented by special ar-
rangement. Let them know when you're arriving and where
you're staying so they can have a bike reserved and ready for
you. The shop is located at the GNC store in the Sunny Isle
Shopping Center near Christiansted. ☎ 340-719-1990;
www.endurancesportsvi.com.

◆ Adventures in the Air

Simply getting to St. Croix is quite an adventure if you arrive
by seaplane. **Seaborne Seaplane Adventures** comes in
low over the water and touches down in Christiansted Harbor
right next to the yachts and people strolling along the boardwalk. Call the office for seasonal schedules, rates and reservations. ☎ 888-359-8687, 340-773-6442; www.seaborne
airlines.com.

ST CROIX

◆ Shopping

Duty-free shopping in St. Croix is not on the same big scale as St. Thomas, and Christiansted's selection and variety aren't nearly as great as Charlotte Amalie's. In order to compete, shop owners have turned to artists for their creative talent, offering one-of-a-kind items. While most of the best shops are found in Christiansted, a few are in Frederiksted, and fewer still are located in museums, hotels or shopping centers scattered around the island.

SHOPPING HOURS

Unless noted otherwise, stores are open 10 am-5 pm, Monday-Saturday. Shops may stay open later during high season or when a cruise ship is in port, and may close entirely during the off season.

Christiansted

The main shopping area in Christiansted is made up of charming narrow passageways running parallel between

King's Alley.

Boardwalk, on the waterfront, and Strand Street. The entire flower-filled, vine-covered area can be scouted on foot in a couple of hours. Serious shoppers will want to linger longer. Look for **Pan Am Pavillion**, **Caravelle Arcade** and **King's Alley**. Other worthwhile stores can be found past Strand Street on King, Company and Queen Streets.

DECODING THE STARS

This guidebook trims the list of shops on St. Croix to a manageable roster of those with special features, outstanding service or superior products. All are recommended, but those with one star deserve particular notice, and two-star award means "you just gotta browse there."

Chic boutiques are tucked into quaint old Danish buildings made of cut coral or old-world bricks held together with molasses mortar. Some of the most expensive high-quality items may be hidden in hole-in-the-wall boutiques. Many businesses are owned and operated by the talented craftsmen or artists that create all the merchandise, and you may be able to watch them at work.

THE BEAUTY OF NO DUTY

Remember, you can bring back $1,200 of goods per person duty-free from the tax-free US Virgin Islands. All goods made on the islands are exempt from duty and don't count toward the $1,200 allowance. Adults over 21 years of age can bring back five bottles of liquor and a sixth, if one is locally produced in the US Virgin Islands.

Jewelry is a big seller throughout the Caribbean, and three excellent Christiansted stores stand out from the others. At **Crucian Gold**, islander Brian Bishop crafts distinctive pieces, including popular knot-button-latch bracelets, Crucian Mill pendants and Conch Pearl creations. He's self-taught and you can watch him work at his shop on Boardwalk at King's Wharf. ☎ 877-773-5241 or 340-773-5241; www.cruciangold.com.

Waterfront Larimar brings the exclusive blue larimar gemstone from its source on a remote Caribbean mountaintop to Christiansted, where it is set in locally crafted sterling silver and 14K gold pieces. Stop by the store at Boardwalk and King's Alley to see this rare stone. ☎ 340-692-9180.

Sonya's ☆ is world-famous, and you'll probably hear the name mentioned in any conversation about jewelry or shopping on St. Croix. Sonya Hough has been making exquisite

ST CROIX

jewelry for 30 years and she originated the popular "Crucian hook" bracelet. According to local tradition, if the C-shaped clasp is worn with the opening facing toward your heart, you're in a committed relationship. If the C faces away from your heart, you're available. Stop by to see Sonya's elegant new signature bracelet. The shop is on the southwest corner of Company and Church Streets. ☎ 340-773-8924; www.sonyaltd.com.

The best place to shop for perfume and cosmetics is at the well-stocked **Violette Boutique**. Pick up cosmetics by makers such as Borghese, Lancôme and Clarins, or fragrances from Lalique, Givenchy and Estée Lauder. In addition, you can browse through a fine selection of Mont Blanc pens, Fendi handbags and Gucci watches. Violette is located in the Caravelle Arcade at 38 Strand Street. ☎ 340-773-2148.

Art and craft items from St. Croix and around the Caribbean can be found at **Folk Art Trader** ☆. Patty and Charles Eitzen travel throughout the region to find baskets, masks, pottery, jewelry and original paintings for their unique shop. Everything is high quality and captivating at this emporium on the east corner of Strand and Queen Cross Streets. ☎ 340-773-1900.

The Royal Poinciana is a unique gift shop. You'll think you've entered an old-time drug-and-department store when you see the assortment of Caribbean teas, herbs, spices, soaps, lotions, candles and decorative household items. Don't be overwhelmed. Simply browse for a few minutes, and don't be surprised if you find something you really must have. If you buy something cumbersome, the store will pack and ship it home for you. Look for this enchanting store at 1111 Strand Street. ☎ 340-773-9892.

Purple Papaya is a relative newcomer to the gift-shop scene, so they try hard to be almost everything to almost everyone. If you're stuck for a gift or souvenir idea, consider a T-shirt or embroidered dress. Located in the Pan Am Pavillion at Strand and Queen Cross Streets. ☎ 340-713-9412; www.shopusvi.com.

Several stores in Christiansted specialize in clothing. **Pacific Cotton**, 36 Strand, has been voted "Best Ladies Clothing on St. Croix" by locals. ☎ 340-773-2125. **From the Gecko**, 1233 Queen Cross Street, offers an eclectic mix of colorful clothes and accessories for men, women and kids, ☎ 340-778-9433. At 1111 Strand Street, **Coconut Vine**, offers clothes with Indonesian designs that are perfect for a tropical vacation.

Around the Island

St. Croix Leap is a hands-on trade school and workshop for those who make fine products from island woods. The St. Croix Life and Environmental Arts Project sponsors the effort, which stresses conservation and self-development. You can order custom-made pieces or select from finished projects such as tables, trays, vases, clocks and frames. The open-air shop is located in the rain forest two miles east of Frederiksted on Route 76 (Mahogany Road) and is open daily from 8 am until 5 pm. ☎ 340-772-0421.

Whim Museum Gift Shop features stunning mahogany furniture reproduced from originals by Baker Furniture. In addition, you can pick up cards, jewelry, maps and books. (An associate gift shop may have opened in downtown Christiansted by the time you read this book. Ask when you visit or call the Plantation gift shop.) Visit the store at the Whim Plantation on Route 70 (Centerline Road) two miles east of Frederiksted. ☎ 340-772-5668.

ST CROIX

◆ Where to Stay

One of St. Croix's many distinctive charms is the selection of excellent small hotels in addition to several splendid resorts. Former plantations, waterfront inns, secluded condos and private homes round out the list of overnight accommodations. If you stay in Christiansted, you'll be near shops, restaurants, daytime activities and after-dark entertainment. Frederiksted properties are quieter and the rain forest is nearby.

Rental Agencies

If you're interested in renting a condo, villa or house, contact one of the following management companies:

- ❖ **Rent-A-Villa**, 26157 Gallows Bay, St. Croix, USVI 00824. ☎ 800-533-6863 or 340-786-87841; www.st-croixrentavilla.com

- ❖ **St. Croix Island Villas**, 340 Strand Street, Frederiksted, St. Croix, USVI 00840. ☎ 800-626-4512 or 340-772-0420; fax 340-772-2958; www.stcroixislandvillas.com.

- ❖ **enjoystcroix.com,** ☎ 800-496-7379 or 340-778-8782; fax 773-2150; www.enjoystcroix.com.

The accommodations listed below are considered among the best on the island judged by location, price and facilities. All hotels have air-conditioned bedrooms, cable TV, telephones and pools.

Use the prices given as a guide to the average high-season rate per standard double room. If the review is for an all-inclusive or all-suites resort, the listed price is the lowest available during high-season for two people sharing a room. During low-season, generally from April 15 through December 14, rates drop 25-50%. Expect to pay an additional 8% tax, year-round.

The **St. Croix Hotel and Tourism Association** is a valuable source for all types of travel arrangements. ☎ 800-524-2026 or 340-773-7117; www.stcroixhotelandtourism.com.

SLEEPING WITH THE STARS

Our suggested list of lodging has been reduced drastically to keep this pocket guide small enough to actually fit in your pocket. You can browse the Internet as well as we can, and we encourage you to do so. Below you'll find only the best possibilities to fit a variety of budgets. Properties marked with one star (☆) are highly recommended. When a single feature or the overall allure is particularly impressive, you'll find two stars (☆☆) beside the name. Three stars (☆☆☆) means, simply, WOW!

In & Near Christiansted

Hotel Caravelle ☆, 44 Queen Cross St, Christiansted, St. Croix, USVI 00820. ☎ 800-544-0410, 340-773-0687; fax 778-7004; www.hotelcaravelle.com. 43 rooms; 1 suite. $135.

© Hotel Caravelle

Expect to be captivated by this intimate hotel with its enviable location overlooking Christiansted Harbor. Guests step directly from the busy core of the historic district into a quiet courtyard lobby dominated by a seahorse-studded fountain surrounded with tropical plants. The old-world, new-world effect is an ideal centerpiece for this modern Euro-Carib inn. Hospitality is a priority, which draws repeat guests year after year.

Protestant Cay's excellent beach and watersports center are just across the harbor, and transportation is by ferry, which leaves every 10 minutes from the nearby dock. Caravelle Arcade adjoins the hotel and other stores, restaurants and attractions are within easy walking distance.

Hotel on the Cay, Protestant Cay, PO Box 4020, St. Croix, USVI 00822. ☎ 800-524-2035 or 340-773-2035; fax 773-7046; www.hotelonthecay.com. 55 rooms and suites. $120.

The tiny islet just across from the wharf in Christiansted Harbor is Protestant Cay, home to this aging hotel with impressive views and an outstanding watersports center. A complimentary ferry zips guests back and forth across the narrow strip of water that separates the cay from town. (Guests of other hotels

© Hotel On the Cay

may take the ferry to the cay for $4, round trip.) The main draw here is the wide sandy beach with its large assortment of water toys. In addition, there's a freshwater swimming pool, beach bar and steakhouse restaurant.

King Christian Hotel, 59 King Street, Christiansted, St. Croix, USVI 00820. ☎ 800-534-2012 or 340-773-6330; www.kingchristian.com. 39 rooms. $100.

© King Christian Hotel

This recently refurbished hotel is located in a three-story building that was once a harborside warehouse. It features both superior and budget rooms, with the difference being view and size. You can save a few dollars if you simply want a clean, comfortable room. It costs a bit more for larger accommodations with two double beds and a balcony overlooking Christiansted Harbor. The nearest beach is on Protestant Cay, a $4 ferry ride across the harbor.

King's Alley Hotel ☆, 57 King Street, Christiansted, St. Croix, USVI 00820. ☎ 800-843-3574 or 340-773-0103; fax 773-4431. 35 rooms. $150.

Ask for one of the new deluxe rooms featuring four-poster beds at this hotel adjoining King's Alley shopping complex on the historic waterfront. All rooms are cooled by both air conditioning and ceiling fans, and second-story rooms have wide French doors that open onto spacious balconies. Guests take the Protestant Cay ferry to the beach.

Pink Fancy Hotel ☆, 27 Prince Street, Christiansted, St. Croix, USVI 00820. ☎ 800-524-2045 or 340-773-8460; fax 340-773-6448; www.pinkfancy.com. 12 rooms. $95.

This popular small hotel has quite a history. The oldest part was built in 1780 as a townhouse for a Danish family and is listed on the National Register of Historic Places. In the

1950s, after it was re-modeled as an inn, writers, actors and artists discovered its charm and moved in for weeks at a time. Today, the owners have restored the entire complex, which now includes 12 guest rooms overlooking flowering gardens, a water fountain and small swimming pool.

© Pink Fancy Hotel

East End

The Buccaneer ☆☆☆☆, Estate Shoys on Gallows Bay (Route 82), PO Box 25200, St. Croix, USVI 00824. ☎ 800-255-3881 or 340-773-2100; www.thebuccaneer.com; 138 rooms and suites. $300.

© The Buccaneer

ST CROIX

This sprawling 300-acre resort on the beach at Gallows Bay has a gripping history that began in 1653 when a Knight of Malta built the manor that now stands beside one of the hotel's swimming pools. The resort has grown to 134 rooms and suites, all set on a beautifully landscaped compound that includes an 18-hole golf course, eight championship-quality tennis courts, three beaches, two swimming pools, a jogging trail, a health spa and fitness facility, a watersports center, beach bars and two full-service restaurants.

© The Buccaneer

Rooms fall into eight categories and are located in the grand main building or one of the attractive low-rise buildings built on the hillside or waterfront. Basic rooms are small, but comfortably furnished. The newest rooms are on the beach and outfitted with four-poster beds and whirlpool tubs. All accommodations have ceiling fans, refrigerator, private safe, data ports and a balcony or patio. A complimentary full breakfast is served each morning.

Villa Madeleine ☆☆, Tague Bay on Route 82, PO Box 3109, St. Croix, USVI 00824. ☎ 800-496-7379 or 340-778-8782; fax 773-2150; www.teaguebayproperties.com. 22 villas. $275 (villa).

The centerpiece of this condominium resort is a hilltop West Indian plantation house with elegant furniture and luxurious decorations that serves as a common area and restaurant. Villas are scattered on the landscaped hillside below. Each unit has its own 11-by-20-foot plunge pool and a full kitchen. The one- and two-bedroom condos are comfortably furnished; bathrooms have oversized pink-marble showers and thick towels. Most of the villas are privately owned and rented by a management company when the owners are off-island. The nearest beach is about a third of a mile away.

Divi Carina Bay Resort, 25 Estate Turner Hole/South Shore Road (Route 60), St. Croix, USVI 00820. ☎ 877-773-9700 or 340-773-9700; www.divicarina.com. 126 rooms, suites and villas. $200.

Rooms at this sprawling resort are decorated in shades of blue to match the sea, which is just steps away. All have a furnished patio or balcony, a wet bar  with a mini refrigerator, microwave and coffee maker. Bathrooms are outfitted with thick towels, bathrobes, hair dryer and deluxe grooming products. Oceanview villas have a separate living area and a fully equipped kitchen.

© Divi Carina

Many guests never leave the resort, which features a watersports center on the 1,000-foot white-sand beach, two freshwater swimming pools, lighted Hard-Tru tennis courts, a 10,000-square-foot casino, three restaurants and a health spa. The activities desk will arrange sightseeing tours, fishing excursions, dive trips and day sails to Buck Island.

Tamarind Reef Hotel ☆, 5001 Tamarind Reef on Route 82, St. Croix, USVI 00820-4230. ☎ 800-619-0014 or 340-773-4455; www.tamarindreefhotel.com. 46 rooms. $180.

If you love settling into a casual well-run hotel with lots of amenities and personal attention, Tamarind Reef will suit you perfectly. This modern resort adjoining Green Cay Marina has several types of accommodations, all featuring custom-made bedspreads and window treatments fashioned from original-design tropical print fabrics signed by the artist.

Ground-floor rooms have landscaped patios while upper rooms open onto private balconies overlooking the sea. Deluxe rooms with a queen-size bed and sleeper-sofa feature

ST CROIX

well-equipped kitchenettes, and the larger junior suites have two queen-size beds.

Guests can use four lighted tennis courts and watersports equipment from the well-stocked beach shack. Snorkeling is good along the reef that begins near shore, and there's also kayaking out to nearby Green Cay. Boats leave from the adjacent marina for fishing and diving trips or day sails to Buck Island.

Deep End Bar, beside the large freshwater swimming pool that overlooks the sea, serves fat burgers, delicious sandwiches, light salads and icy drinks. For more elegant dining, make reservations at The Galleon, a waterfront restaurant overlooking the marina that specializes in gourmet French and Italian cuisine (see the review under *Where to Eat*).

North Shore

Carambola Beach Resort ☆☆☆, Davis Bay on Route 80, PO Box 3031, Kingsmill, St. Croix, USVI 00851. ☎ 340-778-3800; fax 340-778-1682; www.carambolabeach.com. 150 suites. $200.

© Carambola Beach Resort

A description of Carambola sounds like paradise in *America's Paradise*. Laurance Rockefeller built the villas. Robert

Trent Jones designed the golf course. One of the world's best beach-access dive sites is directly offshore.

This casually elegant resort, covering 2,000 rolling waterfront acres between Christiansted and Frederiksted on the sparsely developed north shore, presents St. Croix at its best. Suites occupy 24 two-story villas that spill down 28 acres of green hillsides to Davis Bay. The award-winning 18-hole golf course spreads across a lake-studded valley behind the villa compound.

Guest accommodations are in 500-square-foot units with separate living and sleeping areas that are furnished with Danish-antique reproductions. Each opens onto a private balcony or patio and features a spacious bathroom with oversized shower. A complimentary breakfast buffet is served every morning in one of the three restaurants.

Paths lead from the villas across lush landscaped grounds to a large freshwater swimming pool and two outdoor Jacuzzi tubs. Complimentary watersports equipment is available from the beach shack and the on-site scuba center organizes guided beach and boat dives. Other amenities include a fitness center, four lighted tennis courts and a well-stocked gift shop.

Hibiscus Beach Resort ☆, 4131 La Grande Princesse, St. Croix, USVI 00820. ☎ 800-442-0121 or 340-773-4042; fax 340-773-7668; www.hibiscusbeachresort.com. 38 rooms. $210.

© Hibiscus Beach Resort

The alluring Hibiscus Beach Hotel sits on a lovely stretch of palm-shaded beach at Pelican Cove, just 10 minutes west of Christiansted. Comfortable rooms are tucked into five two-story structures that face the sea and are named for tropical flowers. All accommodations have a pri-

ST CROIX

vate ocean-view patio or balcony and a mini-bar. The Star Bar and H2O Restaurant serve meals.

The Waves at Cane Bay, North Shore Road, Cane Bay, PO Box 1749, St. Croix, USVI 00851. ☎ 800-545-0603 or 340-778-1805; fax 778-4945; www.thewavesatcanebay.com. 12 rooms. $140.

© Waves at Cane Bay

Divers won't find a better location than The Waves. It's built right into the rocks, directly on the water at Cane Bay, with easy beach access to the magnificent coral gardens that form the Cane Bay Wall. Romantics, beach bums and those who want to get away from it all will enjoy this intimate hotel, too.

Each studio unit is outfitted with cooking facilities, a king-size bed, ceiling fans, cable TV and a large screened balcony that overlooks the sea. Some accommodations also have air conditioning, so make a request if that is important to you.

Sugar Beach, 3245 Estate Golden Rock, Route 752, St. Croix, USVI 00820. ☎ 800-524-2049 or 340-773-5345; fax 340-773-1359; www.sugarbeachstcroix.com. 46 villas. $180.

You'll be just a short drive from Christiansted at this beach complex on the north shore. All accommodations are air-conditioned villas with every convenience, including kitchens, patios/balconies and from one to four bedrooms. The remains of an 18th-century sugar mill are incorporated into the lovely swimming pool area, and villas are only a few feet from Sandy Beach.

West End

The Frederiksted Hotel, 442 Strand Street, Frederiksted, St. Croix, USVI 00840. ☎ 800-595-9519 or 340-772-0500; www.frederikstedhotel.com. 40 rooms. $100.

The outside could use an update, but rooms at this four-story waterfront hotel in the heart of Frederiksted are comfortable, clean and budget-priced. Each is air conditioned and outfitted with a TV, microwave and refrigerator. There's a swimming pool and sundeck, the restaurant serves well-priced meals all day, and the courtyard bar often features local entertainers. Location is a big plus here. You're near the tropical forest and some of the best beaches along the north and west coasts.

Cottages by the Sea, 127A Estate Smithfield, Frederiksted, St. Croix, USVI 00840. ☎ 800-323-7252 or 340-772-0495; fax 340-772-1753; www.caribbeancottages. com. 20 cottages. $125.

© Cottages by the Sea

These basic waterfront cottages are scattered on three acres just outside Frederiksted. Each unit has a kitchenette and oversized group patios encourage guests to get together while grilling dinner or watching the sun set during happy hour. The atmosphere is casual, the accommodations are comfortably rustic, and you can't beat the price.

© Sandcastle on the Beach

Sandcastle on the Beach, 127 Smithfield, Route 71, Frederiksted, USVI 00840. ☎ 800-524-2018 or 340-772-1205; fax 340-772-1757; www.sandcastleonthebeach. com. 21 rooms/suites/villas. $130.

This diverse-lifestyle resort is right on the water and many rooms have a view of the sea. Children are not wel-

ST CROIX

come, and most guests are gay couples. Larger villas have full kitchens, smaller rooms and suites have kitchenettes, and every guest is treated to a continental breakfast each morning. On-site amenities include tennis courts, two pools, a restaurant, gym, watersports center and laundry facilities.

◆ Where to Eat

International cuisine and West Indian specialties fill the menus of restaurants scattered across St. Croix. You can feast on familiar dishes or try something new and exotic. The following recommendations are a mix of restaurants in all price ranges. Use the prices given as a guide to the average price of a mid-range meal per person, excluding drinks and tip. There is no sales tax in the Virgin Islands, but restaurants may add a service charge, so check your bill before you figure your tip. Many eateries are in or near Christiansted, but you'll find excellent choices throughout the island.

DINING WITH THE STARS

Some restaurant reviews are marked with stars. One star (☆) indicates that the restaurant is highly recommended, two stars (☆☆) mean you should make an extra effort to eat there, and three stars (☆☆☆) promise an experience to remember. The rating may be for super value or an amazing view or, perhaps, simply the best "cheeseburgers in paradise."

See *Dining*, page 33, for a list of common West Indian food specialties.

> **TIP:** *Restaurants often change their hours or close for extended periods during low season, so call to check.*

In & Near Christiansted

Tutto Bene ☆, Boardwalk Building, Hospital Street, Gallow's Bay, ☎ 340-773-5229; www.tuttobenerestaurant. com. Italian. $20. Nightly 6 pm-10 pm. Credit cards accepted. Reservations suggested.

Everyone's raving about this hot spot. The name means "everything good," and you won't go wrong with any selection. The veal *saltimbocca* is excellent. It's a not-so-basic veal scallopine with proscuitto, fresh sage and assorted cheeses. Other familiar Italian dishes are offered, including osso bucco, or you might try the fresh fish. Just save room for one of the homemade desserts.

Bacchus ☆☆☆, Queen Cross Street, ☎ 340-692-9922; www.restaurantbacchus.com. Continental. $25. Tuesday-Sunday, 6 pm-10 pm. Credit cards accepted. Reservations recommended.

Named for the mythological god of wine, this classy restaurant features the largest wine selection on the island and has received *Wine Spectator* magazine's "Award of Excellence" many times. Superb vintages are offered by the glass, so this is your chance to sample something new. The kitchen turns out superb steaks, lobster and fresh fish. After the wonderfully rich meal, indulge in a cup of French-press coffee.

RumRunners Steaks & Seafood, Queen Cross Street/harborfront, ☎ 340-773-6585; www.rumrunnersstcroix.com. International/American. Breakfast $9, lunch $12, brunch $15, dinner $20. Daily, 7 am-10 pm; Sunday brunch served 10 am-2 pm; Happy Hour daily 4-6 pm. Credit cards accepted. Reservations suggested for brunch and dinner.

From the name, you might expect a trendy bar. And, you'd be right. But, RumRunner is also a popular restaurant with fantastic views of Christiansted Harbor and a crowd-pleasing menu. On Sundays, a steel band plays during brunch, which features Bloody Marys to complement a menu of peel-'n-eat shrimp, eggs Benedict, lobster salad and other popular dishes.

ST CROIX

Monday through Saturday the restaurant offers a varied breakfast and lunch selection, and dinner each evening focuses on prime rib, Caribbean lobster, ribs and steaks.

Elizabeth's at the Palms ☆☆, 4126 La Grande Princess, ☎ 340-719-0735; www.elizabethsatthepalms.com. Continental. Breakfast $10, brunch $12, lunch $12, dinner $22. Monday-Friday, 12 pm-3pm, Monday-Saturday, 5:30 pm-9:30 pm. Credit cards accepted. Reservations recommended for dinner.

New and charming, Elizabeth's is run by husband-and-wife team Jason and Elizabeth Gould. Jason cooks. Elizabeth provides the charm. In just a short time, Jason has earned an

enviable reputation for serving outstanding cuisine. His superb crab cakes have been named "Best on the Island." Although he's known for working magic with all types of seafood, meat lovers praise his steaks and rack of lamb. Elizabeth greets everyone at the door, as if they were invited guests, and offers seating in the lovely dining room that glows with candlelight after dark.

Avocado Pitt, 59 Kings Wharf, King Christian Hotel, ☎ 340-773-9843. Casual/light meals. Lunch/snack $5-10. Daily, 6:30 am-5:30 pm. No credit cards.

If you're going on a picnic or heading for Buck Island, pick up lunch at this popular café next to the pier. Breakfast offerings include pancakes, omelettes and French toast. For lunch, eat in or take out, build your own sandwich or try the chicken breast sandwich doused with hot sauce. Top off with a milkshake.

Fort Christian Brew Pub, 55 A&B Kings Alley, ☎ 340-713-9820; www.fortchristianbrewpub.com. Contemporary

Caribbean. Pub (downstairs) $10, restaurant (upstairs) $25. Monday-Saturday 11 am-11 pm; Sunday 11 am-9 pm. Credit cards accepted.

Nothing more than beer is expected from a brew pub, but this one serves up an impressive list of sandwiches, soups and salads at lunch. Prices are in the moderate range. After  five, you can choose something from the dinner menu, with meals in the $25 range. But, you'll come for the micro-brewed beer, and it is well worth your time. Try a sampling of freshly made brews before you settle on a favorite. Most nights, you'll have some type of entertainment to enjoy along with the food and drinks.

© Fort Christian Brew Pub

Kendrick's ☆☆☆, 51 Company Street at King Cross, ☎ 340-773-9199. Continental. Dinner $28. Monday-Saturday 6 pm-9:30 pm. Credit cards accepted. Reservations recommended.

David Kendrick is the popular and creative chef at this open-air restaurant. Reserve a table in the courtyard and enjoy some of the best cuisine in the Caribbean. House specialties range from roast pork encrusted with nuts, fresh grilled fish and pasta dishes. Pair them with a great wine, sold by the glass or bottle.

East End

Morning Glory Coffee & Tea, Gallows Bay, ☎ 340-773-6620. Coffee, tea, pastries, sandwiches. Breakfast/lunch/snacks $4-8. Monday-Friday, 7 am-6 pm; Saturday, 7 am-3 pm. No credit cards.

Freshly roasted and ground superior coffee is the highlight here. You can add a *beignet* or home-made muffin, but you

ST CROIX

can't walk past this delicious smelling spot without succumbing to a hot cuppa java. At lunchtime, the menu includes salads, sandwiches and wraps. Late afternoon is the perfect time to enjoy a cappuccino, latte or espresso. All types of tea also are available, and you can sit at a table inside or out.

Duggan's Reef ☆☆, Tague Bay/Route 82, ☎ 340-773-9800. Caribbean/American. Lunch $12, brunch $15, dinner $25. Daily, 11:30 am-2 pm and 6-11:30 pm; Sunday brunch, 11 am-3 pm; bar opens at 4:30 pm every day except Tuesday. Credit cards accepted. Reservations required for dinner.

Right on the water at Reefs Beach, this casual open-air restaurant is a longtime favorite with locals and visitors. They close sporadically during the low season, so call if you plan to make a special trip to the East End. Brunch is an eclectic mix of egg dishes, fish, soups and salads. The most popular dish at dinner is the pasta topped with lobster. Other choices include steaks, fresh fish, pastas and just-made desserts.

The Galleon ☆, Green Cay Marina/Route 82, ☎ 340-773-9949; www.GalleonRestaurant.com. Mediterranean. Dinner $38. Daily for dinner, 6 pm-10 pm; Daily Happy Hour in the Piano Bar, 4 pm-6 pm. Credit cards accepted. Reservations recommended.

Arrive early to enjoy a glass of wine and watch the setting sun light up the sailboats in the marina. Then settle in for an excellent dinner of Caesar salad prepared tableside, followed by a French or Northern Italian entrée such as filet gorgonzola or osso buco. Fresh-baked bread and side dishes accompany each meal. Linger over your dessert or wine while the pianist entertains you with relaxing music.

The Case Place, Chandler's Wharf, Gallows Bay, ☎ 340-719-3167. Eclectic. Lunch $15, dinner $25. Monday-Saturday, 11 am-10 pm; Happy Hour daily 4 pm-6 pm. Credit cards accepted. Reservations recommended.

Locals have known about this place for a couple of years, but visitors are just catching on. Lunch is served all day, which is a good thing, if you're eating lighter these days. Happy hour runs from 4-6 pm every afternoon, and many people make dinner from the large selection of appetizers.

Other menu items include pasta, ribs, steaks and a variety of seafood, even lobster. Just to keep things interesting, you also can order a corn dog, so bring the kids.

Cheeseburgers in Paradise ☆, East End Road, Route 82, Estate Southgate, ☎ 340-773-1119. Burgers, etc. $8. Daily, 11 am-10:30 pm. Credit cards accepted.

You know what to expect at a restaurant with cheeseburger in the name. In addition to the best burgers on the island, you'll find barbecue ribs, grilled chicken sandwiches, nachos, terrific fries and ice cold ale. Look for this open-air hangout less than a mile east of Green Cay Marina.

North Shore & West End

Blue Moon, 17 Strand Street/Frederiksted, ☎ 340-772-2222. Cajun/Caribbean/vegetarian. Lunch $12, dinner $25. Tuesday-Friday, 11:30 am-2 pm; Tuesday-Sunday, 6 pm-9:30 pm; Sunday brunch, 11 am-2 pm. Credit cards accepted. Reservations suggested.

An historic landmark building on the waterfront is home to this New Orleans-style bistro. Jazz musicians play during Sunday brunch and on Friday nights, and a crowd often gathers to enjoy the cool moves and hot sounds. The décor can best be described as tacky chic and arty, which goes well with the jazz. Appetizers are the most interesting choices on the menu, but the fresh fish is dependably good and you'll also see some chicken and steak options as well as vegetarian choices.

Off The Wall, Cane Bay/Route 80, ☎ 340-778-4771; www.offthewallstcroix.com. Light meals/drinks. $8. Daily, 8 am-late. Credit cards accepted.

This casual beach shack is named for the popular dive site in Cane Bay. Friendly folks staff the bar and people come in to enjoy the drinks and simple food. It's a great

© Off the Wall

place to meet locals and other travelers. Menu selections include sandwiches, nachos, pizza and fried fish. Try one of the tropical drinks invented by Michelle, the bartender. Musicians provide entertainment several nights each week.

Changes in L'Attitude, La Grange, north of the pier, ☎ 340-772-3090. Casual/Eclectic. $10. Daily, 9 am-9 pm. No credit cards.

Beach bums and watersports enthusiasts love Changes. It's directly on the water, a short walk from the fishing pier in Frederiksted. You can use their beach chairs, lay back and enjoy a sandwich or nachos. On Friday nights, plan on showing up for the catfish fry – a great bargain at $11.50. Breakfast is served only on weekends, but the bar opens every day at 9 am.

H2O ☆☆, Hibiscus Beach Resort/Route 75, ☎ 340-773-4042. American. Breakfast $8, brunch $25, lunch/dinner $20. Daily, 7:30 am-10 pm (midnight on Friday and Saturday); Sunday brunch, 11 am-3:30 pm. Credit cards accepted. Reservations recommended for dinner and brunch.

The views of Buck Island are great from this beachside restaurant. You could eat here every day and never have the same meal twice – and many hotel guests do just that. Breakfast and lunch are fairly common fare, but uncommonly delicious. Dinner entrées are exceptional and feature such delicacies as New Zealand mussels, tuna sashimi and garlic-encrusted filet mignon. Sunday brunch is especially popular, so make reservations well in advance for the all-you-can-drink Bloody Mary event.

© Hibiscus Beach Resort

◆ Nightlife

Pick up a free copy of *St. Croix This Week* (www.stcroix thisweek.com) to check out locations for live entertainment.

Resorts, restaurants and bars regularly feature steel pan, reggae and jazz bands. In Christiansted and Frederiksted, follow the crowd and the music to the liveliest spots.

MOCKO JUMBIES

Mocko Jumbies (costumed stilt entertainers) and heritage dancers often preform at special events. If you aren't visiting during a festival, look for Caribbean-style entertainment offered at resorts and restaurants throughout the week. These colorful cultural shows perpetuate the African traditions that were brought to the islands during the plantation days.

Sunset Jazz is sponsored by the Frederiksted Economic Development Association and held on the third Friday of each month at the park adjacent to Fort Frederik. Beginning at 6 pm, a jazz band plays as the sun sets over the harbor and locals turn out to visit and enjoy the music. There's no charge. The FEDA runs a cash bar and food stands sell snacks. Bring a picnic or plan to have dinner at one of the restaurants in town after the two-hour concert. ☎ 340-277-0692.

Gaming and entertainment run all night at the **Divi Carina Bay Casino**, the only casino in the Virgin Islands. There are hundreds of slot machines, live and video poker, game tables and live music. The casino is open Monday-Friday, noon-4 am; Saturday and Sunday, noon-6 am. ☎ 340-773-7529; www.carinabay.com.

From November through May, local art galleries host **Art Thursday Gallery Walk**. Typically, a group of nine or more Christiansted art galleries stay open later than usual on the first Thursday of each month to offer special exhibitions of work by local and Caribbean artists. Pick up a list of participating galleries at any of the shops in town or call ☎ 340-773-7376 for a list of participating galleries. Strollers are treated to a glass of wine as they meander through the galleries and meet the artists.

ST CROIX

> **TIP:** *Remember that works by local artists are exempt from customs duty when you return to the US. Go ahead and splurge. That wonderful painting or sculpture will not affect your $1,200 exemption allowance.*

Don't miss the opportunity to hear a **steel pan** band or local musician. Check with the concierge at your hotel or look through the entertainment section of *St. Croix This Week* for scheduled performances. The following bars and restaurants regularly feature live entertainment, but call ahead to confirm the dates, times and current lineup of performers.

The **Buccaneer Hotel** features steel pan bands on Sunday evenings, 5 pm-8 pm. ☎ 340-712-2100.

Harbormaster Beach Club at Hotel on the Cay, Protestant Cay, hosts a Beach Barbecue and Caribbean Floor Show on Tuesday nights from 7-10 pm. Make reservations, ☎ 340-719-5438.

Carambola Beach Resort puts on a Pirates Buffet from 7 pm until 9 pm on Friday nights. Live entertainment follows. Call for information about other events. ☎ 340-778-3800.

Island House Restaurant at Chenay Bay has an all-you-can-eat West Indian Buffet on Thursdays from 6:30-9 pm. A live band provides music for dancing, and Mocko Jumbies entertain. ☎ 340-773-2918.

Fort Christian Brew Pub brews up the island's only handmade beer and features live guitar music on Mondays from 6:30-10 pm. ☎ 340-779-2262.

Club 54 on Company Street in Christiansted is a popular multi-level, indoor-outdoor nightclub. Live music plays every weekend and the big-screen TV is always tuned to the biggest sporting events. ☎ 340-773-8002; www.club54.net.

Blue Moon, 7 Strand Street, Frederiksted, hosts love jazz groups on Wednesday and Friday evenings and at their Sunday brunch. ☎ 340-779-2262.

◆ Island Facts & Numbers

AIRPORT: **Henry Rohlsen International Airport** (STX airport code), ☎ 340-778-0589.

AREA CODE: The area code for all US Virgin Islands is 340. You may dial direct from the States.

BANKS, ATMs: Most banks are open Monday-Thursday, 9 am-3 pm and Friday, 9 am-4:30 pm. There are ATMs all over, including at the airport, DIVI and Carambola resorts and Schooner Bay Market Place in Christiansted.

DRIVING: Traffic stays to the left. The speed limit is 35 mph in rural areas, 55 mph on open portions of Route 66, 20 mph in towns.

ELECTRICITY: 110 volts, 60 cycles, as on the US mainland.

EMERGENCIES: ☎ 911 for Ambulance, Fire Department and Police assistance; Virgin Island Search and Rescue, ☎ 340-773-7150; Governor Luis Hospital, ☎ 340-778-6311.

GOVERNMENT: The US Virgin Islands are an unincorporated territory with a non-voting delegate elected to the US House of Representatives. Anyone born on the islands is a US citizen.

INTERNET ACCESS: Many resorts now offer WiFi and data ports. You can check e-mail at **Strand Street Station** in Christiansted, ☎ 340-719-6245.

LAUNDROMAT: **Green Cay Marina,** ☎ 340-773-1453; **St. Croix Marina,** ☎ 340-773-6011.

LIQUOR LAWS: The legal drinking age is 21, as on the US mainland. Minors may not enter bars or purchase liquor.

MONEY: The US dollar is the legal currency throughout the US Virgin Islands. Travelers' checks and major credit cards are acceptable at most locations, but always carry some cash for smaller establishments.

ST CROIX

NEWSPAPERS, MAGAZINES: *St. Croix This Week* features up-to-date information about the island and is available free of charge at hotels and other tourist-oriented sites. *St. Croix Guide Book* is a clever publication put out free of charge by Great Dane, Inc. ☎ 340-776-6922. Pick one up at hotels, restaurants and tourist sites around the island or check out their website at www.stcroixguidebook.com.

Newspapers from some US cities are flown to St. Croix news stands daily. Look for the *Miami Herald* and *New York Times* at resort gift shops. Local news is published in *The Virgin Islands Daily News*, available at newsstands. ☎ 340-774-8772.

POST OFFICE: Post offices are found on Company Street in Christiansted, and at Gallows Bay, Kingshill, Sunny Isle and Frederiksted. Stamps are priced the same as on the US mainland.

TAXES: There is no sales tax or departure tax. An 8% surcharge is added to all hotel bills.

TELEPHONE DIRECTORY INFORMATION: ☎ 913.

TOURIST INFORMATION: In the US, information is available from **The US Virgin Islands Division of Tourism**, 1270 Avenue of the Americas, New York, NY 10020. ☎ 800-372-USVI (800-372-8784) or 212-332-2222; fax 212-332-2223; www.usvitourism.vi.

Also try the **St. Croix Hotel and Tourism Association**, ☎ 800-524-2026 or 340-773-7117; fax 773-5883; www.stcroixhotelandtourism.com.

In Canada, information is available from **The US Virgin Islands Tourism Department**, ☎ 416-233-1414.

In the UK, contact **The US Virgin Islands Tourism Department**, 2 Cinnamon Row, Plantation Wharf, York Place, London SW11 3TW. ☎ 0207-9785262.

On St. Croix, a **Tourist Information** booth is set up at the airport. In addition, a Visitor's Bureau is open in the fort, near the wharf in Christiansted, ☎ 340-773-0495, and at the Custom House Building near the pier in Frederiksted, ☎ 340-772-0357. Both are open Monday-Friday, 8 am-5 pm.

WEBSITES: www.usvi.net; www.st-croix.com; www.gotostcroix.com.

WEDDINGS: It's easy to get married in the USVI. For complete details, call the Department of Tourism for a brochure called *Getting Married in the United States Virgin Islands*, ☎ 800-372-USVI. To apply for a license, write to the Territorial Court of the Virgin Islands, Box 70, St. Thomas, USVI 00804, ☎ 340-778-9750. Wedding arrangements can be made with **Seaside Weddings**, ☎ 340-773-9607; www.seasdiewed.com.

The British Virgin Islands

ANEGADA

The Settlement

Approx. 12 miles (not to scale)

Necker Island

Prickly Pear Island

Mosquito Island

VIRGIN GORDA

Caribbean Sea

Spanish Town

Copper Mine Point

The Dogs

Scrub Island

Fallen Jerusalem

Round Rock Passage

Ginger Island

Atlantic Ocean

Great Camanoe Island

Beef Island

Cooper Island

Salt Island

Guana Island

Carrot Bay

Salt Island Passage

TORTOLA

Sir Francis Drake Channel

Dead Chest

Road Town

Peter Island

BRITISH VIRGIN ISLANDS

Little Jost Van Dyke

Green Cay

West End

Norman Island

Jost Van Dyke

Windward Passage

US VIRGIN ISLANDS

Great Harbor

Great Thatch

Great Tobago

ST. JOHN

Little Tobago

N

HUNTER PUBLISHING

10 MILES

© 2007 HUNTER PUBLISHING, INC.

The British Virgin Islands

The British Virgin Islands are often referred to as "nature's little secrets," and the 50 or so islands, islets and cays that form the archipelago have been successful in protecting themselves from mass tourism, so far. But yachtsmen discovered them years ago and escapists are captivated by them, so the "secrets" can't be safeguarded for long.

With the exception of Anegada, all the British Virgin Islands are exceedingly close to one another and to the US Virgin Islands. Collectively, they are strikingly different from their American siblings, but understandably similar to one another. Each is mountainous, covered in dense foliage, ringed by wide strands of fine white sand and surrounded by incredible reefs beneath clear turquoise waters. Still blessedly underdeveloped and natural due to strict environmental policies, they have just enough lavish creature comforts to make them enjoyable. Most of the BVIs are lined up along both sides of the 18-mile-long **Sir Francis Drake Channel**, which serves as a watery highway for ships, ferries and private yachts. **Tortola** anchors the northwestern side of Drake's Lake (the channel's nickname), and **Virgin Gorda** dominates the eastern end. **Norman, Peter, Salt, Cooper** and **Ginger** line up along the south side of the channel. **Jost Van Dyke** sits just off the western tip of Tortola's north coast, and **Anegada** is 12 miles north of Virgin Gorda. Anegada is flat and the only BVI made up of coral and limestone rather than volcanic debris. It has wonderful attributes and a host of loyal fans who enjoy its isolation, but it is surrounded by shallow coral reefs that make it hazardous for boats. This danger, and its remoteness from the other Virgins, puts it out of the island-hopping loop.

Tortola, Virgin Gorda and Jost Van Dyke are the most developed and most visited islands. They offer travelers a medley of posh resorts, comfortable inns and secluded villas as well as excellent watersports, isolated beaches, unique shops and imaginative restaurants. Cooper Island, Peter Island, Norman Island and Marina Cay are sparsely populated and have limited facilities, but they are extremely popular with day-trippers. Most of the other islands and cays are enchanting spots favored by the yachting crowd.

Tortola

◆ Overview

Tortola means *turtle dove* in Spanish, and the 21-square-mile island is the largest, most populated and liveliest of the British Virgin Islands. Don't expect highrise hotels, glitzy nightclubs and contrived tourist attractions. Nature is the star here, and visitors primarily focus on watersports and sailing.

Sedate little **Road Town**, on the rugged south coast, is the capital of Tortola, which is, in turn, the capital of the BVI. Most of the population lives in or near Road Town, but there are settlements at West End (home to popular restaurants and shops at Soper's Hole) and East End, which is connected by a bridge to Beef Island and the main airport for the BVI. The islands's highest point is 1,700-foot **Sage Mountain**, and the best beaches are along the north shore at **Cane Garden Bay**, **Smugglers Cove** and **Brewer's Bay**.

Opposite: Sailing on Sir Francis Drake Channel

◆ Getting There

By Air

Air service is increasing, but there still are no scheduled direct flights from North America, Canada or Europe to Tortola. You can make easy connections through Puerto Rico, St. Thomas or St. Croix on several small carriers. Flight time from St. Thomas is about 15 minutes and from Puerto Rico it's about 30 minutes. Since the planes fly low, you often get awesome views of the islands as you pass over them.

You'll arrive at the modern **Terrence B. Lettsome Airport** (EIS) on Beef Island, which is linked to Tortola's East End by a new two-lane bridge. The original single-lane toll bridge, named in honor of Queen Elizabeth, remains in place, but the toll booth is closed and shuttered.

> **NOTE:** *The area code for all of the British Virgin Islands is 284.*

American Eagle (☎ 800-433-7300, 284-495-1122; www.aa.com) has frequent daily flights from San Juan.

Cape Air (☎ 800-352-0714, 284-495-2100; www.flycapeair.com) provides hourly service from San Juan and St. Thomas.

LIAT (☎ 800-468-0482, 888-844-5428 or 284-495-1187; www.liatairline.com) flies from several Caribbean islands, including St. Kitts, Antigua, St. Martin, St. Thomas and Puerto Rico.

Air Sunshine (☎ 800-327-8900, 284-495-8900; www.airsunshine.com) has scheduled flights from Puerto Rico and St. Croix.

Clair Aero Services (☎ 284-495-2271) flies from Anegada to Beef Island/Tortola four days per week.

Fly BVI (☎ 284-495-1747; www.fly-bvi.com) runs a charter service between Puerto Rico and the British Virgin Islands.

Seaborne Aviation (☎ 888-359-8687; www.seaborneair lines.com) offers seaplane transportation to West End, Tortola from Charlotte Amalie, St. Thomas and sightseeing flights throughout the USVI and BVI.

Caribbean Star (☎ 800-744-7827 Caribbean, 866-864-6272 US/Can; www.flycaribbeanstar.com) also offers service.

By Ferry

Frequent ferry service connects both Charlotte Amalie and Red Hook (St. Thomas) with Road Town and West End (Tortola). Consult a map and make sure you leave from and arrive at the most convenient docks. Otherwise, you'll be stuck traveling cross-island in a taxi.

The Roadtown Fast Ferry (☎ 340-777-2800 in St. Thomas;

284-494-2323 in Tortola; www.roadtownfastferry. com) links Charlotte Amalie to Roadtown without a stop on St. John.

Native Son (☎ 888-273-3284 or 284-495-4617) provides service from Red Hook, St. Thomas to West End, Tortola, and from Charlotte Amalie, St. Thomas to both Road Town and West End, Tortola several times each day. **Smith's Ferry** (☎ 340-775-7292 in Charlotte Amalie; 340-775-2569 in Red Hook and 284-495-4495 on Tortola) runs daily service to the West End and Road Town on Tortola from Charlotte Amalie, St. Thomas, and to the West End from Red Hook. **Inter-Island Boat Services** (☎ 284-495-4166 on Tortola; 340-776-6597 on St. John) has service from Red Hook, St. Thomas to Cruz Bay, St. John and then goes on to West End, Tortola. Round-trip tickets are approximately $40.

DEPARTURE TAX

You will be charged a departure tax when you leave the BVI. The per person cost is $20 if you leave by plane and $5 if you leave by boat. In addition, expect to pay a $5 security fee when you depart by air.

Tranquil waters and safe harbors attract sailors.

◆ Getting Around

By Car

If you're confident you can handle driving an American-style car, with left-hand steering, on the left side of the road (European style), rent a jeep or car and explore the island on your own. Most of Tortola is rural with good roads, but traffic can be heavy in populated areas, the roundabouts are tricky and mountain roads have steep grades and blind curves. Stick with taxis and tour buses if you're unsure of your skills.

You must have a valid driver's license in order to purchase a mandatory BVI permit, which costs $10 and is good for three months. Car rental agencies conveniently issue these permits when you pick up your car.

Expect to pay about $50 per day or $300 per week for a compact car with automatic transmission and air conditioning. Add 5% for government tax. Four-wheel-drive vehicles are nice, but not necessary, and open jeeps are fun, but can be a security problem. Take the optional insurance if your credit card or personal auto insurance doesn't cover you.

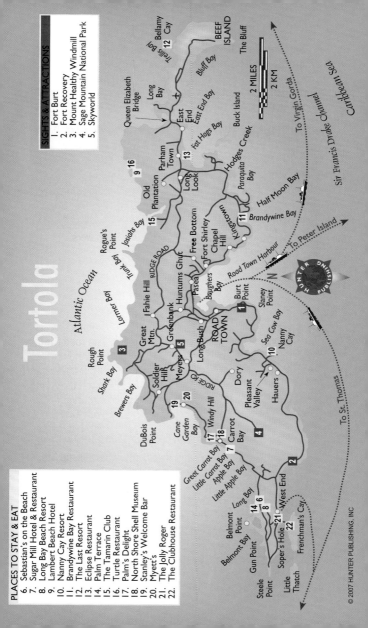

Tortola

PLACES TO STAY & EAT
6. Sebastian's on the Beach
7. Sugar Mill Hotel & Restaurant
8. Long Bay Beach Resort
9. Lambert Beach Hotel
10. Nanny Cay Resort
11. Brandywine Bay Restaurant
12. The Last Resort
13. Eclipse Restaurant
14. Palm Terrace
15. The Tamarin Club
16. Turtle Restaurant
17. Palm's Delight
18. North Shore Shell Museum
19. Stanley's Welcome Bar
20. Myett's
21. The Jolly Roger
22. The Clubhouse Restaurant

SIGHTS & ATTRACTIONS
1. Fort Burt
2. Fort Recovery
3. Mount Healthy Windmill
4. Sage Mountain National Park
5. Skyworld

© 2007 HUNTER PUBLISHING, INC

Locals are friendly and courteous, even behind the wheel. When they honk, it's usually to greet a friend or signal that you may turn in front of them. But, they also stop without warning to pick up friends, and often slow to chat with someone walking. Give yourself plenty of braking time.

RENTAL CAR AGENCIES	
D & D	☎ 284-495-7676; fax 494-8241
Denil Clyne ☆	☎ 284-495-4900; www.islandsonline.com/denzil/
Hertz	☎ 800-654-3080, 284-495-4405; fax 494-6060; www.hertzbvi.com
International ☆	☎ 284-494-2516; fax 494-4715
Itgo ☆	☎ 284-494-5150; fax 284-494-4975; www.itgobvi.com
Jerry's	☎ 284-495-4111; fex 284-495-4114
National	☎ 284-494-3197; fax 494-4085
Tola	☎ 284-494-8652; fax 494-8654

By Taxi

Taxis meet flights at the airport on Beef Island and you'll be sharing the car or van with other passengers unless you make arrangements in advance for a private pick-up. Rates are regulated, but unpublished, so you should ask the fare to your destination before you get into the taxi. Expect to pay about $15 for two in a group van from the airport to a hotel near Road Town and around $25 to a hotel on the West End.

> **TIP:** *Some hotels contract with drivers to pick up guests at the airport and add the fare to the guest's bill at checkout, so don't think the friendly driver who refuses payment at your destination is providing a free service.*

It's easy to find or summon a taxi from most points on the island, and you can arrange for drivers to drop you off and return for you if you want to spend time at a remote beach or other secluded location.

TAXI COMPANIES	
Beef Island Taxi Association	☎ 284-494-1982, 495-2875
Nanny Cay Taxi Service	☎ 284-494-0550
Waterfront Taxi Stand (Road Town)	☎ 284-494-6362

Island Hopping

Once you're in the US or British Virgin Islands, it's relatively easy to hop from one island to another.

You can get to all the major islands, and a few of the smaller ones, by ferry, with the exception of Anegada, which is farther away and surrounded by dangerous shallow reefs. Call or stop by the ferry terminals to check schedules. Service changes seasonally, and sometimes for no apparent reason.

> **TIP:** *Aero flies from Tortola to Anegada.* ☎ 284-495-2271.

Most ferries dock at the main ports of entry in Road Town or West End, but some leave from other marinas or bays, so you need to know which boats leave each dock and where they are destined. Check the listings in *BVI Welcome*, a free publication that's widely available on the island.

Dohm's Water Taxi provides on-demand ferry service point-to-point within the US and British Virgin Islands. You specify the dock and pick-up time. You also can charter one of the three motor-powered catamarans for a private party, wedding or a day of island hopping. Call for rate information and reservations, ☎ 340-775-6501; www.watertaxi-vi.com.

◆ Touring the Island

Guided Tours

Several companies and private guides give excellent tours of Tortola. Their stories and insider information will both entertain and educate you. Expect to pay about $45 for a two- or three-hour tour of Tortola for up to three people.

TORTOLA

The **BVI Taxi Association** (☎ 284-494-2872) provides drivers/guides throughout the island. **Larry Henley**, owner of Cane Garden Bay Superette, is an excellent independent guide with a comfortable van. Contact him at ☎ 284-495-9455. **Travel Plan Tours** (☎ 284-494-2872) conducts island tours and arranges snorkeling trips and sailing or fishing excursions.

Smith Ferry Services (☎ 340-775-7292; fax 340-774-5532 on St. Thomas and 284-494-4495/494-2355 in the BVI) offers a variety of ferry/land tour packages for day trips to Tortola and Virgin Gorda. *Native Son* (☎ 284-774-8685/495-4617 in the BVI; 340-775-3111; fax 340-779-2811 on St. Thomas) has ferry/land day excursions to Virgin Gorda and Tortola from St. Thomas, and will plan customized group trips.

© Lidian Neeleman/iStockPhoto

An island tour offers spectacular views of the coastline.

Independent Island Tour

The best way to see Tortola is to take an up-down-and-over drive along the lofty, twisting roads that meander through the island. Start by traveling the south-shore road that runs from **Frenchmans Cay** and **West End,** around **Road Bay** as it passes through **Road Town**, to **East End**, where it crosses the **Queen Elizabeth Bridge** to **Beef Island**. Then tackle

Ridge Road, which climbs and plummets through the central hills, for stunning views of neighboring islands across the clear turquoise sea. Finally, tour the spectacular north-shore beaches and their funky-to-fabulous bars, restaurants, shops and resorts.

The entire island centers around **Road Town**, the capital of the British Virgin Islands, and its harbor on beautiful **Road Bay**, where ferries, cruise ships and private yachts arrive from international ports. The town wraps around the bay and spreads up into the green hills that form the islands central ridge.

At first glance, Road Town appears to be a sleepy tropical village not quite in step with the 21st century. In reality, it is a thriving center of maritime business, offshore finance and island government. The façade is deliberate. An attempt to distinguish itself from its US sister islands and stay true to its Caribbean culture.

The most interesting area for visitors is the quaint section between Waterfront Drive and Main Street, directly across and just west of the ferry dock. This is a great place to roam on foot, do a little shopping and sample delicious island cuisine. (See *Where to Shop* and *Where to Eat*.)

> **TIP:** *The unofficial local dress code prohibits walking around Road Town in swimsuits or other skimpy attire. No one should go shirtless or shoeless.*

Main Street is wedged against the base of a hillside, which was the only flat land available before much of the harbor was filled in. Most of the street's charm and character comes from the jumble of cars and pedestrians that crowd into the narrow lane lined with historic wooden buildings with red tin roofs.

Get a crash course on Tortola's tropical vegetation by visiting the four-acre **J.R. O'Neal Botanical Gardens**, across from the police station on Main Street. This peaceful garden began early in the 1900s as an agricultural experiment sponsored by the government. Today it is run by volunteers and the BVI National Park Trust. Highlights include a miniature

TORTOLA

rain forest and fern house, 62 varieties of palms and a cactus garden. Many species of birds are drawn to the flowering bushes and brilliant flamboyant trees. Benches along the red-brick pathways tempt you to linger in the shade to watch redlegged tortoises and peach-faced love birds. There's no admission charge and the gardens are open Monday-Saturday, 9 am-4 pm. ☎ 284-494-4997.

As you drive around the island, watch for the following sites:

Historic **Fort Burt** is now a hotel and restaurant, but it was built by the Dutch and rebuilt by the English to guard the entrance to Road Bay Harbor in the 1600s. The foundation and arsenal are the most intact historic ruins on the island, and the view of the harbor from the hillside grounds is awesome. Look for the fort high above Waterfront Drive west of Road Town. (See *Where to Eat* for information about the restaurant.)

Fort Recovery was built by the Dutch in 1660. The unrestored ruins are about eight miles west of Road Town on the grounds of Fort Recovery Estate, a compound of tourist villas. You can walk around the estate and explore the lookout tower with three-foot-thick stone walls, but this isn't set up as a true tourist attraction. (See *Where to Stay* for information about the villas.)

The Martello Tower of Fort Recovery is right on the beach.

The BVI National Park Trust has funded restoration of the **Mount Healthy Windmill**, part of an 18th-century sugar plantation. It is one of the few restored ruins on Tortola, and includes a factory, stables and workers' huts. The national park is open during daylight hours free of charge. Park in the clearing on Brewers Bay Road East, above Brewers Bay on the north coast, and walk through the green picket gate to the ruins.

Sage Mountain National Park is dominated by Sage Mountain, the highest point on Tortola at 1,716 feet. Trails lead up to the peak and through a small tropical forest, all that remains of a larger timberland that has been cut down in past centuries. Several spots offer striking vistas and mountain doves live in the tall old mahogany trees. The temperature at this higher elevation is usually comfortable for hiking and you'll see ferns, vines and flowers that don't grow anywhere else on the island. Visit free of charge during daylight hours. A large placard in the parking area outlines the trails through the park. The turnoff for Sage Mountain Road is on Ridge Road, west of Joe's Hill Road, which leads uphill from Road Town.

Skyworld, a restaurant situated at 1,337 feet in the hills above Road Town, has an observation deck that offers a 360° panorama of Tortola, the Caribbean Sea and islands as far away as St. Croix (40 miles) and Anegada (20 miles). Follow the signs on Ridge Road, west of Joe's Hill Road, to a sharp right turn that takes you uphill past a school to the parking lot. Arrive late in the afternoon to watch a spectacular sunset. (See *Where to Eat* for information about the restaurant.)

As you travel along Ridge Road, watch for the mural painted on a retaining wall east of Skyworld. Locals painted beautiful scenes of Tortola's early days.

TORTOLA

◆ Adventures on Water

Best Beaches

Cane Garden Bay is the star of Tortola's dazzling north-side beaches. It's only a 15-minute drive from Road Town. Take Joe's Hill Road up the mountain to Ridge Road, then take Cane Garden Bay Road down to the north shore. A long stretch of white sand shaded by palm trees faces a calm bay filled with colorful sailboats. Buoys mark a swimming area and you can rent kayaks, Hobie Cats, boogie boards and pedalboats from **Pleasure Boats** (☎ 284-495-9660, 495-9528). A complete line of watersports equipment is available for rent on the beach at **Baby Bull** (☎ 284-495-9627).

Several popular restaurants and bars are set back from the water and their music can be heard from every point on the beach. (See *Where to Eat*.) **Callwood's Rum Distillery** is across the road at the west end of the beach. Michael Callwood still produces rum the old-fashioned way – from sugar cane grown on the island. Take the tour and buy a $5 bottle to bring home.

If you take a right turn to the east off Cane Garden Bay Road, you'll find the less developed **Brewer's Bay**. You'll find good snorkeling around the rocks on the west end and out a short distance from the middle of the beach. Beware of strong currents along the outer points on each end of the bay. A small campground is on the west end of the beach. If you're in the mood for a hike, walk up to the restored mill on Mount Healthy above the east end of the bay.

West of Cane Garden Bay, the North Coast Road passes the drowsy fishing village of Carrot Bay and arrives at **Apple Bay**. The beach here is popular with surfers, especially in the winter when big waves roll in from the Atlantic. During the summer, the water tends to be calmer and is perfect for swimming and body surfing.

Long Bay Beach, farther west on North Coast Road, is a picturesque span of sand that stretches for a mile to Belmont Point. Storms in the North Atlantic sometimes create rough

Opposite: Cane Garden Bay.

View of Apple Bay.

surf here during the winter, but at other times the water is calm and excellent for swimming.

A rugged unpaved road leads from Long Bay to **Smuggler's Cove**, around the west side of Belmont Point. You'll wish for a four-wheel-drive jeep to navigate the road, but it's worth the trouble to get to this lovely crescent-shaped white-sand beach. The water is calm, clear and turquoise. Snorkeling is good along the close-in reef, which is visible from the beach.

Josiah's Bay can be seen from the east end of Ridge Road. Just follow Josiah's Bay Road down to the beautiful, sometimes deserted, beach. Rocks hidden just below the surface of the water makes body surfing dangerous and the waves often are too rough for novice swimmers.

Lambert Bay, on the remote eastern end of the north shore, has a striking white-sand beach lined with palms and backed by steep cliffs. The Lambert Beach Resort is set back from the water. Make a left turn off Ridge Road, near the police station in Long Look, onto Blackburn Road, then turn left again at Lambert Estate and follow the signs to the beach and resort.

Long Bay Beach East is across the Queen Elizabeth Bridge on Beef Island. Locals favor this beach because of its long stretch of sand and calm water for swimming. It's on a dirt road off Beef Island Road just past the salt flats.

Trellis Bay on Beef Island is home to the BVI Boardsailing School that teaches windsurfing. Steady trade winds provide near-perfect conditions for windsurfers, who hang out at the nearby bar named de Loose Mongoose. A free ferry leaves from the dock for **Marina Cay**, where you can dine at Pusser's and snorkel along the rocks off the sandy beach.

TORTOLA

Scuba Diving & Snorkeling

The British Virgin Islands rank among the top 10 dive destinations in the world and the wreck of *RMS Rhone* is considered one of the best wreck dives in the Caribbean.

The BVI has an abundance of dive sites, many within the Underwater National Park System, where conservation is the primary concern. Over 60 dive sites are charted and countless reefs still are unexplored. Favored spots feature thriving coral gardens, stunning canyons and intriguing tunnels and caverns teaming with underwater creatures.

Horseshoe Reef, the third largest reef in the world, stretches 11 miles from Anegada's southeastern coast. Hundreds of ships have wrecked and sunk here over the centuries and their remains provide unlimited possibilities for wreck diving. Many divers use Tortola or Virgin Gorda as a base for boat diving along the south side of the Sir Francis Drake Channel. Norman, Peter, Salt, Cooper and Ginger Islands separate the channel from the Caribbean and their underwater world features a variety of canyons, pinnacles and shallow reefs for snorkelers and divers of every skill level.

© Walker Mangum

Horseshoe Reef.

Non-divers staying on Tortola can join a resort course or go on a guided snorkeling tour of the more shallow sites. Snorkeling also is good off the beach at **Brewer's Bay**, unless winter storms are stirring up the North Atlantic and causing rough surf on the northern shore. **Marina Cay**, a five-minute ferry ride from the east end of Beef Island, also offers good snorkeling.

The Indians is a popular site near tiny Pelican Island, off the north shore of Norman Island. Snorkelers can float above the jagged pinnacles that some say resemble Indian feathers

Colorful corals below the water's surface.

and tower 50 feet above the water's surface. Divers usually circle the rocks at depths of 30 to 50 feet, passing healthy growths of coral and sponge. A canyon known as The Sunken Indian and a formation called The Fish Bowl host abundant sea creatures.

The Caves at Norman Island are popular with snorkelers and swimmers, and divers often use the site as a rest stop between descents. Visitors come here in a never-ending search for hidden pirates' treasure. The far northern cave is the most magnificent and extends about 70 feet into the mountainside. If pirates left treasure in the BVI, this is the most likely hiding place.

Both **Sandy's Ledge** and **Angelfish Reef** are popular snorkeling and easy-dive sites off Norman Island. Sandy's beauty starts at depths of five feet, so snorkelers can easily view the coral and young fish just below the water's surface. Angelfish Reef, off the southwest end of Norman, rises to about 20 feet below the surface at some points, allowing experienced snorkelers to observe from the surface while divers go to 60-foot depths.

Norman is 2½ miles long and the largest uninhabited island in the British Virgin Islands. It is the most western of the

TORTOLA

Norman Island.

small islands that line up across the Sir Francis Drake Channel about five miles south of Tortola. Locals call it Treasure Island because of age-old legends of buried pirates' loot on the island.

NORMAN ISLAND TREASURE

A letter dated 1750 refers to recovered treasure that was buried on Norman, and Robert Louis Stevenson based his famous 1883 novel, *Treasure Island*, on ruthless characters living on an island that sounds very much like Norman. In the early 1900s, a family from Tortola found a large stash of pirates' booty in one of Norman's caves.

A large sheltered harbor at Norman has been called **The Bight** since pirate days. The western tip of this harbor, where the famous **caves** are located, is named **Treasure Point**. Once you see the three watery caves and explore their dark musky depths, you'll agree that they are an excellent place to store up earthly treasures. Lofty **Spy Glass Hill** on the island's central ridge is the perfect lookout point from which to spot enemy pirates and vulnerable Spanish galleons. If you

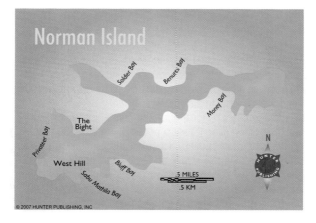

hike up the hill, be aware that the goats are wild and known to have nasty tempers.

Spy Glass is a popular wall dive off the northeast side of Norman near Benures Bay. The top is in fairly shallow water, so snorkelers can watch schools of colorful fish that feed among the coral and sea fans. Divers go to 60 feet, where the wall meets a sand bottom and turtles, rays and tarpon feed.

If you're checking out as a new diver, chances are you'll make your first dive at **Coral Gardens** off Deadman's Bay east of the resort on Peter Island. Snorkeling is excellent when the water is calm, and divers get a look at brain, star and sheet corals growing in the garden at 20 to 35 feet.

Deadman's Bay.

TORTOLA

DIVE OPERATORS

The following dive shops on Tortola offer first-class PADI instruction, multi-level certification, guided dive trips and equipment rental. Most operators schedule two boat trips daily and arrange instruction courses to meet students' vacation plans. In addition, many of the dive boats will rendezvous with private yachts to pick up divers.

Expect to pay $70 for a one-tank dive and $95 for a two-tank dive. Snorkeling trips are priced in the $20-$30 range.

Bring your internationally accepted certification card if you want to rent equipment, get air fills or participate in guided tours designed for experienced divers. Introductory dives and resort courses are available and priced at about $100.

Sail Caribbean caters to small groups so that each diver receives special attention. Their two full-service dive shops are located at Hodges Creek, between Road Town and East End on Tortola, and on Maya Cove. Custom-outfitted boats rendezvous with private charters and pick up at Marina Cay, as well as at the two dive shops. ☎ 284-495-1675, fax 284-495-3244; www.sailcaribbeandivers.com.

UBS Dive Center has three custom-outfitted boats and specializes in diving and snorkeling trips for private groups. Gather your family or friends for a day of cruising the islands, swimming, diving and snorkeling. You choose the sites, or let owners Tony and Katheryn Brunn and their experienced

© UBS Dive Center

crew guide you to their favorite wrecks, walls and lesser-known eco spots. ☎ 284-494-0024 (office), 284-496-8475 (cell); fax 284-494-0623; www.scuba bvi.com.

Dive BVI is an inveterate favorite among scuba enthusiasts. Joe Giacinto has owned the business since 1975 and now operates from three locations: Marina Cay (a free ferry ride from Trellis Bay, Beef Island); Leverick Bay on Virgin Gorda; and Virgin Gorda Yacht Harbor. Each PADI 5-star shop is fully equipped and staffed by a friendly crew of skilled instructors. They now offer Nitrox. ☎ 800-848-7078, 284-495-5513; fax 284-495-5347; www.divebvi.com.

Aquaventure, at Village Cay Marina in Road Town, has an impressive 35-foot Striker dive boat configured for 16 divers. Even more impressive, they limit the number of divers on each trip to eight. That means lots of room under the big bimini awning and out front on the sunny, cushioned deck. While you sprawl out in all that comfy space, the crew readies your state-of-the-art

Wreck diving.

equipment, and the boat (aptly named Aqua Venture) speeds you to the ideal dive site. Book your reservations early. ☎ 284-494-4320, fax 284-494-5608; www. aquaventurebvi.com.

Blue Water Divers started small in 1980 and is an award-winning operator with two shops (at the marinas in Nanny Cay and Soper's Hole), four dive boats and a large staff of PADI-qualified instructors. The owners Keith and Muffy Royle and crew take satisfaction in training new divers and showing experienced divers the best scuba sites in the islands. ☎ 284-494-2847 (Nanny Cay) or 284-495-1200 (Soper's Hole); www.bluewaterdiversbvi.com.

TORTOLA

Dive Tortola sits on the dock at Prospect Reef Marina, just west of Road Town. The dedicated staff goes that extra step to provide unbeatable service to divers, especially those who sign up for multiple dives over several days. Clients store their gear at the shop after their first dive, then return each day to find all their equipment rinsed and set up on the boat, ready to go. Depending on water clarity, boats go out mornings and afternoons to all the most popular sites. Night dives and open-water certification are a specialty. ☎ 800-353-3419 (US), 954-453-5040 (outside the US), 284-494-9200 (Virgin Islands); fax 954-351-9740; www.divetortola.com.

Boating & Sailing

With steady easterly trade winds, an average year-round temperature of 85°, clear-to-the-bottom turquoise seas and a lineup of pristine islands, the British Virgin Islands are considered the best cruising waters in the world. Every visitor wants to get out on the water, and since the BVI is a major yachting center, there are several ways to do it.

If you can handle a boat, consider renting a small craft for the afternoon or chartering a live-aboard for your entire stay. If you can't handle a boat, but want to learn, sign up for sailing school. If you prefer to leave the piloting to someone else, reserve a spot on one of the many full- or half-day sailing excursions.

Scheduled outings often go to secluded coves on outer islands for snorkeling, swimming and picnicking. Others make day trips to popular sites such as The Baths on Virgin Gorda. Call a few operators before you book to ask how many passengers the boat is licensed to carry and how many are expected at the time you want to go. Also, find out if snorkeling equipment and refreshments are included.

Rates for a full-day excursion with lunch run about $85-100 for adults and $50 for kids. Prices for half-day and sunset sails vary widely depending on the types of refreshments served and the length of the trip, so shop around before you make a reservation.

While dozens of operators offer a long menu of boat-related services, the following are recommended as some of the best on Tortola.

SAILING SCHOOLS

Offshore Sailing School is run by Steve and Doris Colgate, award-wining leaders in the sailing industry, with over 90,000 satisfied graduates. Their instructors and boats meet the highest standards. ☎ 800-221-4326; fax 239-454-1191; www.offshore-sailing.com.

Full Sail Sailing School teaches everything from basics for beginners to advanced techniques for experienced sailors who want to improve their skills. Full Sail encourages students who want to become good crew members, those who hope to captain their own boat and those who are simply curious about sailing. Contact them at the marina on West End, ☎ 284-494-0512, fax 494-0588; www. fullsailbvi.com.

A Full Sail boat going by Peter Island.

Sail Caribbean is a Tortola-based school for teens 13 to 18 years of age. Students start with windsurfing and move on to sailing two to five hours each day. Every night is spent moored at a different island. Students also have the opportunity to learn other sports such as scuba diving, water skiing and kayaking. Call for a catalog and information, ☎ 800-321-0994 or 284-495-1675; fax 284-495-3244; www.sailcaribbean .com.

Swain Sailing School is under the direction of Rob Swain, a former professional racer, US Coast Guard Master and certified sailing instructor. For more than 10 years, Swain and his crew of dedicated instructors have taught the basics to beginners and advanced techniques to experienced sailors. Call the Tortola-based school for a schedule of classes,

TORTOLA

☎ 800-948-SAIL (US), 284-495-9376 (Tortola); www. swainsailing.com.

Upper Bay Sailing School is a well-known facility started by Captain Keith Binnersley and based in Chesapeake Bay. Now, from November through July, the school offers multi-level sailing instruction in Tortola. The cruiser/racers are docked at Nanny Cay Marina, and the Drake Channel serves as a picturesque training ground. ☎ 888-302-7245; www.upperbay sailing.com.

© Upper Bay Sailing School

A Leopard 45 Cat available for charter.

CREWED DAY-TRIPS

© Aristocrat Charters

Aristocrat
under full sail.

Aristocat, captained by John and Sandra, is a 48-foot French-built catamaran. Sit under the sun-blocking awning or out in the open on one of the foredeck trampolines. Aristocat leaves Soper's Hole, heads out into Drake Channel, and sails for Norman and Peter islands, where you can swim or snorkel. Scheduled cruises accept a maximum of 14 guests to avoid crowding; private charters can accommodate up to 30 passengers. ☎ 284-499-1249 (cell); www.aristocatcharters.com.

Patouche Charters, in Road Town, offers full- and half-day sailing and powerboat trips. On all excursions, you go to great snorkeling sites and enjoy refreshments onboard. The full-day trips include a gourmet lunch. Boats are in top shape and the crews are friendly, safe and knowledgeable. ☎ 284-494-6300; www.patouche.com.

White Squall II is a lovely classic schooner that sails daily from Village Cay Marina in Road Town to The Baths on Virgin Gorda and the beach at either Cooper or Norman Island. You'll get a full day of island-sighting, snorkeling, refreshments and lunch. ☎ 284-494-2564; www.whitesquall2.com.

Chocolat Blanc sails out of Fat Hogs Bay on the East End for day sails and weekly charters that include swimming, snorkeling and drinks. This 39-foot catamaran is as sweet as its name, which translates as "white chocolate." Call to schedule a trip with Captain Dan. ☎ 284-495-1266 or 284-496-6600 (cell); www.chocolat blanc.com.

© Chocolat Blanc

Chocolat Blanc.

© Kuralu

Kuralu is a great boat for families. The 50-foot catamaran is ultra-stable, has 1,000 square feet of deck, a wide platform for getting into and out of the water and plenty of shade. The boat leaves daily from the West End and goes to various islands for swimming and snorkeling. Lunch, drinks and snorkeling equipment is provided. Contact owner/captain Robin Pinfold, ☎ 284-495-4381; www.kuralu.com.

TORTOLA

CREWED & BAREBOAT CHARTERS

Bareboat Charters ☆ represents a select group of catamarans, monohulls and motor yachts. This company knows the BVI well and will help you as much or as little as you wish when planning your vacation. ☎ 284-495-4168; www.bareboatsbvi.com.

Sunsail is a huge chartering operation that started in the Mediterranean. The base at Frenchman's Cay Marina, West End, has catamarans and monohulls in numerous sizes that rent crewed or bareboat. Contact the office for information on the many services they provide. ☎ 888-350-3568; www.sunsail.com.

The Moorings runs a full-service yachting resort with about 200 boats, the 44-room Mariner Inn, a dockside restaurant, scuba equipment and extensive support services. Contact them at Wickhams Cay in Road Town ☎ 888-952-8420 or 284-494-2332; fax 494-2226; www.moorings.com.

Conch Charters ☆, in Road Town, has a large fleet of charter boats in various sizes. They've been in business since 1986 and have a reputation for excellent boats and dedicated service. ☎ 800-521-8939 (US), 800-463-6625 (Canada), or 284-494-4868 (Tortola); fax 494-5793; www.conchcharters.com.

Cuan Law ☆☆ is a 105-foot luxury trimaran featuring 10 double air-conditioned cabins with private baths, the largest sailing trimaran in the world. The vessel is outfitted with all types of watersports equipment, including scuba gear. For information about this deluxe cruise contact, ☎ 800-648-3393 or 284-494-2490; www.bvisailing.com.

POWERBOAT RENTALS

Sheppard's Powerboat Rentals and Water Taxis out of Soper's Hole, West End, offers rentals and water taxi transportation to outlying islands. ☎ 284-495-4099; fax 284-495-4792.

Pleasure Boats on the beach at Cane Garden Bay rents small motor boats and offers drop-off service to three beaches on Jost Van Dyke and guided tours to Jost and Virgin Gorda. ☎ 284-495-9660; fax 284-495-9984.

WATER TAXI

Dohm's Water Taxi provides on-demand ferry service point-to-point within the US and British Virgin Islands. You specify the dock and pick-up time. You also can charter one of the three motor-powered catamarans for a private party, wedding or a day of island hopping. Call for rate information and reservations, ☎ 340-775-6501; www.watertaxi-vi.com.

Happy Girl Scouts, Tortola.

Fishing

You'll need a $35 permit if you want to do any recreational fishing in the BVI. Charter companies usually supply them, or you can apply for one at the Department of Natural Resources and Labour on the second floor of the Government Administration Complex, near the dock in Road Town. ☎ 284-494-3701.

> **NOTE:** *Spear fishing is prohibited in the BVI. Also, it's against the law to fish within the boundaries of a marine park or to capture or remove any underwater creatures while scuba diving.*

Expect to pay about $800 per day or $400 per half-day to charter a fully equipped and crewed fishing boat. The following operators have proven records as excellent fishermen and friendly guides.

TORTOLA

Caribbean Fly Fishing Outfitters ☆, out of Nanny Cay, will pick you up in *After You*, their 28-foot Bertram, then transfer you to an 18-foot poling boat for a day of fly fishing. ☎ 284-494-4797 (office), 284-499-1590 (cell); www. caribflyfishing.com.

> **TIP:** *If you want to fish off a dock or right from the beach at your resort, rent equipment from **Caribbean Fly Fishing Outfitters**, ☎ 284-494-4797.*

Pelican Charters runs trips from Prospect Reef Harbour near Road Town on a 45-foot ChrisCraft Sportsfisherman, the M/V *Whopper*. Full- and half-day charters include all equipment, drinks and lunch or snacks. *The Whopper* is available for deep-sea fishing, whale watching, snorkeling or just cruising to various islands. ☎ 284-496-7386.

Watersports

Last Stop Sports is located at Wickham's Cay II in Road Town and owned by Chris Guiorse s. Rentals include single and double ocean kayaks, windsurfers come in many styles and sizes and surfboards. Call for rates and information about instruction. ☎ 284-495-0564; fax 284-494-0593; www. laststopsports.com.

BVI Watersports HQ, owned by Jeremy Wright, rents windsurfers, kiteboards, boogie boards, surfboards and sea kayaks by the day or week. On-site instruction is offered and the shop will deliver equipment anywhere on Tortola. Ask about the windsurfing trips to Anegada. Offices are located at Trellis Bay on Beef Island, ☎ 800-880-7873; 284-495-2447; fax 284-495-1626; www. windsurfing.vi.

HIHO (Hang In Hold On) has a store in Road Town and rents kayaks, surfboards and windsurfers from various marinas around the island.

Contact the store for information, ☎ 284-494-7694; www.go-hiho.com.

Hobie cats racing on the aqua waters around Tortola.

Pleasure Boats on the beach at Cane Garden Bay rents kayaks, pedal boats, boogie boards, canoes and windsurfers as well as motor boats. They also offer drop-off service to three beaches on Jost Van Dyke and guided tours to Jost and Virgin Gorda. ☎ 284-495-9660; fax 284-495-9984.

Parasail BVI with Jim Frey and Tanys Waldron at Soper's Hole is an exciting way to see the BVI from an altitude of 600 feet. No experience is necessary, you won't get wet unless you want to, and kids are welcome. They will pick you up at your hotel or rendezvous with your boat. ☎ 284-494-4967.

British Virgin Islands Watersports Center at Sea Cows Bay rents dinghies, keelboats and kayaks. ☎ 284-494-1669; fax 284-494-0663; www.bviwatersports.com.

TORTOLA

◆ Adventures on Foot

Hiking

Tortola offers ample opportunity for casual walks and rugged hikes. One of the most popular hikes is along the trails that wind through **Sage Mountain National Park**. In addition, picturesque hamlets along the coast provide ideal spots for leisurely strolls. Beaches are popular for romantic walks at sunset and dedicated ramblers will enjoy poking around historic Road Town.

Sage Mountain National Park covers 92 acres on the rugged slopes of Tortola's highest mountain. Even non-hikers can enjoy the fantastic views from the parking lot located off Ridge Road. The vista takes in Jost Van Dyke, Sandy Cay, Tortola's north shore and St. Thomas.

Hiking Tortola's coastal trails often rewards you with great views.

The national park is open daily from dawn to dusk. For information about the park or trails, contact the BVI National Park Trust, ☎ 284-494-3904; fax 494-6383; www.bvi nationalpark.com.

A large placard in the parking area illustrates the park's three interconnecting trails. The central path, known as the

Rain Forest Trail, presents the easiest hike, while the **Mahogany Trail** leading to the top of Sage Mountain is the most difficult. The **Henry Adams Loop Trail** is short, but fairly steep, and passes through the best preserved old-growth forest.

Foliage along the well-maintained **Rain Forest Trail** is labeled. Pay special attention to the white cedar tree, which is honored as the national tree of the BVI, and the mountain guava, which is used to make the islanders' favorite Christmas-season rum drink. You may hear hermit crabs scampering in the undergrowth. Once a year, thousands of them rush down the mountain to the sea to mate and find a new shell to call home, then return to the forest.

Count on about 20 minutes to leisurely cover the entire Rain Forest Trail, which is less than a mile. When you reach a large old fig tree at the end of the path, retrace your steps and pick up the **Henry Adams Loop Trail** near the gate that crosses the entrance into the park.

The Loop Trail is a short, steep path that tends to be slippery after a rain. A 10-minute uphill hike past giant philodendron vines (aka elephant ears) will take you deep into a stand of tall old trees called bulletwoods, which supply timber that resembles mahogany.

A third path, called the **Mahogany Forest Trail,** branches off from the main Rain Forest Trail at the entrance gate. Allow about a half-hour to hike the rather short distance, because you'll be traveling a steep ascent/descent most of the way. The path can be quite slippery after a rain, so it's a good idea to wear shoes with heavy tread or hiking boots. You'll be hiking through old plantation grounds to the top of Sage Mountain, the highest point in all the US and British Virgin Islands. A sign points the way to a side trail with an observation area on the 1,710-foot-high peak.

Tennis

Long Bay Beach Resort features a racquet club and tennis program under the direction of Peter Burwash International. There are two lighted championship courts with artificial grass plus a hard-surface court. Non-guests may make reservations for play or instruction with the on-site pro. ☎ 284-495-4252 or 495-4306.

◆ Adventures on Wheels

Cycling

Biking is a popular sport on Tortola and the **BVI Cycling Federation** has more than 40 members, including an impressive team of international competitors. The National Cycling Series includes approximately 10 races between February and September, and visitors to the islands may see cyclists training early each morning. If you're interested in current race information, contact the BVI Cycling Federation, ☎ 284-494-3567; fax 495-9546; www.bvicycling.com.

If you're a recreational biker you'll want to stick to leisurely rides on paved level roads along the coast. More experienced riders and adventure cyclists will enjoy rugged trails that lead to secluded beaches and steep roads that wind around scenic hills. There are many routes, including a 10-mile stretch of flat coastal road from Road Town to West End.

Bike Rental

Last Stop Sports runs a bike shop at Port Purcell in Road Town that rents a large selection of mountain bikes. Owner Chris Guiorse and his staff have years of experience riding on the islands, so they are well qualified to outfit you and suggest routes that match your riding skills.

Multi-gear bikes rent for around $30 per day or $120 per week. Front- and full-suspension bikes cost slightly more. Helmets, locks and racks are supplied at no charge. If you plan to ride on nearby islands, your bike can go along on the ferry at no charge. ☎ 284-494-1120; fax 494-0593; www.laststopsports.com.

◆ Adventures on Horseback

One of the best ways to tour secluded beaches and remote hilltops is on horseback. **Shadow Stables**, on Ridge Road east of Skyworld Restaurant, and the **Ellis Thomas Riding School**, at the race track on Sea Cow Bay, offer rides on Sage Mountain, along the island's central ridge and down to the north-shore beaches. Contact Shadow at ☎ 284-494-2262; Ellis Thomas can be reached at ☎ 284-494-4442.

◆ Shopping

Tortola doesn't try to compete in the duty-free shopping wars. The island offers a few good deals on items imported from the United Kingdom, but the real finds are locally made products and one-of-a-kind arts and crafts. Often, the shabbiest looking shops hold the most unusual treasures. So, overlook peeling paint and rusting metal on the exterior. Even the most meticulous shopkeepers can't keep up with the assaults of salt air, tropical storms and the Caribbean sun.

A vendor's market is set up just east of the ferry dock. You can pick up sunglasses, T-shirts, tote bags, sarongs, spices and local crafts at the open stands. Hours vary, but most merchants open around 9 am and close about 4 pm. When cruise passengers are in town and during peak tourist season, stalls open earlier and stay later. Many close for several weeks or keep shorter hours during low season. You may find some good bargains, if you visit at the right time.

SHOPPING HOURS
Unless noted otherwise, stores are open Monday-Friday, 9 am-4 pm; Saturday, 9 am-1 pm.

Road Town

Sunny Caribbee Herb and Spice Company, 119 Main Street, is the best place to buy gifts and, perhaps, a little treat for yourself. You'll be tempted to spend hours in this large shop filled with fragrant herbs and spices, attractively packaged baskets of assorted beauty potions and medicinal cures, locally made ceramics and island cookbooks. ☎ 284-494-2178, fax 494-4039; www.sunnycaribbee.com.

Sunny Caribbee Art Gallery ☆ is next door to the Herb and Spice Company. You'll find original paintings, prints, sculpture, pottery and handcrafted jewelry. The quality is excellent. You can arrange to have your purchases shipped home. ☎ 284-494-2178, fax 494-4039; www.sunnycaribbee. com.

Sea Urchin has a shop across from the ferry dock as well as at Wickham's Cay and Soper's Hole. You'll find stylish beachwear, sandals and casual clothing in all sizes. The phone number for the waterfront store is ☎ 284-494-7366. For Wickham's Cay, ☎ 284-494-4108, and for Soper's Hole, ☎ 284-494-6234.

Bolo's, at the in-town traffic circle next to Bobby's Supermarket, is a popular variety store with a little bit of everything for sale. Check here if you need things such as notebooks, batteries, film, skin cream or household items. They also do one-hour film processing. ☎ 284-494-2867.

Latitude 18 carries embroidered and printed polo shirts and T-shirts, shorts, tops, hats and sandals for men and women. In addition, this trendy shop has a collection of dresses and sarongs for women, and the island's largest selection of Kipling bags and luggage. Look for the blue store at 116 Main Street, ☎ 284-494-4807, where the road makes a 90° turn. A second store is at Soper's Hole, ☎ 284-494-7807.

Flamboyance Duty Free Gift Shoppes, on Waterfront Drive facing the harbor, sells a fine selection of perfumes, watches and jewelry. ☎ 284-494-4099.

Samarkand features gold and silver jewelry handcrafted by artisans Sally and Richard Bibby. The BVI-map charm makes a wonderful souvenir. Visit the shop at 94 Main Street, ☎/fax 284-494-6415.

Caribbean Handprints ☆ offers fabric and clothing in lovely silk-screened designs. All clothing is handmade by local craftspeople, so each piece is a wearable souvenir of the

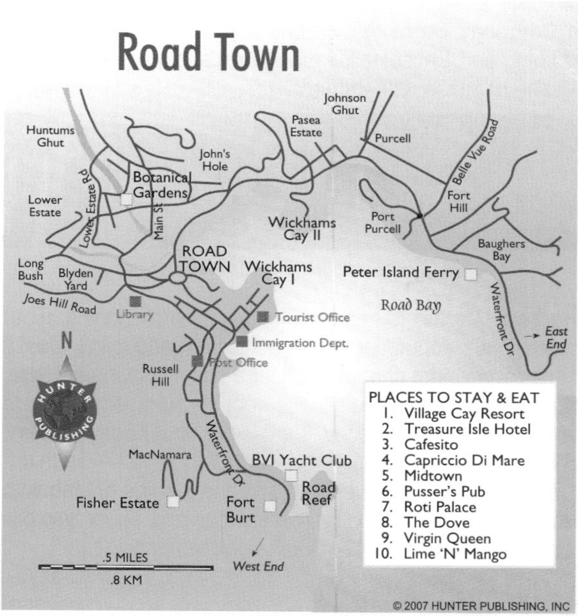
Road Town
Huntums Ghut
Lower Estate
Lower Estate Rd
Botanical Gardens
Main St
John's Hole
Pasea Estate
Johnson Ghut
Purcell
Belle Vue Road
Fort Hill
Port Purcell
Wickhams Cay II
ROAD TOWN
Wickhams Cay I
Peter Island Ferry
Baughers Bay
Long Bush
Blyden Yard
Joes Hill Road
Library
Tourist Office
Immigration Dept.
Post Office
Road Bay
Waterfront Dr
East End
N
Russell Hill
MacNamara
Waterfront Dr
BVI Yacht Club
Road Reef
Fisher Estate
Fort Burt
West End
.5 MILES
.8 KM
PLACES TO STAY & EAT
1. Village Cay Resort
2. Treasure Isle Hotel
3. Cafesito
4. Capriccio Di Mare
5. Midtown
6. Pusser's Pub
7. Roti Palace
8. The Dove
9. Virgin Queen
10. Lime 'N' Mango
© 2007 HUNTER PUBLISHING, INC

island. Located on Main Street near the back entrance to Pusser's Company Store. ☎ 284-494-3717.

Pusser's Company Store opens onto Waterfront Drive across from the ferry dock and exits onto Main Street. You can walk in one door and out the other. On your way through, pick up some nautical-theme clothing and a bottle of their famous rum. ☎ 284-494-2467.

Soper's Hole

Soper's Hole is a marina on **Frenchman's Cay**, which is connected to Tortola near West End by a bridge. The picturesque wharf features colorful pastel shops (shown above) newly designed to look like a traditional West Indian village. **Pusser's Landing** is the two-story focal point with two restaurants, a bar, an outdoor terrace overlooking the water,and a **Company Store** that carries their private-label nautical clothing and British-sailor rum. The Landing is open daily, 11 am-10 pm. ☎ 284-495-4554.

Picturesque Soper's Hole.

Harbour Market is nearby. This luxury provisioning outlet has a great reputation with yachtsmen who can't face a cruise across the channel without a supply of vintage wine, French bread and aged cheese from the Hamper. The store is open Monday-Thursday, 8 am-4 pm, and Friday-Sunday, 8 am-7 pm. ☎ 284-495-4541.

B.V.I. Apparel features 100% cotton T-shirts printed with island designs, top-quality resort wear and exotic jewelry. ☎ 284-494-5511; fax 494-3867; www.bviapparel.com.

Trellis Bay

Trellis Bay is a unique little stretch of shops and cafés along a sandy beach north of the airport on Beef Island. Grab lunch at **De Loose Mongoose** (☎ 284-495-2303, 8 am-10 pm, closed Mondays) or the **Cyber Café** (☎ 284-495-2447, 7 am-11 pm daily) then browse through the studios of artists Aragon Dick-Read and Roger Ellis.

Aragorn's Studio ☆☆ is a rambling shop full of Aragorn Dick-Read's exceptional sculptures and paintings. A pottery studio is located in one area, and you'll find some of the local artisans' works for sale. Another section of the shop offers jewelry, pottery, wood carvings and baskets crafted by native Caribs living on other islands. Some of Aragorn's original art is available on high-quality tee shirts, which make excellent souvenirs. On your way out, browse through the large selection of Caribbean spices and teas. ☎ 284-495-1849; www.aragornsstudio.com.

❋ coconut choppers ❋

© Aragorn's Studio

Aragorn's T-shirts feature his own designs, such as this one.

Flukes ☆ is the showcase for art and maps created by Roger Ellis, a world-renowned designer, cartographer and conservationist. His fine art is remarkable for capturing the colors of the Caribbean, and his work is often seen in murals and exquisite fabrics. Prints of his amazingly accurate hand-drawn maps are wonderful souvenirs. If you like his work, but don't see exactly what you want, Ellis accepts commissions. ☎ 284-495-2043; www.caribbeanarts.com.

Around the Island

Skyworld Gift Shop is below the observation deck at Skyworld Restaurant in the hills above Road Town. The best reasons to come here are the view and Jim Cullimore's cooking, but take time to poke around the little gift shop. You'll find original island art, mini paintings, cards and pottery. Watch for signs to the restaurant/shop on Ridge Road. ☎ 284-494-3567.

TORTOLA

Arawak ☆, on the dock at Nanny Cay Marina, has a fine selection of Indonesian-style batik clothing designed in the BVI. There's also other tropical apparel, silver jewelry and T-shirts, as well as crafts from around the world. The shop's open daily, 9 am-5 pm. ☎ 284-494-5240; www.arawakbvi. com.

Nan's Gallery in Apple Bay is the place for original water-color prints, exquisite bowls made from Calabash gourds and Moko Jumbee masks. Look for the shop on the North Coast Road where it intersects with Zion Hill Road. Take time to browse. You'll find brightly painted birdhouses, Christmas ornaments and planters. ☎ 284-495-4887.

◆ Where to Stay

If you're not sleeping onboard ship, your lodging choice will set the tone for your entire stay in the British Virgin Islands. Tortola is an excellent home base because it has every convenience and service as well as easy access to all the other islands and cays.

There is a handful of luxurious full-service resorts, a dozen fine hotels and numerous deluxe to rustic guest houses and villas. Don't expect glitz and extravagance like that found at behemoth resorts in the USVI. Most accommodations in the BVI put more value on serenity and simplicity.

The accommodations listed below are chosen for their unique character, optimum location and essential creature comforts. Use the prices given for accommodations as a guide to the average high-season rate per standard double room. If the review is for an all-inclusive or all-suites resort, the listed price is the lowest available during high-season for two people sharing a room. During low-season, generally from April 15 through December 14, rates drop 25-50%. Expect to pay an additional 10% service charge and 7% tax year-round.

SLEEPING WITH THE STARS

To keep this *Pocket Adventures* book to a reasonable size, our list of lodgings has been kept to a minimum. You can browse the Internet as well as we can, and we encourage you to do so. Here you'll find only the most recommended possibilities to fit a variety of budgets. Properties marked with one star (☆) are highly recommended. When a single feature or the overall allure is particularly impressive, you'll find two stars (☆☆) beside the name. Three stars (☆☆☆) means, simply, WOW!

Rental Agencies

If you want to rent a house or private villa, contact one of the follwing agencies:

- ❖ **Areana Villas**, ☎ 284-494-5864; www.areana villas.com.
- ❖ **Caribbean Way**, ☎ 877-953-7400; www.caribbeanway.com.
- ❖ **Caribbean Realty LTD.**, ☎ 284-494-3999; www.caribbean realtybvi.com.
- ❖ **BVI Villas**, ☎ 284-494-2442; www.british virginvillas.com.

CAMPING

Campgrounds are located on Brewers Bay. Twenty two-man tents rent for $40 per night; bare sites cost $15 for two people. Facilities include toilets, showers, cookout areas, a casual restaurant/bar and windsurfer rentals. For reservations, contact **Brewers Bay Campground**, ☎ 284-494-3463. No credit cards.

In & Near Road Town

Village Cay Hotel, Village Cay Marina, PO Box 145, Road Town, Tortola, BVI. ☎ 284-494-2771; fax 494-2773; www.villagecay.com. 21 rooms. $125.

You're within walking distance of Road Town's shops, restaurants, charter boats and ferry docks when you stay at this hotel overlooking Village Cay Marina. All rooms are air condi-

TORTOLA

tioned, comfortably furnished in rattan and outfitted with cable TV. Laundry facilities, a small swimming pool and a watersports center with a dive shop are on site. A waterside restaurant is open for all meals and the bar often hosts live entertainment.

© Village Cay Hotel

Treasure Isle Hotel, Waterfront Drive, PO Box 68, Road Town, Tortola, BVI. ☎ 800-223-1108 (US), 0800-894057 (UK) or 284-494-2501; fax 494-2507; www.treasureislehotel. net. 40 rooms and suites. $170.

You can't miss this brightly-colored hotel perched on a landscaped hillside east of Road Town. The spacious air-conditioned rooms are equally as bright, with colorful island

© Treasure Isle Hotel

art on white stucco walls that contrast with tile floors. Each unit has satellite TV and a private tub/shower bathroom. Guests enjoy a freshwater swimming pool, complimentary sailing and transportation to various beaches. An on-site dive shop is convenient for those who want to scuba or snorkel. The open-air Lime and Mango Restaurant and Spy Glass bar are popular gathering spots for locals and visitors to the island. (See *Where to Eat.*)

Fort Burt, Waterfront Drive, PO Box 3380, Road Town, Tortola, BVI. ☎ 284-494-2587; fax 494-2002. 19 rooms and suites. $135.

Dutch settlers built Fort Burt in the 1600s to defend the island against foreign armies and pirates. Today it's a modern hotel conveniently located near the west side of Road Town, across the south-coast road from the BVI Yacht Club and within walking distance of the ferry dock and town attractions.

Renovated rooms and suites are air conditioned, comfortably furnished in rattan and feature cable TV, small refrigerators and private balconies with views of the water. If you don't splurge on one of the two deluxe suites with a private pool, you can swim in the lovely hotel pool, which overlooks the harbor. (See *Independent Touring* and *Where to Eat* for more information about the grounds and restaurant.)

North Shore

Sebastian's On The Beach Hotel and Villas, Little Apple Bay, PO Box 441, Road Town, Tortola, BVI. ☎ 800-336-4870 or 284-495-4212; fax 495-4466; www.sebastiansbvi.com. 26 rooms, 8 villas. $110.

Kick off your shoes and enjoy this friendly barefoot beach hotel on shady Little Apple Bay. All rooms are cozy, nicely decorated and outfitted with a small refrigerator and private

© Sebastian's Hotel

bath. Oceanview rooms have private balconies or patios, while garden units open onto a lushly landscaped courtyard. Rooms are situated in three buildings and vary significantly, so ask about noise, views and location in relation to the water and road when you make a reservation.

New seaside villas offer more room and luxury. Each one- and two-bedroom air-conditioned unit has a kitchen and is equipped with ceiling fan, TV, VCR, and Internet access. The living area has a sleeper-sofa and opens onto a large private balcony. Deluxe villas have oversized bathrooms with whirlpool tubs.

Sugar Mill Hotel ☆☆, Little Apple Bay, PO Box 425, Road Town, Tortola, BVI. ☎ 800-462-8834 or 495-4355; fax 495-4696; www.sugarmillhotel.com. 21 rooms and suites, 2 villas. $325.

This elegant hideaway is built around the ruins of a 17th-century sugar mill and rum distillery nestled in a garden overlooking the sea. It is superbly serene. The perfect retreat. Owners Jeff and Jinx Morgan are writers who specialize in travel and food, so they are well acquainted with the de-

mands and expectations of vacationers. Spacious rooms and suites have one king or two twin beds, a private balcony and kitchenettes with refrigerators. All have ceiling fans, and some are air conditioned. The air-conditioned two-bedroom villa has a full kitchen, cable TV with VCR and sea views. Guests often gather around the shady circular swimming pool during the day and at the romantic gazebos beside the bar in the evening before dinner in the fabulous Sugar Mill Restaurant. Lunch is served at Islands Restaurant on the beach. (See *Where to Eat* for a full review.)

Long Bay Beach Resort ☆, Long Bay Beach, PO Box 433, Road Town, Tortola, BVI. ☎ 800-943-4699 or 495-4252; fax 495-4677; www.longbay.com. 122 rooms and villas. $320.

The mile-long white-sand beach on Long Bay is one of the prettiest on Tortola, and this full-service resort spread across 52 acres provides everything you need to enjoy it. Recently updated rooms are tucked into the lush tropical vegetation that grows up the hillsides. Each spacious unit is air conditioned and outfitted with a ceiling fan, small refrigerator and cable TV. All have large balconies or patios with dramatic ocean views.

Beachfront cabanas that are built on stilts have extra luxuries such as VCRs, hammocks on the deck and deluxe bathrooms. Larger family-style rooms have sitting areas, oversized balconies, separate shower rooms and walk-in closets. Luxurious homes and apartments with up to five bedrooms are available, also. Guests in all accommodations may use two fresh-

water swimming pools with a swim-up bar and waterslide, the fitness center, tennis courts with complimentary clinics and a nine-hole pitch-and-putt golf course. Surfboards, sea kayaks and snorkeling equipment may be rented on the beach. The Garden Restaurant and the Beach Café provide meals throughout the day, and bands perform a couple of nights each week.

Lambert Beach Hotel, PO Box 534, East End, Tortola, BVI. ☎ 284-495-2877; fax 495-2876; www.lambertbeachresort .com. 38 rooms, suites and villas. $160.

This quiet retreat is located on eight acres along a half-mile-long white-sand beach at the bottom of a steep road that keeps curious explorers away. Although the resort doesn't attempt to be plush or extravagant, the comfortable air-conditioned Mediterranean-style bungalows have an air of sophistication. Each unit has a ceiling fan, hair dryer and wet bar. Guests enjoy free use of snorkeling equipment, boogie boards and kayaks on the beach. In addition, there's a tennis court, a huge swimming pool with a swim-up bar and a club-house with satellite TV.

South Shore

Nanny Cay Marina & Hotel, PO Box 281, Road Town, Tortola, BVI. ☎ 866-284-4683 or 494-4895; fax 494-0555; www.nannycay.com. 40 studio rooms. $160.

If you like to stay busy during vacations, this hotel between West End and Road Town is right for you. Scuba diving, sailing lessons, boat charters, watersports equipment and bikes all are available on the dock at Nanny Cay. You can stay in one of the air-conditioned rooms overlooking the marina and

schedule a different activity every day. Each unit has a kitchenette – excellent for keeping picnic supplies handy – and there's an on-site swimming pool and tennis court in case you have a free block of time. Peg Leg Landing Restaurant, Plaza Café, several shops and a supermarket also are in the marina area.

Fort Recovery Beachfront Villas ☆, West End, Tortola, BVI. ☎ 800-367-8455 or 284-495-4354; www.fortrecovery. com. 17 villas. $260.

Driving from Road Town toward the West End, you'll spot this little resort tucked among the palms and bougainvillea on the south shore. Ruins of the Dutch fort that was built here in the 1600s are still standing and provide a commendable view of the channel and nearby islands. The one- to four-bedroom villas are directly on a small beach and have air-conditioned bedrooms, a spacious living area, a full or partial kitchen and an ocean-view patio. There's no restaurant, but a complimentary continental breakfast is served in the villas each morning, and you can arrange to have dinner served each evening.

◆ Where to Eat

The dilemma on Tortola is whether to eat West Indian rotis on a sandy patio at the water's edge or enjoy international cuisine at a romantic little restaurant tucked into the hills overlooking the Sir Francis Drake Channel. There are more than 60 restaurants on the small island and no fast-food chains. Every establishment has its own personality and each chef takes great pride in preparing competition-level meals. In fact, Tortola is home to several local and international award-winning cooks.

> **TIP:** *Restaurants often change their hours during low season, and some close for several weeks during the summer. Call ahead to avoid disappointment.*

DINING WITH THE STARS

The following restaurants are recommended for their excellent food, charming ambience and friendly service. One star (☆) indicates that the restaurant is highly recommended, two stars (☆☆) mean you should make an extra effort to eat there, and three stars (☆☆☆) promise an experience to remember. The rating may be for super value or an amazing view or, perhaps, simply the best "cheeseburgers in paradise."

Don't make the mistake of shunning a restaurant because of its outside appearance. As with the shops, sometimes the best offerings are hidden behind the shabbiest exteriors. If you see local people eating there, give it a try. Tortola also has a fine selection of upscale restaurants with elegant dining rooms and exquisite cuisine. In the mid-range, there are lovely family-owned cafés that serve Caribbean specialties made with fresh produce and mysterious seasonings.

Use the prices given here as a guide to the average price of a mid-range meal per person, excluding drinks and tip. There is no sales tax in the Virgin Islands, but restaurants may add a service charge, so check your bill before you figure your tip.

In & Near Road Town

C & F Restaurant, Purcell Estate, ☎ 284-494-4941. Caribbean. $20. Open nightly, 6:30 pm-11 pm. Credit cards accepted. Reservations recommended in high season.

TORTOLA

Chef Clarence and his wife, Florida, run this popular restaurant that draws a crowd of loyal clients with specialties such as barbecued ribs, seafood curry and grilled fish. Try the conch with lime butter sauce. It's excellent. Homemade cakes and pies make up the dessert offerings. C & F is tricky to find, so call for detailed directions or consider taking a cab. It's off Purcell Road, which is just past the Riteway store, east of Road Town.

Cafesito, Wickham's Cay, ☎ 284-494-7412. West Indian/International. $25. Daily, 10:30 am-11 pm. Credit cards accepted.

Start with sangria or a frozen tropical drink at this open-air café in Romasco Place pavilion facing Waterfront Drive. The cool drink will go well with Spanish tapas. Then move on to coconut shrimp or blackened fish. Everything is good, even the pasta dishes. Live music plays on Wednesday and Saturday nights. Happy hour runs daily from 4:30 pm until 6:30 pm.

Capriccio Di Mare ☆, Waterfront Drive, ☎ 284-494-5369. Italian. Breakfast $6, lunch $9, dinner $12. Monday-Saturday, 8 am-10:30 am and 11 am-9 pm. Credit cards accepted.

This will become your favorite restaurant after one meal. It's owned by Davide and Cele Pugliese, owners of the elegant Brandywine Bay Restaurant. While you may not be able to afford Brandywine on a daily basis, Capriccio fits almost anyone's budget. The pizza is excellent, the pasta dishes divine. The focaccia sandwiches are perfect for lunch. Specials change daily and are always a good choice. In the morning, start with an authentic cappuccino. In the evening, order a Bellini made with fresh peaches. You sit outside on a patio facing the ferry dock and harbor, so the atmosphere is super-casual, but the food is as good it gets anywhere on the island.

Midtown Restaurant, Main Street, ☎ 284-494-2764. Caribbean. Breakfast $6, lunch $10, dinner $15. Monday-Saturday, 7 am-10 pm; Sunday, 7 am-5 pm. No credit cards.

This restaurant isn't for everyone, but if you want to try down-home cooking island-style, come on in. Gloria is the owner/cook who stirs up *souse* (pig's feet stew), cow-foot soup and curried mutton. She also makes a tasty johnnycake and the conch fritters are excellent.

Pusser's Pub, Waterfront Drive, ☎ 284-494-3897; www. pussers.com. English pub food. Lunch $8, dinner $15. Open daily, 11 am-10 pm. Credit cards accepted. Reservations recommended for dinner.

You can't miss the landmark building facing the ferry dock. It's a convenient and dependable place for a meal when you're in town or waiting for the ferry. The menu includes giant burgers, deli sandwiches and meat pies. English ale is available on draft and the bartender whips up wonderful drinks using Pusser's rum. Other Tortola locations are at Soper's Hole on the West End (☎ 284-495-4554), and Marina Cay, by ferry from Trellis Bay (☎ 284-494-2174).

Roti Palace, Main Street on Russel Hill above Samarkand Jewelers, ☎ 284-494-4196. Sandwiches. Breakfast $6, lunch/dinner $12. Monday-Saturday, 7 am-9:30 pm. No credit cards.

First-time visitors to the islands quickly learn that a roti is a wrap, similar to a Mexican burrito, that was introduced to the Caribbean by India. Flat, pan-fried bread is wrapped around various fillings, usually some type of meat, often curried. At Roti Palace, fillings include vegetable, seafood, beef, chicken and goat. Some are served with a side condiment, such as lime-butter sauce or mango chutney. Most customers pick up their rotis to go, but the tiny restaurant has a few tables and chairs for communal dining in. To get there, walk north on Main Street with the harbor to your right, round the corner, then take the next left onto Abbot, which runs below the big purple Bougainvillea Clinic. Roti Palace is tucked into a small building on the left.

Village Cay Restaurant, Village Cay Marina, ☎ 284-494-2771; www.villagecay.com. International. Breakfast $10, lunch $15, dinner $30. Daily, 7:30 am-10 pm. Credit cards accepted. Reservations recommended at dinner.

Join the sailing crowd at this waterfront pub and restaurant. The bar is jammed each afternoon during happy hours, and many patrons stay on for dinner. Dinner is on the pricey side, but breakfast and lunch is reasonable, and the food is dependably good. Steaks and seafood are the most popular items on the menu, and the deli has to-go meals to enjoy on your boat or back at your hotel.

The Dove Restaurant and Wine Bar ☆☆☆, Main Street, Road Town. ☎ 284-494-0313; www.dovebvi.com. Fusion/Continental. $35. Tuesday-Thursday, 6:30 pm-10 pm; Friday-Saturday, 6:30 pm-11 pm; Saturday brunch 10:30 am-2:30 pm. Credit cards accepted. Reservations highly recommended for dinner.

The buzz about this classy new restaurant started the moment it opened. Business people began stopping by for champagne happy hour after work (Tuesday-Saturday, 5-7 pm, champagne cocktails $3), and singles showed up to listen to jazz at the bar or mingle on the shady terrace. Word spread about the 20-plus wines served by the glass (more than 100 served by the bottle), and locals began booking tables to try the dinner offerings. Now, you best call early if you want reservations most any night of the week. The place is small, intimate, eclectic. Look for the Dove signs on Main Street (front entrance) and Waterfront Drive (back terrace).

Virgin Queen, Fleming Street, Road Town, ☎ 284-494-2310. Pizza, West Indian. Lunch/dinner $12. Monday-Friday, 11 am-10 pm; Saturday, 6 pm-10 pm. Credit cards accepted. Reservations suggested for weekend evenings.

Winner of the "Best in the BVI" award for its cheesy pizza, the Queen is understandably popular with families and sports teams, but the menu includes much more. Generous servings of island-style chicken and pork are especially good, and the baby back ribs are a four-napkin treat. If you're in the mood for something a bit more gourmet, try the baked brie or grilled shrimp. Look for the casual eatery on the upper floor of the building across Fleming Street from Rite Way Grocery, a block north of Waterfront Drive. The dining room gets crowded on weekend nights, so call for a reservation to avoid a wait.

Lime 'N' Mango, Treasure Isle Hotel/Waterfront Drive, ☎ 494-2501. Mexican/Caribbean. Breakfast $9, lunch $12, dinner $25. Daily, 7 am-11 pm. Credit cards accepted. Reservations recommended.

You can get surprisingly authentic Mexican dishes such as quesadillas and fajitas at this trendy spot in the Treasure Isle Hotel. Other menu standouts include coconut shrimp and pepper steak. On Saturday nights, a steel pan band plays during the Caribbean barbecue. The restaurant is set in an open garden with dazzling views of the Sir Frances Drake Channel.

Skyworld ☆, Ridge Road, in the hills above Road Town, ☎ 284-494-3567; fax 495-9546. Continental/Caribbean. Lunch $15, dinner $35. Open daily, 10 am-11 pm, kitchen closed 2-5:30 pm. Credit cards accepted. Reservations recommended.

Skyworld sits on one of Tortola's highest peaks, offering a fantastic 360° view from the observation deck. Plan to arrive well before sunset so you can enjoy the panorama from 1,337 feet above Road Town Harbour. Then, settle inside the charming circular dining room for excellent drinks, food and service. Jim Cullimore, the owner and chef, is a fabulously friendly guy and a shameless perfectionist – two desirable traits in a restaurateur. Proper dinner attire is required in the fancier section of the restaurant (collared shirts and long pants for men, dresses or long pants for women) but, if you arrive in shorts, you can order from the same menu and sit in the more casual area. Enjoy one of Jim's specialty drinks from the bar while you watch the sun set beyond the large windows. Then select from the superb menu that includes creative dishes such as conch-stuffed mushrooms, grilled seafood with ginger-butter sauce, chicken breast with mango-hazelnut stuffing and a Key lime pie that is reportedly the best in the BVI.

East End

Brandywine Bay Restaurant ☆, Blackburn Highway/Brandy Wine Bay, ☎ 284495-2301. Northern Italian. $30. Monday-Saturday, 6:30 pm-9 pm. Credit cards accepted. Reservations strongly recommended.

When visitors ask a resident where to go for a romantic dinner, Brandywine will often be the answer. Davide and Cele Pugliese have built an enviable reputation for themselves and their restaurant. Chef Davide is from the Tuscany region of Italy and grew up among excellent cooks. His Australian wife, Cele, is the restaurant's gracious hostess and manager. Together they provide exquisite food in a quixotic setting. The menu changes daily, but always features an ample choice of carefully prepared and artistically seasoned appetizers, entrées and desserts. Main courses center around grilled specialties such as beef, portobello mushrooms, veal chops and fresh fish. Do not miss the homemade tiramisu for dessert. Follow Waterfront Drive east out of Road Town and watch for signs on the south-shore road indicating the turnoff at Brandy Wine Bay, about three miles outside town.

The Last Resort, Trellis Bay/Bellamy Cay, ☎ 284-495-2520. English. Lunch $15, dinner $30. Daily, 12:30 pm-2 pm (lunch), 5 pm-7 pm (happy hour), 7:30 pm (dinner), 9:30 pm (show); the bar is open all day. Credit cards accepted. Reservations strongly suggested.

Book your front-row table well in advance so you won't miss a moment of Tony Snell's nautical entertainment. The Englishman is a legend and every BVI visitor should spend an evening at his after-dinner comedy show. Use the hotline on shore to request a five-minute free ferry ride from Trellis Bay to tiny Bellamy Cay, where you enjoy a huge buffet feast before the show. If you can't make the dinner show, zip over for lunch or just a drink at the bar.

Eclipse Restaurant, Penn's Landing Marina, Fat Hog's Bay, ☎ 284-495-1646. Fusion/International. $30. Daily, 5 pm-10 pm; bar opens at 4 pm. Credit cards accepted. Reservations highly recommended.

You'll drive right past this little hideaway if you're not on the lookout for the "Penn's Landing" sign tucked into the shrubbery on the coast road just west of the bridge to Beef Island. Eclipse is on the water, behind the trees and bushes. It's well worth the hunt. While the restaurant has been an island favorite for years, a couple of new chefs have worldly epicureans raving. Menu offerings include a wide variety of appetizers, including calamari, mussels and tuna carpaccio.

Vegetarians will find a few meatless dishes, including Thai curries, but most entrées feature fresh seafood or tender beef. Splurge on a flaming dessert, then end the evening by sipping an after-dinner drink in the new wine garden.

North Shore

Palm Terrace, Long Bay Beach Resort, ☎ 284-495-4252. International. Lunch $15, dinner $30. Daily, 6:30 pm-9:30 pm. Credit cards accepted. Reservations suggested.

This is the main restaurant for the luxurious Long Bay Beach Resort on the north coast. As you would expect, the atmosphere is casually elegant and the ocean views are enchanting. The menu changes nightly and features nicely spiced Caribbean-style entrées, seafood and grilled steaks, all dressed in savory sauces and accompanied by creative side dishes. Sunday brunch, served 11 am-3 pm, is a popular and leisurely event that includes specialties such as grilled lobster and spicy jerk-seasoned pork steaks.

If you want to dine more casually, opt for a meal at the resort's **1748 Restaurant and Bar** set in a seaside sugar mill. The menu offers luscious scallops in coconut sauce, spicy fish fritters and grilled steaks with innovative sauces. Breakfast is served daily from 7:30 am-11 am and lunch service runs from noon until 3 pm.

The Tamarind Club ☆, Josiah's Bay/Tamarind Club Hotel, ☎ 284-495-2477. International. Breakfast $10, brunch $20, lunch $18, dinner $35. Daily, 8 am-10:30 am; 11 am-3 pm; 6 pm-10 pm; Sunday brunch, 11 am-3 pm; Happy Hour, 4 pm-7 pm. Credit cards accepted. Reservations highly recommended for dinner and Sunday brunch.

Since Chef Dwight took over the kitchen in early 2005, this casual restaurant has consistently received superb reviews. The breakfast and lunch menus hold few surprises, but the dinner offerings, which change daily, are innovative and diverse. On a recent visit, our table shared several seafood appetizers, passed around one of the homemade soups, then dug into a varied selection of main courses, including crab-stuffed chicken breast and freshly-caught snapper with a spicy creole sauce. No one had room for dessert, but we ordered crème brulée, anyway. Good decision. Clint, the bartender, mixes wonderful drinks, so arrive early to watch the sun set before dinner. Even better, come out any afternoon to enjoy the Tamarind Club pool with swim-up bar. The Sunday brunch has become very popular, so if you want a reservation, call early.

Turtle Restaurant ☆, Lambert Bay/Lambert Beach Resort, ☎ 284-495-2877. Caribbean/International. Breakfast $10, lunch $20, dinner $30. Daily, 7:30 am-3 pm and 7 pm-10 pm. Credit cards accepted. Reservations suggested.

Come to the Turtle in the evening for sea-view romance. During the day, this is a casual, friendly, open-air restaurant and bar that caters to resort guests and beach visitors with standard American-style breakfast and lunch fare. But, as the sun begins to set each evening, the dining pavilion turns sensual with lighted candles and torches and chicly-dressed patrons gazing starry-eyed at the lovely view of the sea and palm trees turning deep shades of purple. Dinner guests tend to be a mix of in-the-know locals and tourists who've heard about the fine cuisine featuring Italian specialties and fresh seafood. If you're looking for a place to sample a large variety of island dishes, you can't go wrong with the Sunday brunch buffet. There's a nice selection of cold salads and appetizers, a couple of hot meat selections that are carved to order, several side dishes, and enticing homemade desserts. Call early for reservations because this buffet has become a popular after-church gathering spot for locals.

Palm's Delight ☆, Carrot Bay, ☎ 284-495-4863. West Indian. $20. Monday-Saturday, 6 pm-10 pm.

You're going to love Iona Dawson and her down-home cooking. She used to work at Long Bay and Skyworld Restaurants, but had a dream of opening her own business. So, in 1994, she and her son, Tony, started cooking, and fans haven't let them stop. The menu includes sautéed shrimp, grilled fish, barbecue and rotis. One of her best creations is the chicken breast in ginger-wine sauce. In addition to excellent meals, the waterside restaurant serves up fantastic views and friendly ambience. Most of the staff are family members, and many customers are friends – or they will be before they leave. Look for Palm's Delight under the swaying palms across from two churches in the center of Carrot Bay.

North Shore Shell Museum, Carrot Bay, ☎ 284-495-4714. West Indian. Breakfast $12, lunch $18, dinner, $35. Daily, 8 am-10 am; 10:30 am-3 pm; and 6 pm-10 pm. Reservations recommended for dinner.

Egbert and Mona Donovan run the most unusual restaurant on the island. The open-air building has a restaurant and bar on the upper level and an odd but interesting museum on the lower level.

A dirt path meanders through tables displaying coral, shells and other beach findings. Most of the exhibits are for sale. The restaurant features hearty breakfasts, island-style lunches and gourmet dinners spotlighting grilled fresh lobster and fish. All entrées come with island-style side dishes such as rice and beans. Happy hour, 4 pm-6 pm daily, is a great time to browse through the museum.

Sugar Mill Restaurant ☆☆☆, Little Apple Bay, ☎ 284-495-4355. International. Lunch $18, dinner $35. Daily, noon-2 pm and 7 pm-9 pm. Credit cards accepted. Reservations required for dinner.

This romantic restaurant, set in a beautifully restored 340-year-old sugar mill, has a long list of admirable accolades, and owners Jeff and Jinx Morgan recently published a cookbook full of recipes. Check with your local bookstore or order *The Sugar Mill Caribbean Cookbook* (Harvard Common Press) through the restaurant's website at www.sugarmillhotel/restaurant. The menu changes daily, so you can return several times to try different dishes. Favorites include wild mushroom bisque, curried banana soup, scallops in puff pastry with roasted red pepper sauce, Jamaican jerk pork roast and desserts such as banana-almond mousse. A lovely gazebo bar overlooks the bay and the candle-lit main restaurant is decorated with Caribbean art and lush plants.

TORTOLA

During the day, lunch is served in the beachfront **Islands Restaurant**. The innovative menu there features salt fish fritters, vegetarian pita sandwiches, burgers and nachos.

Stanley's Welcome Bar, Cane Garden Bay, ☎ 284-495-9424. Casual grill. Lunch $10, dinner $18. Daily, 10 am-late.

Stanley's was one of the first bar/cafés built on the fabulous stretch of sand that lines Cane Garden Bay and has built up a loyal following over the years. Drop in for one of the best burgers in the BVI. Other choices include fried chicken, baby back ribs, fresh fish and pasta. A band often plays on weekend nights, when the music can be heard all along the beach.

Myett's, Cane Garden Bay, ☎ 284-495-9649; www.myettent.com. International. Lunch $12, dinner $20. Daily, 10 am-10 pm. Credit cards accepted. Reservations suggested for dinner.

Myett's tropical garden is hidden among seagrape trees and palms, but when you venture into the lush growth, you find a gorgeous restaurant pavilion and terrace. Lunch and dinner are served daily. The menu features fresh seafood, chicken, veggies, and steaks cooked by chef Luigi on an outdoor grill. A luscious aroma drifts through the trees and out onto the sandy beach, drawing a hungry crowd. A live band plays on weekends and Monday evenings. Look for Sandman, the owner, at the bar, whipping up frozen treats with the local Callwood rum. Happy hour runs from 5-7pm daily.

West End

The Jolly Roger, Soper's Hole, ☎ 284-495-4559; www.jollyrogerbvi.com. West Indian/International. Breakfast/lunch $10, dinner $15. Daily, 8 am-midnight (closed in September).

Credit cards accepted. Reservations suggested for dinner.

This popular sailor hangout overlooks the passage between the tiny island of Frenchman's Cay and the main island of Tortola, near the West End ferry dock. It's a great place for boat-watching. On weekends the nautical restaurant hosts a barbecue with live music for dancing. A regular menu includes well-prepared and reasonably priced meals, with blackboard specials in the evening. Fish chowder, conch fritters, grilled seafood and inventive pizzas top the crowd-pleaser list.

The Clubhouse Restaurant, Frenchman's Cay Hotel, ☎ 284-495-4844; www.frenchmans.com/restar.htm. Caribbean/Continental. Breakfast $10, lunch $15, dinner $25. Open Tuesday-Saturday, 8 am-10:30 am, 11:30 am-2:30 pm and 6:30 pm-9 pm; Sunday, noon-3 pm and 6:30 pm-9 pm. Credit cards accepted. Reservations suggested for brunch and dinner.

An added perk when you dine at this hotel restaurant overlooking the Sir Francis Drake Channel is complimentary use of the beach, pool and tennis court. The regular menu features fresh seafood specialties such as escargot and Caribbean lobster; the Sunday barbecue buffet is especially popular. West Indian dishes and the signature chocolate mousse are exceptional.

◆ Nightlife

Pick up the current issue of *Limin' Times* (☎ 494-2413; www.limin-times.com) at most any hotel to find out what entertainment is available for the week. Bands and solo musicians play at many restaurants and hotels on weekend nights and Sunday afternoons, and you stand a good chance of seeing live entertainment somewhere on the island any evening of the week.

LIMIN'

The *Dictionary of the Virgin Islands English Creole* defines the verb "to lime," as meaning *to hang around idly* or *to go out on the town*. Be sure to do a lot of limin' while you're in the BVI.

Try to see the **Heritage Dancers**, a 22-member group that performs traditional dances celebrating historical island events, such as emancipation. They dance at hotels on a rotating schedule, so ask at the activities desk of your hotel or check *Limin' Times* for performance dates and locations.

Bomba's Beach Shack is best known for its all-night full-moon parties, where the house punch is spiked with a "secret" ingredient rumored to be hall-ucinogenic mushrooms, but is probably homemade rum. A full moon and weird punch

© Bomba's Shack

isn't required to make Bomba's a truly unique experience. The tumble-down shanty owned by Bomba Smith is open every day from 10 am to midnight, and top-notch bands play during the all-you-can-eat barbecue dinner on Wednesday and Sunday evenings. The Shack is on the beach at Cappoon's Bay, next to Apple Bay. ☎ 284-495-4148.

Quito's Gazebo serves as the stage for local recording star Quito Rymer and his band, The Edge. Call ahead or check *Limin Times* for scheduled performances, but you'll find Quito sings solo or with his group at this casual bar on most weekend nights. Other local musicians perform at the Gazebo at various times, also. If you're looking for a good meal, try the Friday night fish fry or Sunday evening Caribbean buffet. The food is good, the atmosphere is jovial, and you can't beat the entertainment. Quito's is on the beach at Cane Garden Bay. ☎ 284-495-4837.

Jolly Roger offers a variety of bands and music styles on Friday and Saturday nights beginning around 8 pm. Drop by for dinner, then stay to enjoy the music. The restaurant/bar/inn is near the ferry dock at West End. ☎ 284-495-4559.

Pusser's Landing has a pig roast with live entertainment starting at 6 pm on Fridays. Local bands often play on Wednesday, Thursday and Saturday nights as well. The bar turns out excellent drinks, such as their famous Painkiller, made with Pusser's rum. Happy hour runs every afternoon from 5 pm until 7 pm, and Thursday is nickel beer night 8 pm-10 pm. Pusser's is located across Waterfront Drive from the ferry dock in Road Town. ☎ 284-494-4554.

The Last Resort is known for the after-dinner entertainment of Tony Snell. He dishes out a cabaret-style comedy show geared toward the yachting crowd every night. Happy hour starts at 5 pm, a buffet dinner begins at 7:30 pm, and Tony takes center stage at 9:30 pm. A free ferry provides transportation from the dock at Trellis Bay on Beef Island to The Last Resort on tiny Bellamy Cay. Call well ahead for a front-row table. ☎ 284-495-2520.

Trellis Bay holds a family-friendly **Fireball Full Moon Party** on Beef Island each month. A West Indian barbeque dinner gets things rolling around 7pm, followed by live music, dancing, fire-juggling and entertainment by costumed stilt-walking Mocko Jumbies. About 9 pm, artist Aragorn Dick-Read (owner of Aragorn's Studio, page 308) lights his famous fireball sculptures on the beach. Trellis Bay is on the north coast of Beef Island, behind the airport as you drive east on the main road; look for signs to the secondary road. For information about the party, call one of the sponsoring businesses: **Trellis Bay Cyber Café**, ☎ 284-495-2447, or **Aragorn's Studio**, ☎ 284-495-1849.

Bat Cave is one of the most popular dance clubs and night-meet spots on the island. It is designed to resemble Batman's cave, with music and laser lights cutting through the mechanized haze surrounding the raised, circular dance floor. Black lights create a nightclub atmosphere around the well-stocked bar, and the crowd spills out onto the two-tier outdoor deck, the only place where smoking is allowed. Jazz plays several nights each week, happy hour is 5 pm-7 pm daily, and music plays late into the night. Look for the cave next door to Spaghetti Junction on Waterfront Drive, east of town. ☎ 284-494-4880.

Virgin Gorda

Necker Island

Pajaros Point

Eustatia Island

Prickly Pear Island

Mosquito Island

Mountain Point

Great Dog

Long Bay

Nail Bay

Blunder Bay

Little Leverick Bay

North Sound

Great Leverick Bay

Biras Creek

Gun Point

Gun Creek

South Sound

South Sound Bluff

Gorda Peak National Park

Mountain Trunk Bay

Mahoe Bay

Pond Bay

Savannah Bay

Black Point

NORTH SOUND ROAD

Little Dix Bay

Casey Bay

Colison Point

St. Thomas Bay

Taylor's Bay

Spanish Town (The Valley)

Little Fork Nat'l Park

Spring Bay

The Baths

Stoney Bay

Crooks Bay

Copper Mine Point

PLACES TO STAY & EAT
1. Little Dix Bay
2. Old Yard Village
3. Biras Creek
4. The Bitter End
5. Leverick Bay Resort
6. NailBay Resort
7. Top of the Baths
8. Mad Dog
9. Giorgio's Table
10. Mineshaft

N

HUNTER PUBLISHING

1 MILE

1 KM

© 2007 HUNTER PUBLISHING, INC

Virgin Gorda

◆ Overview

Virgin Gorda is a long, skinny island with a fat middle. From a distance, the mountain dominating its wide center makes it look a bit like an ample reclining woman or, perhaps, a pregnant woman. Thus, an explanation for Columbus's Spanish name for the island, Virgin Gorda, meaning "the fat virgin."

The southern end of the island is an arid parcel known as **The Valley**. Its western shore is famous for an area called **The Baths**, which is covered by huge granite boulders that form an intriguing network of seawater pools and cave-like passageways. **Devil's Bay**, another boulder-enclosed cove to the south, is linked to The Baths by a coastal trail.

Granite boulders at The Baths.

Spanish Town is the main settlement and home to **Virgin Gorda Yacht Harbor**, which has dock space for 150 boats, a dive center, restaurants, a grocery store and various shops. A narrow strip of land connects this rather flat southern section to a broad, mountainous area in the middle of the island, which is topped by 1,500-foot **Gorda Peak**, the centerpiece of **Virgin Gorda National Park**.

A second narrow strip of land branches off the "fat" central section to form the **North Sound**, a water-lover's paradise and one of the world's most sheltered coves. Most of the resorts and restaurants scattered along the Sound are accessible only by boat.

> **NOTE:** You may see "The Valley" and "Spanish Town" used interchangeably on maps, ferry schedules and brochures. In this book, The Valley refers to the entire southern portion of the island; Spanish Town refers to the settlement encompassing the dock and Yacht Harbour.

◆ Getting There

By Air

A short landing strip east of Spanish Town has received small aircraft for many years. However, the government recently took control of the airfield and warned that it may close the facility due to safety concerns. Ferry service is far more reliable.

By Ferry

Most visitors arrive by boat from Tortola. **Speedy's Ferries** (☎ 284-495-5240) and **Smith's Ferries** (☎ 340-775-7292) offer daily service between Road Town, Tortola and The Valley on Virgin Gorda. The trip takes about 35 minutes and round-trip tickets are $25 for adults, $15 for seniors and children. Speedy's also makes runs between St. Thomas and Virgin Gorda on Tuesday, Thursday and Saturday. Round-trip tickets are $60 for adults, $40 for children.

North Sound Express (☎ 284-495-2138) provides powerboat service between the dock on Beef Island, near the airport, to Leverick Bay and The Bitter End Yacht Club on North Sound, and to Spanish Town on Virgin Gorda. The 30-minute trips cost $40 round trip to North Sound and $30 to Spanish Town.

◆ Getting Around

By Taxi

Taxis meet the ferries when they arrive at the dock near Spanish Town. Drivers will drop you off anywhere on the island or take you on a guided tour. If you want to eat or shop at Yacht Harbour, you can walk there along a path through a fenced, but public, field to the right of the dock.

Taxis are easy to find at Yacht Harbour and The Baths, but if you want to arrange for transportation or a tour, phone one of the following: **Mahogany Taxi**, ☎ 284-495-5469; **Andy's Taxi**, ☎ 284-495-5252; **United BVI Taxi Federation**, ☎ 284-494-2743. Expect the fare to be about $3 per person anywhere in The Valley and about $20 to Leverick Bay or Gun Creek for up to four passengers.

By Car

You'll enjoy Virgin Gorda more if you have a car for touring and exploring on your own. Expect to pay around $50 to $60 per day for a car or jeep, but you sometimes can get a better deal off-season.

RENTAL CAR AGENCIES	
Speedy's Car Rental	☎ 284-495-5240; fax 495-5755
Andy's Car & Jeep Rental	☎ 284-495-5252
L & S Jeep Rental	☎ 284-495-5297
Mahogany Car Rental	☎ 284-495-5469; fax 495-5072

◆ Touring the Island

The Virgin Gorda Tours Association will pick you up at the ferry dock and take you on a tour of the island for about $30 per person. Make arrangements by calling Andy Flax (of Andy's Car and Jeep Rental and Andy's Taxi) at ☎ 284-495-5252.

Independent Driving Tour

Touring on your own is easy, since one main road runs from the southern tip of the island, over the central mountain, to Gun Creek and Leverick Bay on the North Sound. Most of the North Sound is not accessible by land, but you can get to Biras Creek and the Bitter End Yacht Club by ferry from Gun Creek.

> **TIP:** Pick up maps and brochures at the **BVI Tourist Board** office at Yacht Harbour in Spanish Town. ☎ 284-495-5182.

The Baths ☆☆, a majestic creation of nature, is an area on the southwestern shore filled with huge, precariously balanced boulders that form a maze of warm sea-water pools and interconnecting tunnels. This premier tourist attraction is about 15 minutes by car from the ferry dock. It is part of a 682-acre site protected by the BVI National Parks Trust

Opposite: The Baths © Sjm1123/Dreamstime

(www.bvinationalparkstrust.org) that includes **Devil's Bay**, **Spring Bay** and the **Copper Mine Point**.

Take the main road south to the signed entrance to The Baths, park in the circular lot and follow the twisting path down to the beach. The walk takes less than 10 minutes; although the hike down isn't difficult, it becomes so when you're loaded down with beach gear and snorkeling equipment. Wear good shoes, watch for slick rocks and leave non-essentials locked in your car. The sometimes-rocky path winds through a patch of cactus and shrubs, ending in a shady palm thicket near the boulder-strewn white-sand beach.

Snorkeling is good along the reefs offshore, and it's great fun climbing around the towering weather-worn boulders.

> **TIP:** *If the surf is rough, as it can be in the winter, avoid the open water and wander through the boulders at the south end of the beach until you find a calm pool in a deserted grotto.*

Adventurous types will want to pick their way over the slippery boulders, through magnificent little caves, to **Devil's Bay** ☆☆. A few unobtrusive ropes and wooden ladders have been placed at the most perilous points, but wear some type of shoe for traction.

Turbulent sea at Devil's Bay.

Devil's Bay is less dramatic and less crowded than The Baths, and you'll find good snorkeling sites off the north end of the white-sand beach. If you don't want to tackle the coastal route over the boulders, you can hike to Devil's Bay on an inland path that begins in the parking circle. A trail map is posted in the gazebo-like shelter near Top of the Baths Restaurant. Allow about 15 minutes to make your way along the path to the beach. You'll hike through an arid area filled with lovely sage, frangipani, tamarind and cactus.

Watch for ground lizards, small geckos and harmless little snakes.

Copper Mine Point is the site of a deserted mine that was first excavated by the Spanish more than 400 years ago. All that remains today are the ruins of a smokestack, boiler house and cistern used by Cornish miners who abandoned the area in 1867. The structures sit on a dramatic bluff that juts out above the Atlantic. Views from here are stunning, but the ruins are fragile and dangerous to climb.

Copper Mine Point ruins.

Little Fort National Park, off the main road about a half-mile south of Yacht Harbour, is a 36-acre wildlife sanctuary. The remains of an old Spanish fort are hidden among vegetation and bounders in the park. You can cool off with a swim-and-snorkel break at a site just offshore known as the **Aquarium** or **Fischer's Rocks**. You'll see colorful fish along a shallow sponge-and-coral reef. This site also is a good beach dive, if

VIRGIN GORDA

you have your own equipment. Be careful about boat traffic; always use a floating flag to mark your presence.

◆ Adventures on Water

Best Beaches

In addition to **The Baths** and **Devil's Bay**, a string of less-crowded beaches line the west coast south of the ferry dock near Spanish Town. All the beaches are reached most easily by boat, but you can reach **Spring Bay** and **The Crawl** on Lee Road, a signed secondary road off the main road, less than two miles south of Spanish Town. Beautiful Spring Bay has a white-sand beach and The Crawl, a seawater pool formed by rocks, is fun for snorkeling.

Savannah Bay and **Pond Bay** are north of Spanish Town on the narrow strip of land that joins The Valley to the wide portion of the central island. Watch for a secondary road to

Savannah Bay.

Savannah Bay a short distance past Olde Yard Inn. The turn off for Pond Bay is marked by a sign for Mango Bay Resort. Both bays have beautiful sandy beaches that often are deserted.

Long Bay offers excellent snorkeling. It's located farther along the partly-unpaved secondary road that leads to Pond Bay. You'll drive about 15 minutes after you turn off the main road. Once you arrive, you'll find a long stretch of sand and calm water.

Leverick Bay is at the end of the main road and the last beach that can be reached by land on the North Sound. Pusser's Resort, Leverick Bay Watersports and Dive BVI are located here, and there's plenty of activity, especially on weekends.

Scuba Diving & Snorkeling

Dive boats based on Virgin Gorda often take passengers to the same dive sites in the Sir Frances Drake Channel that are

Looking out toward the Dog Islands.

popular with divers from Tortola. Additional favorites are located around the uninhabited **Dog Islands** off the northwest coast of Virgin Gorda. The islands are protected by the BVI National Parks Trust as nesting grounds for birds.

The Coral Gardens off the south end of Great Dog is a good dive for beginners. Coral, of course, is the star attraction here, and you may spot lobsters and fish such as snappers and spotted drums as you swim along the reef at depths of 10 to 60 feet. Stingrays and turtles are seen in sandy areas. Nearby, you may spot an airplane wreck in about 40 feet of water. It was deliberately sunk to form an artificial reef.

The Chimney is very popular with divers of all levels. It's at a depth of 15 to 45 feet in a gorgeous bay on the west side of

Spanish hogfish, The Chimney

Great Dog. Snorkeling is excellent along the shore and novice divers enjoy the Fish Bowl that's directly below the moorings. Various types of colorful fish congregate here, waiting for handouts from divers. The Chimney, north of the Fish Bowl, is a wall covered in white sponges in a narrow opening between two large boulders.

Bronco Billy offers coral arches, canyons and boulders off the northwest coast of George Dog. Skilled snorkelers find interesting coral and fish near the shore.

DIVE OPERATORS

The two dive operators on Virgin Gorda offer two-tank dives for $85-$95, one-tank dives for around $70. They also arrange night dives, snorkel trips and training courses. Bring your internationally accepted certification card if you want to rent equipment, get air fills or participate in guided tours designed for experienced divers. Introductory dives and resort courses are available if you're not certified.

Kilbrides Sunchaser Scuba is on the dock at the Bitter End Resort, but the custom-outfitted dive boats will rendezvous with private yachts or pick up divers anywhere in the North Sound area. They also make trips to Anegada and Saba Rock. Snorkelers are welcome to come along. ☎ 800-932-4286 or 284-495-9638; fax 495-7549; www.sunchaser scuba.com.

Dive BVI has locations at Yacht Harbor in Spanish Town and at Leverick Bay on the North Sound, as well as at Marina Cay off Beef Island. They are a PADI 5-star center with instruction at all levels. Custom-designed dive boats from both locations rendezvous with private yachts and the Leverick Bay boat picks up divers on North Sound. Weekly trips go to Anegada. ☎ 800-848-7078 or 284-495-5513; fax 495-5347; www.divebvi.com.

Boating & Sailing

The Bitter End Yacht Club offers a variety of boating excursions. Call about snorkeling trips on the 40-foot *Ponce de Leon*, motorboat jaunts to Anegada on the 50-foot *Prince of Wales* and cocktail cruises around the North Sound. You can also rent sailboats, motorboats and dinghies. ☎ 284-494-2746 or 800-872-2392; www.beyc.com.

Leverick Bay Watersports offers full-day trips to Anegada on a 33-foot cigarette boat. The center also rents Hobie cats, powerboats, Sunfish and kayaks. ☎ 284-495-7376; www.watersportsbvi.com.

Spirit of Anegada takes passengers on guided half- and full-day sightseeing and snorkeling tours to various islands, including Anegada. The traditional gaff-rigged schooner also is available for private charter. ☎ 284-499-0901; www.spiritofanegada.com

Spice Charters arranges sailing-snorkeling trips on a 51-foot sloop out of Leverick Bay. ☎ 284-495-7044.

Euphoris Cruises and **Powerboat Rentals**, based at Yacht Harbour, offers rentals and water-taxi service on a variety of boats, including a captained 49-foot Albin Trawler, a 28-foot Bertram and 21- to 24-foot Makos and Robalos with awnings. ☎ 284-494-5511; www.boatsbvi.com.

North Sound Watersports offers a 30-foot Bertram glass-bottom boat, either crewed or self-charter, for day-trips, snorkeling and diving. ☎ 284-495-7558.

Watersports & Sportfishing

Bitter End Yacht Club (☎ 284-494-2746) and **Leverick Bay Watersports Center** (☎ 284-495-7376) offer all types of boats and equipment for virtually any watersport that's enjoyed in the North Sound area. Sportfishing is available through **Charter Virgin Gorda**, ☎ 284-495-7421.

The Nick Trotter Sailing School, at the Bitter End Yacht Club, teaches beginning and advance courses in sailing. ☎ 284-494-2745.

© Spirit of Anegada

VIRGIN GORDA

◆ Adventures on Foot

Hiking

Gorda Peak is the highest point on the island at 1,500 feet. Its the centerpiece of the 265-acre **Virgin Gorda Peak National Park**. Two connecting hiking trails to the summit are maintained by the BVI National Park Trust. Both begin on the west side of the main road north of the narrow strip of land that connects The Valley to North Sound. Although the trails are rated moderate, you make a steep ascent on a rocky path and shoes with good tread are essential. Allow about 45 minutes to reach the peak, where you will find an observation deck that's elevated 30 feet above the ground to provide a panoramic view over the treetops. Bring along binoculars and a camera with a zoom lens.

◆ Shopping

Spanish Town

Virgin Gorda Yacht Harbour (☎ 284-495-5500) in Spanish Town is the island's hub and has a small selection of stores surrounding an open-air atrium called **The Courtyard**. You'll find other shops and vendor stalls at the large resorts and in the parking circle at The Baths.

Located at Yacht Harbour Courtyard are the following:

Fill your picnic hamper or refrigerator with fresh produce and frozen foods from **Buck's Food Market**. They also carry a selection of beer, wine and liquor and the deli center prepares sandwiches and take-out meals. ☎ 284-495-5423; fax 495-7493.

The Wine Cellar and Bakery stocks a complete range of spirits and has its own bakery that turns out bread, cookies and pastries. Most days, the bakery staff prepares outstanding take-out sandwiches. ☎ 284-495-5250.

Spanish Town
& The Valley

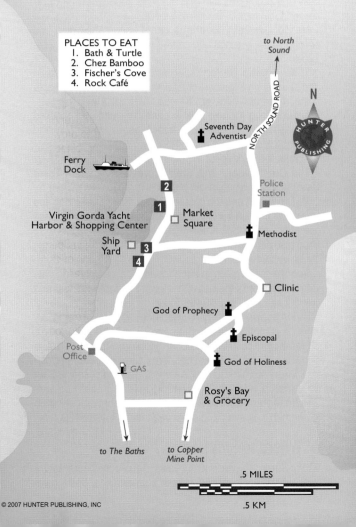

PLACES TO EAT
1. Bath & Turtle
2. Chez Bamboo
3. Fischer's Cove
4. Rock Café

to North Sound

NORTH SOUND ROAD

N

HUNTER PUBLISHING

Seventh Day Adventist

Ferry Dock

Police Station

Virgin Gorda Yacht Harbor & Shopping Center

Market Square

Methodist

Ship Yard

Clinic

God of Prophecy

Episcopal

Post Office

God of Holiness

GAS

Rosy's Bay & Grocery

to The Baths

to Copper Mine Point

.5 MILES

.5 KM

© 2007 HUNTER PUBLISHING, INC

The Virgin Gorda Craft Shop displays the work of local artisans and features items such as jewelry, shell crafts and straw works. ☎ 284-495-5137.

Kaunda's Kysy Tropix is a camera and music store that sells and processes film and stocks a good selection of recorded local music. ☎ 284-495-5638.

Margo's Jewelry Boutique offers handcrafted gold and silver jewelry, sarongs and carved wood sculptures. ☎ 284-495-5237.

Thee Artistic Gallery specializes in luxurious 14k gold and sterling silver pieces, crystal, museum items, collectable coins, maps and gifts. ☎ 284-495-5104; fax 495-5761.

Island Drug Centre has a pharmacy and well-stocked shop selling cosmetics, paperback books, toys, film and greeting cards. ☎ 284-495-5449.

Across the parking lot at Yacht Harbor are:

The Commissary and Ship Store (aka **Spanish Town Café**) is a combination gift shop/deli/grocery. It's owned by Little Dix Resort and the chef *there* prepares sandwiches and salads for the deli *here*. You can eat inside in air-conditioned comfort or enjoy the harbor view from the outdoor tables. The shop also carries groceries, ice, some clothing and a few gift items. ☎ 284-495-5834.

Scoops is the place to shop for unusual clothing and gifts with Virgin Gorda themes. Check out the "lucky lizards" and colorful sarongs. ☎ 284-495-5722.

BVI Apparel Factory Outlet does custom embroidery work on polo shirts and T-shirts. ☎ 284-494-5511.

Flamboyance has additional shops in Road Town and Soper's Hole on Tortola. The stores carry a variety of duty-free luxury items such as watches, perfumes and leather goods. ☎ 284-494-4099; fax 495-5947.

Pelican Puch Boutique is the island's most elegant shop for women's clothing and swimwear. ☎ 284-495-5599.

◆ Where to Stay

Virgin Gorda caters to water-loving, eco-conscious, nature buffs who value peaceful, simple surroundings, basic comforts and individual attention above all else. There are few accommodations in the budget range, since the BVI is an upscale destination, but you can save on your overall vacation by renting a unit with cooking facilities.

SLEEPING WITH THE STARS

You can browse the Internet as well as we can, and we encourage you to do so. Here you'll find only the best possibilities to fit a variety of budgets. Properties marked with one star (☆) are highly recommended. When a single feature or the overall allure is particularly impressive, you'll find two stars (☆☆) beside the name. Three stars (☆☆☆) means, simply, WOW!

The accommodations listed below are recommended for location, value and comfort. Use the prices given as a guide to the average high-season rate per standard double room. If the review is for an all-inclusive or all-suites resort, the listed price is the lowest available during high-season for two people sharing a room. During low-season, generally from April 15 through December 14, rates drop 25-50%. Expect to pay an additional 10% service charge and 7% tax year-round.

Rental Agencies

If you want to rent a villa or private house, contact:

❖ **Priority Property Management** ☎ 284-495-5201; fax 495-5723; www.priorityproperty.com.

❖ **Virgin Gorda Villas** ☎ 800-848-7081 or 284-495-7421; www.virgingordabvi.com.

In & Around The Valley

Little Dix Bay ☆, West Coast/The Valley, PO Box 70, Virgin Gorda, BVI. ☎ 888-767-3966 or 284-495-5555; fax 495-5661; www.littledixbay.com. 98 rooms and suites. $625.

Some say this resort built by Laurance Rockefeller and managed by the elite Rosewood Company is pretentious and overpriced. However, fans return here year after year for the understated elegance and peaceful atmosphere. Designed

to be as one with nature, the resort emphasizes responsible use of resources and strives to function with minimal disturbance of the environment. But don't imagine a campground; this place is opulent.

Recently renovated rooms are grouped two or four to a cottage and tucked among lush vegetation on a hillside above a dazzling bay. Each spacious air-conditioned unit has a private terrace overlooking the sea or landscaped grounds. Exotic furnishings, stone walls, oversized showers and walk-in closets are some of the features that make the rooms unique. The one-to-one ratio of staff to guests guarantees excellent attention.

There's no pool, which disappoints and surprises some guests, but the sea at magnificent Little Dix Bay is calm enough for swimming and floating aimlessly on an air mattress. Guests have complimentary use of watersports equipment, seven all-weather tennis courts and a fitness center.

Olde Yard Village, Main Road/Valley, Virgin Gorda, BVI. ☎ 800-653-9273 or 284-495-5544, fax 284-495-5986; www.oldeyard village.com. 26 studios and condominiums. $270.

Return visitors to the island won't recognize Olde Yard. It used to be a fine inn. Now it's a fabulous three-building village of individually-owned condominiums with ocean views. The nearest beach is about a mile away at Savannah Bay, but there is a large pool, two tennis courts and a fitness center on site. Each condo has a fully-equipped kitchen, and the Village Café serves meals from early morning through dinner.

Nail Bay Resort, Nail Bay, Virgin Gorda BVI. ☎ 800-871-3551 (US), 800-487-1839 (Canada), 284-494-8000, fax 284-495-5875; www.nailbay.com. 21 rooms and condominiums. $125.

© Nail Bay Resort

You have a wide choice of accommodations at Nail Bay, but whether you stay in a hotel-style room or elegant hillside villa, you're guaranteed a fabulous view and plenty of privacy. The 146-acre resort abuts two beaches on the northwest coast, down a rutted dirt road at the base of Gorda Peak. All units have some type of kitchen or kitchenette, and the pool-side Dog and Dolphin Restaurant serves meals throughout the day. Watersports and tennis are on site.

North Sound

Biras Creek ☆☆☆☆, North Sound, PO Box 54, Virgin Gorda, BVI. ☎ 800-223-1108 or 284-494-3555; fax 494-3557; www.biras.com. 30 suites. $810.

© Biras Creek

Elegant suites at Biras Creek are tucked into lush greenery and have sitting rooms, separate air-conditioned bedrooms, garden showers, minibars and private furnished patios – but no TV. The secluded resort is nestled between hills on a 140-acre peninsula that is inaccessible by land and surrounded on three sides by three different bodies of water. Guests arrive by boat. Walking/biking trails wind through the resort's "nature preserve" property crowned by a

VIRGIN GORDA

© Biras Creek

hilltop stone "castle" that serves as a lobby, library, TV room and meeting lounge. Bercher's Bay beach (shown here) is a walk away.

All meals are included in the room rate, and the Pavilion restaurant serves up splendid views as well as extraordinary meals. Facilities include a freshwater swimming pool, two tennis courts, a watersports center and two private beaches. Biras Creek is a member of the distinguished Relais & Chateaux, an international group that accepts only the most exceptional country inns, hotels, resorts and restaurants.

The Bitter End Yacht Club ☆☆☆, John O'Point/North Sound, PO Box 46, Virgin Gorda, BVI. ☎ 800-872-2392 or 284-494-2745; fax 312-506-6206; www.beyc.com. 85 suites and villas; 3 yachts. $630.

Guests arrive by private ferry from Beef Island, near the airport on Tortola, to begin a vacation devoted to watersports.

© Bitter End Yacht Club

Like summer camp, except with gourmet food, the resort's focus is go-go-go fun from dawn to well after dark. Located on a fabulous deep-water harbor, it features three beaches, a pool, hiking trails, daily outings and unlimited use of kayaks, windsurfers, sailboats and snorkeling gear.

Island-style villas and air-conditioned suites have private verandas with hammocks, refrigerators, ceiling fans, showers with views of the sea and large dressing areas. Meals are served in the Clubhouse Steak and Seafood Grille or the

English Carvery, and live entertainment is presented several times each week.

Leverick Bay Resort, North Sound, PO Box 63, Virgin Gorda, BVI. ☎ 800-848-7081 (US), 800-463-9396 (Canada) or 284-495-7421; fax 495-7367; www.leverickbay.com. 16 rooms and 4 condos. $150.

If you can't stretch the budget to fit one of the top-dollar, arrive-by-boat resorts, Leverick Bay is a good alternative. It's the last stop before  the road ends at North Sound, and you can enjoy most of the bay's attractions from here. Modern, fashionable rooms decorated in pastel colors and island art have balconies that overlook the Sound. Villas, some with private pools, are individually designed with one or two bedrooms, living areas and full kitchens. Pusser's Restaurant sits poolside overlooking the marina and small beach where you may rent watersports equipment.

© Leverick Bay Resort

◆ Where to Eat

DINING WITH THE STARS

Every restaurant we review is recommended, and you will find some marked with stars. One star (☆) indicates that the restaurant is highly recommended, two stars (☆☆) mean you should make an extra effort to eat there, and three stars (☆☆☆) promise an experience to remember. The rating may be for super value or an amazing view or, perhaps, simply the best "cheeseburgers in paradise."

Use the prices given here as a guide to the average price of a mid-range meal per person, excluding drinks and tip. There is no sales tax in the Virgin Islands, but restaurants may add a service charge, so check your bill before you figure your tip.

VIRGIN GORDA

Spanish Town

Bath and Turtle, Yacht Harbour/Spanish Town, ☎ 284-495-5239. International. Breakfast $8, lunch $12, dinner $20. Daily, 7:30 am-10:30 pm. Credit cards accepted. Reservations recommended.

Join the crowd for live entertainment on Wednesday nights at the most popular pub on the island. Any day of the week, courtyard tables are full day and night because of the dependably good and reasonably priced pizzas and burgers. At dinner, the menu includes grilled steaks and fish, lobster, pasta and seafood specialties.

The Baths

Top of the Baths, The Baths, ☎ 284-495-5497. Caribbean/International. Breakfast/lunch $10, dinner $18. Daily, 8 am-10 pm. Credit cards accepted.

Located in the parking area at the island's most popular attraction, this casual restaurant has indoor and outdoor seating, a freshwater swimming pool for customers and fabulous views of the beach and Sir Francis Drake Channel. Burgers and sandwiches are top sellers during most of the day, and Caribbean lobster, grilled fish and filet mignon are on the dinner menu. Many visitors to The Baths enjoy a drink on the patio near the pool after a day on the beach and boulders.

Mad Dog's, The Baths, ☎ 284-495-5830. Light meals and snacks. Breakfast/lunch/snacks $5. Daily, 9 am-7 pm.

With a name like this, no further explanation is necessary. Find this popular bar on the main road just before The Baths. Burgers and sandwiches are available, but most people stop in for the piña coladas. Bring cash because credit cards are not accepted.

The Valley

Chez Bamboo ☆, Main Road/The Valley, ☎ 284-495-5752. French/Creole. $30. Daily, 6 pm-9:30 pm. Credit cards accepted. Reservations recommended.

Look for the colorful latticework on this classy indoor/outdoor restaurant just north of Yacht Harbor. The specialty here is Carib/Creole food with a French twist. Try the bouillabaisse, Louisiana penne or snapper *en papillote*. Be sure to save room for homemade dessert. During high season, live jazz is played for theme-night dinners. Call for scheduled events.

Fischer's Cove Restaurant, Main Road/The Valley, ☎ 284-495-5252. Caribbean/International. Lunch $12, dinner $25. Daily, 8 am-10 pm; Sunday brunch, 11:30 am. Credit cards accepted.

The ocean view is wonderful from this casual open-air restaurant at Fisher's Cove Beach Hotel. Fresh grouper in mustard sauce and mango chicken top the menu, but everything tastes especially delicious in this lovely veranda setting.

The Rock Cafe & Sports Bar, Main Road/The Valley, ☎ 284-495-5482. International/Caribbean. Lunch $15, dinner $25. Daily, 4 pm-midnight. Credit cards accepted. Reservations accepted.

Plan to sit on the gorgeous back deck surrounded by dramatic boulders at this trendy restaurant located just south of Spanish Town. The varied menu features such items as pasta, lobster baked in basil sauce and Mexican specialties. Caribbean bands perform most nights, and you can sample top-brand tequilas and margaritas in the upstairs bar.

Giorgio's Table ☆, Mahoe Bay/The Valley, ☎ 284-495-5684. Italian. Lunch $15, dinner $30. Daily, noon-3 pm, 6:30-9 pm. Credit cards accepted. Reservations recommended for dinner.

This charming restaurant overlooks the Sir Francis Drake Channel from Katitche Point, which separates Pond Bay from Tetor Bay in an area known simply as Mahoe Bay. Get there by taking the secondary road toward the west (left coming from Spanish Town) off the main road. The menu ranges from pizza to veal scaloppine and represents all the regions of Italy. Homemade bread, pasta, sauces and desserts are enhanced by a selection of fine wines.

Mineshaft Café and Pub, Coppermine Road/The Valley, ☎ 284-495-5260. International. Lunch $12, dinner $25. Daily, 11 am-3 pm, 5-10 pm. Credit cards accepted.

Don't miss this entertaining café/bar/golf course run by the Sprauve family. Golf is played on a nine-hole mini-course set among boulders. Great fun for families and groups of friends. The views are fantastic, especially at sunset, when you'll want to meander over to the pub that's built like a mine shaft. A bucket hanging from a pulley on the center ceiling beam is filled with the makings of the bar's signature drink, The Cave In. You can win one free by making a hole-in-one on the golf course. Burgers, sandwiches and other light fare is featured on the café menu.

North Sound

Recommended dining on North Sound is limited to the restaurant at **Leverick Bay** (☎ 284-495-7154, $10), where you can get burgers and sandwiches at the lower-level café beginning at 11 am or grilled fish and island specialties in the evening at the upper-level restaurant, open until 10 pm. You may also catch the ferry at Gun Creek for a ride over to **The Bitter End** (see *Where to Stay*) or call **Biras Creek** (see *Where to Stay*) to request a boat ride from Gun Creek to enjoy the fixed-price gourmet dinner.

◆ Nightlife

After a full day in the sun, most visitors turn in early, but the island has much to offer after dark, especially during high season. Check out the *What's Happenin'* section of **Limin' Times** and the *Entertainment* page in **Welcome** (☎ 284-494-2413; www.bviwelcome.com) for current events and scheduled entertainment. Both publications are widely available free of charge at tourist-oriented businesses.

> **TIP:** *Call the following establishments to confirm their live music schedule, especially during low season.*

Live Music

On weekends nearest the full moon, visitors join locals at **The Mineshaft Café** (☎ 284-495-7154) for an especially jovial celebration, similar to Bomba's Full Moon Party, on Tortola. Throughout the month, the popular restaurant-bar features local bands during Fridays' Ladies Night. Be sure to try the signature drink called The Cave In. The Mineshaft Café and Pub is on Coppermine Road in The Valley, ☎ 495-5260. (For additional information, see *Where to Eat*.)

Elsewhere in The Valley, **Rock Café and Sports Bar** hosts live bands and special menus on Wednesdays and Sundays. It's on the main road and open until midnight all week, ☎ 284-495-5482. The **Bath and Turtle**, at Yacht Harbour in Spanish Town, has a live band during its all-you-can-eat buffet on Wednesdays, ☎ 284-495-5239. **Chez Bamboo**, ☎ 284-495-5752, on the main road, offers a variety of live music during the week. Stop by Fridays for jazz; call for other events. **Fischer's Cove**, ☎ 284-495-5252, has a band playing on Fridays and Tuesdays.

Little Dix Bay, on the west coast, often features live entertainment during the high tourist season. Call for information, ☎ 495-5555. On North Sound, the restaurant at **Leverick Bay** has music by local bands on Fridays and Saturdays. The terrace is a popular spot for sunset drinks every night of the week, ☎ 284-495-7154.

VIRGIN GORDA

Jost Van Dyke

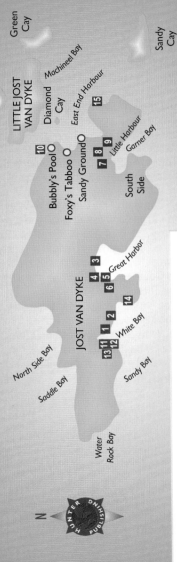

Green Cay

Sandy Cay

LITTLE JOST VAN DYKE

Machineel Bay

Diamond Cay

East End Harbour

15

Bubbly's Pool ○ **10**

Foxy's Tabboo ○

Sandy Ground ○

Little Harbour

7 8 9

Garner Bay

South Side

JOST VAN DYKE

3

4

6 5

Great Harbor

1 2

14

White Bay

13 11

12

Sandy Bay

North Side Bay

Saddle Bay

Water Rock Bay

N

1 MILE

1 KM

© 2007 HUNTER PUBLISHING, INC

PLACES TO STAY & EAT
1. White Bay Sandcastle & Soggy Dollar Bar
2. White Bay Campground & Local Flavor Beach
3. Foxy's Tamarind Bar
4. Corsairs
5. Ali Baba's
6. Rudy's
7. Sidney's Peace & Love
8. Harri's Palace
9. Abe's by the Sea
10. Foxy's Taboo
11. Jewel's Snack Shack
12. Gertrude's
13. One Love Bar
14. White Bay Villas & Seaside Cottages
15. Sandy Ground Estates

Jost Van Dyke

◆ Overview

Little four-mile-long Jost is a sparsely populated barefoot wonderland off the northwest tip of Tortola. *New Horizon* (☎ 284-495-9278; www.jostvandykeferry.com), takes passengers on the 20-minute ride between West End, Tortola and Great Harbor, Jost Van Dyke. One-way tickets are $10 for adults, $6 for children. Call for the schedule, which includes five round-trips each day.

◆ What to Do

Once you arrive in **Great Harbor**, the main settlement, grab a land or water taxi and head for the best beach at **White Bay** on the southwest end of the island. Three friendly locals – George, Bun and Gregory – are usually at the dock when the ferry arrives. **George's Taxi** (☎ 284-495-9253) and **Bun's Taxi** (☎ 284-495-9281) charge $5 to $7 per person for a car ride to White Bay. **Gregory's Brat Water Taxi** and **Bun's Tequila Sea Taxi** charge about the same for a ride over in a motor boat.

> **TIP:** Dorsey Chinnery owns *Jost Van Dyke Safari Services* and gives island tours in a bright red open-air bus. ☎ 284-495-9267.

You can hike to White Bay in 20 or 30 minutes, but it's a long trek if you're carrying snorkeling equipment and beach gear. However, if you want to try **hiking to White Bay**, turn left onto the main road in front of the white Customs Building when you walk off the ferry dock.

Dock leading into Great Harbour.

Continue on this partially-paved road, which has little traffic due to the fact that fewer than 200 people live on the island and fewer than that have cars. You'll go through the little settlement of Great Harbour and up a fairly steep hill. Watch for a sign pointing to a path leading to **White Bay Campground** (see below). It will be the second left. Take it down the hill to the **Local Flavor Bar** (see below) at the campground, where you can stop for lunch or a drink. Then continue along the coast, over a rocky outcropping, to the white-sand beach in front of **Soggy Dollar Bar**.

You also can walk along the road all the way to White Bay. It's not as scenic as the coastal path and you must walk uphill for a few extra minutes before you head down to the bay. But this road may be quicker and easier than the trail, especially if you're carrying a heavy load or wearing sandals.

Snorkeling is not as good as it once was at White Bay. However, you may want to explore **Pull and be Damn' Point** at the campground. Notice where the pelicans are diving, then snorkel out to their feeding ground to watch the fish. Another area with abundant fish is around the rocks at **Changes Point** on the west end of the bay (on your right as you face the water with your back to Soggy Dollar). The reef is almost dead due to careless visitors.

◆ Adventures on Land & Water

Jost Van Dyke Watersports, Great Harbour, ☎ 284-495-0271 (office) or 284-496-7603 (cell); www.jvdwatersports.com. This fairly new operation is run by nature-loving pros who enjoy showing off their island. You have the option of renting a variety of equipment or taking a guided tour. Choices include scuba diving, snorkeling, fishing, kayaking, surfing, mountain biking, hiking and eco-tours. Call the office or reserve online to guarantee the time, equipment and activity you want.

© JVD Watersports

Sea and Land Adventure Sports, White Bay, ☎ 284-499-2269 or 284-495-4966; www.bviadventure.com. On the far end of White Bay Beach, you'll find all types of water toys and sports equipment, including jet boats, skis, paddle boats, water bikes, windsurfers and kayaks. If you prefer to stay on land, try taking an all-terrain vehicle up into the steep hills that rise more than 1,000 feet above the bay, or rent a bike to ride along the coast.

◆ Where to Stay, Eat & Play

Use the prices given here as a guide to the average high-season rate per standard double room. Restaurant prices represent the cost of an average meal for one person, excluding drinks and tip. There is no sales tax in the Virgin Islands, but restaurants may add a service charge, so check your bill before you figure your tip.

SLEEPING & DINING WITH THE STARS

Our suggested list of lodging and restaurants has been kept to a minimum in this book. You can browse the Internet as well as we can, and we encourage you to do so. Here you'll find only the best possibilities to fit a variety of budgets. Properties marked with one star (☆) are highly recommended. When a single feature or the overall allure is particularly impressive, you'll find two stars (☆☆) beside the name. Three stars (☆☆☆) means, simply, WOW!

White Bay

Sandcastle Hotel ☆☆ and **Soggy Dollar Bar** ☆, White Bay, ☎ 284-495-9888; fax 495-9999; www.sandcastle-bvi. com. 6 rooms. White Bay, $225; Soggy Dollar lunch $12, dinner $38.

© Sandcastle Hotel

This is a fantastic casual inn, beach bar and restaurant. A well-known rum drink, the Painkiller, was born here, and the story of its creation is posted beside the bar. There's no dock at White Bay; the bar was named for customers who wade or swim ashore from chartered yachts and arrive with wet money in their pockets. The property is owned and operated by Americans Debby Pearse and Bruce Donath.

All six cottages are within 25 yards of the water and feature king-sized beds, ceiling fans and private bathrooms. Four *rondel* cottages have a daybed to accommodate a third person and a garden shower outside the bathroom with hot water heated by the sun in rooftop tanks. Two recently completed units have indoor showers and air conditioning. Telephones, radios and TVs are conspicuously missing from the rooms, and guests are asked to refrain from using any type of noise-generating appliance.

Soggy Dollar serves breakfast and lunch on the beach every day with eggs and pancakes in the morning and lunch selections ranging from burgers to chicken rotis to flying fish sandwiches.

© Soggy Dollar Bar

The Sandcastle Restaurant serves a four-course fixed-price dinner by candlelight in a lovely upper-level dining room. You must make a reservation before 4 pm so the kitchen can prepare enough meals. Credit cards are accepted.

Coco Locos (☎ 284-495-9401), originally located at Great Harbour, is now selling jewelry and clothing at White Bay, just up the beach from Sandcastle.

Jewel's Snack Shack (☎ 284-495-9286, lunch/snacks $8), a short distance from Soggy Dollar, sits on the sand near the water's edge and is open daily for burgers, hot dogs and snacks.

Gertrudes's (☎ 284-495-9104, lunch $8, dinner $15), serves rotis, lobster salad and burgers every afternoon. The dinner menu includes soups, grilled seafood and chicken, and lobster.

One Love Bar (☎ 284-495-9829, lunch $10, dinner $15) is owned by Seddy Callwood (the famous Foxy's oldest son) and his wife, Raquel. You can't miss the place. It looks like a tumble-down shack held up by car fenders, boat parts and discarded children's toys. This is a family place, and you'll probably see the cute Callwood kids running around, but it's known for serving the best adult-only Bushwhackers in the islands.

White Bay Campground ($70 cabin, $50 tent) and **Local Flavor Beach Bar**, White Bay. ☎ 284-495-9312.

Find this popular campground on the beach just east of Sandcastle. Ivan Chinnery is the friendly and talented islander who owns the campground and occasionally sings and plays guitar at night spots in Great Harbour. He has basic cabins and prepared campsites with electricity.

Local Flavor Beach Bar is known as the on-site "Stress-Free Bar" and operates on an honor system if Ivan isn't around. Call about live entertainment by musicians from throughout the Caribbean and theme-night dinner specials.

White Bay Villas and Seaside Cottages, White Bay, ☎ 800-778-8066 (US) or 284-495-9268, fax 410-571-6693; www.jostvandyke.com. 3 villas, 3 cottages. Rates range from $200 per night to $2,000 per week, depending on facilities, number of bedrooms and location.

White Bay Beach.

A short walk up a hill from the beach, these individual one- to three-bedroom units have full kitchens, decks with sweeping views, and creature comforts such as DVD players and cable TV. Rates are based on weekly rentals. The smallest cottages are perfect hideaways for couples and the largest villa has enough bedrooms and baths for up to eight people. Restaurants and bars on White Bay are within walking distance.

Great Harbour

If you want more excitement than laid-back White Bay can offer, go into Great Harbour. It has an international reputation

The famous Foxy Callwood.

as a beach-party town, largely due to Foxy Callwood at **Foxy's Tamarind Bar**, a casual restaurant and happenin' pub.

Foxy's Tamarind Bar ☆☆, Great Harbour, ☎ 284-495-9258. Lunch $12, dinner $20. Credit cards are accepted. Reservations are expected before 5 pm.

Foxy plays guitar and sings, sometimes made-up-on-the-spot jingles about patrons. His T-shirts are seen around the world; buy one at **The Fox Hole Boutique** (☎ 284-495-9275) next to the open-air restaurant/bar. It's run by Foxy's friendly wife, Tessa.

Foxy's is closed annually from late August through September, but open for lunch Monday-Friday the rest of the year. However, call for hours before you make the trip over, especially during low season. Dinner is served nightly. The menu features barbecue, rotis, burgers, steaks and local lobster.

Several times each year, Foxy throws big events that end in a wild all-night party. These celebrations draw visitors from every island in the Caribbean and most countries around the world. The Halloween Cat Fight is a catamaran race that ends with a Halloween Party. He also hosts a Wooden Boat

Regatta in May, but his New Year's Eve bash is the most popular event of the year.

Corsairs (☎ 284-495-9294, lunch $10, dinner $20) is a fairly new beach bar and restaurant on the coast road at Great Harbour. Vinny is the friendly owner of the bright-pink eatery; Lena tends bar; chef Tom Warner turns out fabulous Mexican, Italian, American and West Indian dishes that include quesadillas stuffed with seafood, pasta tossed with vegetables, homemade French fries and spicy jerk chicken. The restaurant opens for breakfast every morning at 7 am, and the doors don't close until the last patron leaves at night.

Ali Baba's (☎ 284-495-9280, breakfast $5, lunch $10, dinner $25) is the rustic, open-air restaurant next to the Customs house at the dock. It's run by a man named Ali whose family name is, no kidding, Baba. You'll probably meet him if you stop by for breakfast, lunch or dinner. And do stop by. The food is good. All the meals come with side dishes, so you'll get plenty to eat at a reasonable price, and credit cards are accepted. Dinner reservations required.

Rudy's Mariner Inn (☎ 284-495-9282, rooms $90, lunch $12, dinner $25) sits west of the dock, or to the left as you pull into Great Harbour, next door to the Methodist church. This five-room inn is popular with sailors who want to stay in one spot for a day or two, then provision their boat from the stock in Rudy's small store. The restaurant often features live entertainment, and the food is dependably good.

> **TIP:** *Christine's Bakery (☎ 284-495-9281) on the main road in Great Harbour has terrific coconut and banana breads.*

Little Harbour

Little Harbour, on the east end, is popular with charter boats because of the good anchorage and three casual waterfront restaurants it offers. The shore is rocky, so there's virtually no beach. However, hikers may want to take a land or water taxi over and trek up the mountain trail. It's a rough 1,000-foot ascent, but the views are stunning.

The road from Great Harbour is now paved and follows the shoreline. Views are magnificent.

Restaurants at Little Harbour include: **Sidney's Peace & Love** (☎ 284-495-9271, breakfast/lunch $10, dinner $25), open at 9 am and serving all meals all day with live entertainment on Monday and Saturday nights; **Harris' Place** (☎ 284-495-9302, breakfast/lunch $10, dinner $25), famous for the Monday night Lobstermania, serves breakfast, lunch and dinner daily; and **Abe's By the Sea** (☎ 284-495-9239, breakfast/lunch $10, dinner/barbecue $22), holds a pig roast on Wednesday nights and serves breakfast, lunch and dinner daily from 9 am-10 pm. You can pick up ice and a few picnic items at Harris' or Abe's, which also has car rentals.

Sandy Ground Estates, Bakers Bay/East End Harbour, ☎ 284-494-3391, fax 284- 495-9379; www.sandyground. com. 8 villas. Rates begin at $2,000 per week, per villa.

These two- and three-bedroom villas are the perfect escape. Perched on a hillside above a secluded white sand beach between Little Harbour and Diamond Cay, each unit has a fully-equipped  kitchen, living area and a terrace with marvelous views. Dinghies and kayaks are available for rent and provide ideal water transportation to restaurants and bars at Little Harbour and Long Bay. Rates are based on weekly rental.

Long Bay/Diamond Bay

Until recently, the eastern coast north of Little Harbour was all but inaccessible by land. Now, the East Coast Road has been paved almost to Long Bay, which means you can get to some amazing sites without a boat. Leaving Little Harbour, follow the road northeast until you come a sharp turn that leads to a dirt road. Continue to bump along until you spot a red-roofed building on the beach. This is Foxy Callwoods' new venture, **Foxy's Taboo Restaurant and Bar** ☆ (lunch $10, dinner $25).

Taboo has a dock for those arriving by boat, and a boutique/gift shop run by Foxy's wife, Tessa. The restaurant is open-air and serves fat burgers (about $12) and gourmet pizzas that start at $13 and go up quickly as you add ingredients. Like Foxy's Tamarind Bar and the Fox Hole Boutique in Great Harbour, this is an easygoing place that lends itself to lazy afternoons, friendly conversation, and entertaining evenings. Closed Mondays. ☎ 284-495-9605.

Expect more development at Long Bay in the near future. Now that the road is paved, locals and visitors will want to spend more time on the northeast side of the island, which is just across the bay from Little Jost and even closer to Diamond Cay. In 1991, **Diamond Cay** became a national park and official bird sanctuary; a nesting ground for terns, pelicans and other Caribbean species. (Nearby Sandy Cay and Sandy Spit are privately owned, but scheduled to become protected sanctuaries for endangered species of turtles and lizards.)

Perhaps the most exciting thing about this end of the island is the **Bubbly Pool** ☆☆, a geological phenomena created by rocky boulders that trap the surf to produce a natural Jacuzzi. It's about a half-mile from Taboo; you can hike there in less than 15 minutes. Wear good walking shoes and bring along a swimsuit, snacks and a camera.

Anegada

◆ Overview

Anegada is unlike any of the other British Virgin Islands. It sits alone, about 14 miles north of Virgin Gorda and 30 miles northeast of Tortola, sheltered by one of the world's largest coral reefs, 18-mile-long **Horseshoe Reef**. While the other Virgins are made of volcanic mountains, Anegada is a narrow, flat, coral atoll measuring about 12 miles from **East Point** to **West End Point**.

The highest spot on the island is just 28 feet above sea level. Spanish explorers called it Anegada, or drowned land, because storms easily cause ocean waves to engulf the beach. Over the past centuries, many sailors, unable to see the level island on the horizon, have crashed against Horseshoe Reef and sunk offshore. Their wrecked ships lie on the ocean floor attracting shoals of sea creatures and providing excellent adventures for snorkelers and scuba divers.

CHARTER BOAT RESTRICTIONS

Charter companies don't allow their boats to be taken to Anegada. The reef is hard to see unless the sun is directly overhead, and approaches to the two anchorages are tricky, even for skilled captains with local knowledge.

Archeologists have uncovered evidence of Indian villages on Anegada well before Columbus sailed past in 1493. Later, pirates took advantage of the protective reefs to hid themselves and their treasures. The first European settlers came to Anegada to hunt for pirate treasure and pillage galleons that wrecked coming through the Anegada Passage.

Friendly fishermen and their families now inhabit the island and the British Virgin Island National Park Trust protects much of it as a bird and wildlife sanctuary. Creatures living on preserved land include flamingos, herons, ospreys, terns, wild donkeys and feral goats. Spectacular coral-sand beaches line the coast, especially on the north and west shores. With fewer than 200 permanent inhabitants, you can always find a secluded stretch of sand with no footprints.

A local fisherman with fresh lobster.

◆ Getting There

Clair Aero Services offers flights to the airport near **The Settlement** on Anegada's south coast. The 15-minute flights from Beef Island leave regularly on Mondays, Wednesdays, Fridays and Sundays. It's possible to fly from St. Thomas to Beef Island in time to connect with afternoon flights to Anegada. Call the airline for information and reservations. ☎ 284-495-2271.

Fly BVI offers a day-trip package for two for $125 from Beef Island and $175 from Virgin Gorda, which includes an island tour and lunch. ☎ 866-819-3416, 284-495-1747; www.fly-bvi.com.

Island Birds will fly you to Anegada in a Piper Aztec or Navajo, both twin-engine craft that cruise at about 180 mph. For information, call the office on Beef Island. ☎ 284-495-2002; www.islandbirds.com.

Most visitors arrive by boat from Tortola or Virgin Gorda.

The Bitter End offers motorboat jaunts to Anegada on the 50-foot Prince of Wales, ☎ 284-494-2746.

The Spirit of Anegada takes passengers on guided half-and full-day sightseeing and snorkeling tours to various islands, including Anegada, on a traditional gaff-rigged schooner. ☎ 284-496-6825; www.spiritofanegada.com.

Double D Charters has full-day excursions on a 43-foot powerboat. Captain Dave's trips leave from Yacht Harbour and include beer, soft drinks and snorkeling equipment. ☎ 284-495-6150 or 499-2479; www.doublebvi.com.

◆ Getting Around

Call **Anegada Taxi** (☎ 284-495-0228) or **Tony's Taxi** (☎ 284-495-8027) for a ride anywhere on the island. If you want to rent a jeep or car, call: **D. W. Jeep Rentals**, ☎ 284-495-8018 or 495-9677; or **The Anegada Reef Hotel**, ☎ 284-495-8002.

> **TIP:** *The Anegada Reef Hotel runs shuttle-bus service to the northern beaches for $6 per person.*

◆ Adventures on Water

Visitors must bring their own equipment or sign on with an outfitter that offers day trips to Anegada, because there are no full-service dive shops on the island. Snorkelers and divers usually can count on calm seas with excellent visibility, although the Atlantic can be rough during the winter months.

Horseshoe Reef extends into the Atlantic off the north coast and much of the coral is beaten to stubs by pounding surf every winter. However, if you know where to look, you will find superb elkhorn coral and interesting shipwrecks. Check with Anegada Reef Hotel about air fills and tank rentals, ☎ 284-495-8002; fax 495-9362.

> **TIP:** *Both Neptune's Treasure and the Anegada Reef Hotel rent various watersports equipment. See contact information below.*

◆ Adventures on Wheels

Anegada is flat and ideal for biking. Rent from **T&A Bike Rental** in The Settlement (☎ 284-495-8047).

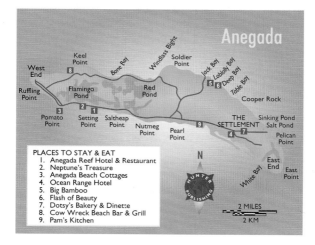

PLACES TO STAY & EAT
1. Anegada Reef Hotel & Restaurant
2. Neptune's Treasure
3. Anegada Beach Cottages
4. Ocean Range Hotel
5. Big Bamboo
6. Flash of Beauty
7. Dotsy's Bakery & Dinette
8. Cow Wreck Beach Bar & Grill
9. Pam's Kitchen

◆ Where to Stay

The Anegada Reef Hotel ☆, Setting Point/South Shore, ☎ 284-495-8002; fax 495-9362; www.anegadareef.com. 20 rooms. $175 (room only), $250 (meals included).

This informal hotel offers simple rooms furnished with rattan and decorated in bright island colors. Each air-conditioned unit has a ceiling fan, private tiled bath and coffee maker, but no TV or phone. Although the hotel accommodates only a few guests, passengers from boats at the nearby marina increase the number for dinner each night at Anegada Reef Restaurant. Guests look forward to fresh swordfish, lobsters and chicken cooked on grills made from 55-gallon barrels and served at tables set up by the water's edge. Often, there is music for dancing under the stars. Since

© Anegada Reef Hotel

all meals are included in the price of a double room, the hotel package is very reasonable.

Neptune's Treasure, South Shore, ☎ 284-495-9439. 20 rooms, $150, www.neptunestreasure.com.

© Neptune's Treasure

"Simplicity" is the keyword at this guesthouse and campground run by the Soares family. The rooms are so close to the beach that you are lulled to sleep by the gentle sound of the surf. The clean, modern units are basic but comfortable, and each has a private bath and air conditioning.

Anegada Beach Cottages, Pomato Point, ☎ 284-495-9466, www.anegadabeachcottages.com. $125.

© Anegada Beach Cottages

If you want to really get away from the world, rent one of these three beachfront cottages on the island's west coast. The one-bedroom cabins are spaced well apart on five acres to assure privacy. Furnishings are basic, clean and comfortable.

Ocean Range Hotel, The Settlement, ☎ 284-495-9522 or 495-2019. 6 rooms. $125.

Visitors who prefer to be near the main village should check into one of the six basic and inexpensive units at this hotel overlooking the inland reef. All rooms are air conditioned, modern and decorated in bright tropical colors. Each is outfitted with a queen-size bed, TV, private bathroom, private balcony and a kitchenette.

Anegada Seaside Villas ☆, Pomato Point/West End, ☎/fax 284-495-9466; www.anegadavillas.com. 7 units. $150.

You'll be just steps from the water in one of these modern one-bedroom villas with separate living areas and full kitchens. There's no air-conditioning, TVs or phones. The sea and seclusion are the draws here.

◆ Where to Eat

Anegada Reef Hotel Restaurant ☆☆, Setting Point/South Shore, ☎ 284-495-8002. Outdoor grilled specialties. Breakfast/lunch $10, dinner $25. Daily, 7 am-9 pm. Credit cards accepted. Reservations for dinner must be made before 4 pm.

Locals and return visitors look forward to sitting outdoors and enjoying a dinner of just-caught spiny lobster cooked over a flaming grill. This is the tradition made famous by hotel owner Lowell Wheatley, who recently died in an accident. His wife, Sue, and children, Lawrence and Lorraine, are continuing his work and welcome guests to the restaurant daily for breakfast, lunch and dinner. Breakfast is traditional hearty fare, lunch centers around sandwiches, burgers and lobster salad. If you don't want lobster for dinner, try the barbecued baby back ribs or chicken, grilled lamb chops, or cooked-to-order steak.

Big Bamboo ☆☆, Loblolly Bay/North Shore, ☎ 284-495-2019. Lunch only, $15.

Stop for lunch at this colorful pavilion set among the seagrapes on the beautiful beach at Loblolly Bay. The specialty is lobster served with veggies, but other seafood and sandwiches are available. Bamboo is also a popular beach bar known for rum drinks and icy beer.

Flash of Beauty, Loblolly Bay/North Shore, ☎ 284-495-8014. West Indian. Lunch $10, dinner $20. Daily, 10 am-9 pm.

Located at the east end of the bay on a beach with the same name, this casual beach bar is sometimes open only for lunch. The menu centers around sandwiches, but you can also order Anegada lobster and a couple of other seafood dishes.

Dotsy's Bakery and Dinette, The Settlement, ☎ 284-495-9667. West Indian. Breakfast/snack $8, lunch/dinner $12. Daily, 9 am-7 pm. Just down the street from the town square, this delicious-smelling café turns out bread, pastries and cakes. They also make sandwiches using fresh-baked bread.

Cow Wreck Beach Bar and Grill, Cow Wreck Bay/North Shore, ☎ 284-495-8047. West Indian. Lunch $10, dinner $20. 11 am-9 pm.

This cozy family-run beach bar offers a shady retreat, cold rum drinks and great meals. Fritters made from fresh-caught conch are outstanding; many patrons come for the grilled lobster dinners. Cool off in the afternoon with the specialty drink, Wreck Punch.

Pam's Kitchen, South Shore, ☎ 284-495-8031. Bakery. Breakfast/snacks $8.

You can start your day with fresh-baked goodies and hot coffee at Pam's, which is part bakery and part condiment shop. In addition to great breads, muffins, pies and pizzas, Pam prepares jams, chutneys, salsas and hot sauces that are made with 100% natural ingredients.

Neptune's Treasure Restaurant and Bar ☆, South Shore, ☎ 284-495-9439; www.neptunestreasure.com. West Indian. Breakfast $8, lunch $10, dinner $25.

The Soares family can guarantee they serve the freshest seafood – they catch it themselves. Try the swordfish, conch or spiny lobster, which also is cooked by family members. Everything is delicious. Add to your dining experience with one of the creative bar drinks. The piña coladas are said to be the best on the island.

Pomato Point Restaurant, Pomato Point/West End, ☎ 284-495-8038. West Indian. Dinner $30. Credit cards accepted. Dinner reservations required.

Wilfred Creque oversees the cooking and artifacts at this comfortable waterside restaurant. Breakfast, lunch and dinner are served, 9 am-9 pm. The menu includes burgers and lobster, steak or chicken for dinner. Take time to look over the owner's collection of Arawak pottery and maritime memorabilia.

Single-Resort Islands

◆ Marina Cay

Marina Cay is a tiny six-acre chunk of land tucked between Great Camanoe and Scrub Island a mile off the north shore of Beef Island. A free ferry shuttles (☎ 284-494-2174) passengers the short distance from the dock at Conch Shell Point on **Trellis Bay**, out to Marina Cay at 10:30 am, 11:30 am and 12:30 pm, then on the hour 3 pm-7 pm.

> **TIP:** Call or see the ferry schedule in BVI Welcome to confirm times.

Once out there, you can snorkel, dive, kayak, swim and relax on the white-sand beach. **Dive BVI** has a small scuba and watersports center on the island, and arranges one- and two-tank boat dives at 9 am and 2:30 pm daily. Contact Scott or Kathleen for information and reservations. ☎ 800-848-7078 or 284-495-5513, www.divebvi.com/marina_cay_facility.htm.

Marina Cay.

Diamond Reef

Diamond Reef is located between Marina Cay and the south-east side of Great Camanoe, a private island that is off-limits to visitors. Novice divers and snorkelers of all levels enjoy exploring the reef, which lies in 10 to 35 feet of crystal-clear water. It's too far from shore to be a beach dive, so check with Dive BVI if you want to go out by boat.

American author Robb White and his wife, Rodie, lived on the island in the 1930s and their house is still standing and open for visitors. White's book, *Our Virgin Island,* was a 1953 best seller that became a movie starring Sidney Poitier and John Cassavettes. Much of the movie, which is about life on Marina Cay, was shot on the island.

Pusser's owns the hotel, restaurant and shop on the island, so when you tire of watersports, you can browse through the **Company Store**, enjoy a Painkiller made with Pusser's rum, and dine in the open-air pavilion that overlooks Sir Frances Drake Channel.

Four rooms and two two-bedroom villas can accommodate up to 16 overnight guests. They are perched on a bluff overlooking the sea and each is furnished with king-size beds and ceiling fans. Villas have a sitting room and an oceanview terrace. Rates, including continental breakfast, run $195 for a double room and $450 for a villa in high season.

One number will connect you to the inn, restaurant and store. ☎ 284-494-2174; fax 494-4775.

◆ Saba Rock ☆☆☆

You reach this tiny speck of land by **North Sound Water Taxi** (☎ 284-495-9966) from any dock on the North Sound. Just call for a free ride. When you arrive on single-resort Saba Rock, you'll find a brand new property on a nearly-deserted island surrounded by **Eustatia Reef**, a snorkelers' paradise.

You may ferry over for the day or stay overnight at the resort. While you hide out there, enjoy sailing, windsurfing, diving, fishing and total relaxation.

> **TIP:** *Don't confuse Saba Rock with Saba Island, a five-square-mile Dutch isle southwest of St. Barts.*

Saba Rock Restaurant is a string of A-frame pavilions overlooking North Sound and the Bitter End Yacht Club. Ceiling fans draw cool sea breezes into the attractive exposed-beam restaurant that features sandwiches and salads at lunch and a $25 all-you-can-eat international buffet for dinner. On Sundays, a West Indian buffet, priced at $20, features johnnycakes, curry, jerk chicken and fresh fish. Live entertainment is provided by a local steel band.

The small resort is super-friendly. Kim, the bartender, whips up extravagantly delicious drinks. Head chef Shelford Tucker, who won a gold medal at the Taste of Caribbean Culinary Olympics for his famous chocolate mousse, works the carving station during the buffets.

Overnight accommodations are in eight rooms ($125) and suites ($350), and rates include continental breakfast. The hotel-type rooms are attractively furnished with one or two double beds. The two-bedroom suites have a king-size bed in one room, two twin-size beds in the other, a full kitchen, living room, dining room and a wrap-around porch.

For information and reservations contact the resort at ☎ 284-495-7711 or 284-495-9966; fax 495-7373; www.sabarock.com.

◆ Cooper Island

Cooper Island Beach Club, Manchioneel Bay/Cooper Island, ☎ 800-542-4624 or 284-494-3111; www.cooper-island.com. 12 rooms. $400.

Catch the ferry in Road Town, Tortola (☎ 284-494-3311) and spend the day at this typical, laid-back beach resort. Ferry service is variable, so call the resort for a schedule. The fare is complimentary for hotel guests and $10 per person each way for day visitors.

Rooms here are open and breezy with kitchenettes and a living area. Water comes from cisterns full of rainwater, electricity is generated by solar units and cooking is done over outdoor grills or gas-powered stoves.

The **Beach Club Restaurant** is popular with boaters, divers and hotel guests. Menu options include fresh fish, conch fritters, pasta dishes and West Indian curries. At lunch, most beachgoers enjoy cold drinks, burgers and fish sandwiches. Reservations are required for dinner and credit cards are accepted.

Sail Caribbean Divers (☎ 284-495-1675; fax 495-3244; www.sailcaribbeandivers.com) has a dive shop and scuba operation on Cooper Island Beach. Dive packages are set up with the hotel, but non-guests also may rent equipment and arrange dive trips. Kayak, powerboats and snorkel equipment are available for rent.

Cistern Point, on the south end of Manchioneel Bay, is a superb diving and snorkeling site. The area is sheltered and usually enjoys calm waters with great visibility. Borrow or rent a dinghy from The Beach Club or walk along the beach to the point. The best fish and formations are around the south side of the point.

Boat dives from Cooper include **Alice In Wonderland**, a 40- to 80-foot dive off nearby Ginger Island, that gets its name from the larger-than-man mushroom-shaped coral heads. Some of the healthiest corals in the BVI are found at this popular site.

◆ Peter Island

Peter Island Resort, across Sir Francis Drake Channel from Road Town on Tortola, recently underwent a $20 million renovation and the 52 rooms and cottages are now magnificent. All units are air conditioned and have a private bath and a private balcony or patio. Luxurious extras include plush terry robes, a mini-bar, hair dryer and private safe.

Beachfront suites are carved into a bluff over Deadman's Bay and feature sitting areas, oversized bathtubs, king-sized beds and walk-in closets. Large ocean- and garden-view rooms near the lobby overlook Sprat Bay Yacht Harbor on one side and a garden swimming pool on the other. A 10,000-square-foot first class spa opened in January 2005. It offers a full men of services for men and women.

The resort's **Deadman's Beach Bar and Grill** is a peaceful spot for a lunch of coconut shrimp or lobster salad. The more formal dining option is **Tradewinds Restaurant**, which requires resort-style dress for dinner (collared shirts and long pants for men, with women dressing to match). The five-course dinner here features fresh seafood, steaks, fine wines and all the trimmings. Live music is played for dancing most evenings. Meals are included in the room rates for overnight guests, but non-guests may ferry over to spend the day and have lunch ($25) and/or dinner ($45). The ferry leaves from the resort's dock on Baughers Bay on the east side of Road Bay; the fare is $30, round-trip. Contact Peter Island Resort for rate information and reservations, ☎ 800-346-4451 or 284-495-2000; fax 495-2500; www.peterisland.com. $865.

BVI Facts & Numbers

AIRPORT: Terrence B Lettsome Airport (EIS), Beef Island, Tortola, ☎ 284-494-3701 or 495-2525.

AREA CODE: The area code for all British Virgin Islands is 284. You may dial direct from the States. To call within the BVI, dial only the seven-digit phone number.

BANKS, ATMs: Most banks are open Monday-Thursday, 7:45 am-4:30 pm, and Friday from 7:45 am until 5:30 pm. ATMs are located in shopping areas and at the following banks: **Banco Popular**, Main St, Road Town, Tortola, ☎ 284-494-2117; **Chase Manhattan Bank**, Wickhams Cay 1, Road Town, Tortola, ☎ 284-494-2662; and **First Caribbean International**, The Valley, Virgin Gorda, ☎ 384-495-5217.

DRIVING: Traffic stays to the left. The speed limit is 20 mph in towns and 35 mph in the countryside. A $10 temporary license is required;you can purchase one at the car rental agency.

ELECTRICITY: 110 volts, 60 cycles, as on the US mainland.

EMERGENCIES: Dial ☎ 999 for ambulance, fire department or Police; Virgin Island Search and Rescue, ☎ 284-494-4357; Pebbles Hospital, ☎ 284-494-3497; Hyperbaric chamber for divers (St. Thomas), ☎ 340-776-2686; Medicure Health Center (Virgin Gorda), ☎ 284-495-5479.

GOVERNMENT: The British Virgin Islands are a Crown Colony with a governor appointed by England.

MONEY: The US dollar is the legal currency throughout the Virgin Islands. Travelers' checks and major credit cards are acceptable at most locations, but always carry some cash for smaller establishments.

NEWSPAPERS, MAGAZINES: *The BVI Beacon* is published on Thursdays. *The Island Sun* comes out on Fridays.

The BVI WELCOME Tourist Guide and *Limin' Times* are free publications that are available island-wide at the airports, ferry docks, hotels, restaurants and tourist attractions.

POST OFFICE: The main post office is in Road Town, ☎ 284-468-3701. Branches are found at the airport, Cane Garden Bay, Carrot Bay, East End and West End on Tortola, and in Spanish Town on Virgin Gorda.

TAXES: There is no sales tax in the BVI. The Departure Tax is $20 if leaving by airplane and $5 if by boat. There is also a $5 airport security fee. A 7% government tax is added to all hotel bills.

TIME: The BIV are on Atlantic Standard Time (EST + 1 hour) and do not observe daylight savings.

TOURIST INFORMATION: In the US, information is available from the **British Virgin Islands Tourist Board**, 370 Lexington Avenue, New York, NY 10017, ☎ 800-835-8530 or 212-696-0400; fax 212-949-8254.

In the British Virgin Islands, contact the **British Virgin Island Tourist Board** in Road Town, Tortola, ☎ 284-494-3134: fax 284-494-3866; www.bvitourism.com.

You also may get information from **The Caribbean Information Office**, ☎ 800-621-1270 in the US and ☎ 847-699-7570 outside the US; fax 847-699-7583.

In the UK, contact **The BVI Tourist Board,** 55 Newman Street, London W1P 3PG, ☎ 0207-947820.

WEBSITES: www.britishvirginislands.com; www.ultimatebvi.com; www.bvivacations.com; www.b-v-i.com.

WEDDINGS: Apply for a marriage license at the Registrar's Office, Main Street, Road Town, ☎ 284-494-3701. Take note:

❖ If you've never been married, you need only a passport. However, if either person has been married they must provide the original divorce decree or death certificate for their former spouse. If these documents are not in English, a certified translation must be included.

❖ A three-day residency requirement must pass from the time you submit your documents to the day you get married.

❖ A $110 marriage tax is collected by the government and it, along with your passports and divorce decree (if applicable), is submitted to the Attorney General.

❖ The Registrar charges $100 to perform the ceremony, which may be held at a location of your choice.

❖ You must appoint two witnesses to sign for you, and they must be present at the wedding.

Weddings are made simple by contacting a wedding service at your hotel or elsewhere on the island. One to consider is **BVI Weddings** in Road Town. ☎ 284-494-5306; www.bviweddings.com.

Index